MODERN
ELITE
FORCES

Section editors:
United Kingdom/Dr John Pimlott   United States/Dr Ian Beckett
Europe/Gary Sheffield   Middle East/Dr Colin McInnes
Southern Africa/Dr Francis Toase

Picture research: Staszek Gnych and Andrea Stern

The contributions of the following authors are gratefully acknowledged:
Max Arthur, Tony Banks, Ed Blanche, Ashley Brown, Lt.-Col. David Chaundler, Major The Reverend David Cooper, Col.
William H. Dabney, Ronnie Daniel, Maj.-Gen. Rafael Eitan, Gen. Sir Anthony Farrar-Hockley, Dr V. Keith Fleming,
Nigel Foster, Adrian Gilbert, Col. James Hamilton-Russell, James D. Ladd, Jonathan Reed, Brigadier E. D. Smith,
Maj.-Gen. John Strawson, Frank Terrell, Leroy Thompson, Lt.-Col. Patrick Turnbull, Col. Nick Vaux, Ian Westwell,
Lt.-Col. Andrew Whitehead, Major Louis Williams

Photographic Acknowledgments
Audio Visuele/Dienst KM, Bamahane, Black Star, Cassidy and Leigh, C.O.I., *Daily Telegraph* Colour Library, Eshel
Dramit, Gen. Farrar-Hockley, M. Flament, Col. J. Hamilton-Russell, John Hillelson Agency, Imperial War Museum,
Wally Insch, Israel Sun, Major Kealy, Charles Lawrence, London Express News and Features Services, Tom Mangold,
Novosti, Capt. D. Oakley, John Penycate, Photographers International, Photo Press, Photo Source, Photri, H. Pike,
Popperfoto, Press Association, David Rubinger, Rex Features, Lt. Col. Sheridan, *Soldier* magazine, Frank Spooner
Pictures, Frank Terrell, Leroy Thompson, Times Newspapers, Robert Young

MODERN ELITE FORCES

Consultant editor Dr John Pimlott

St Michael

CONTENTS

This edition first published for Marks and Spencer plc
in 1986 by Orbis Book Publishing Corporation Limited
A BPCC plc company
Greater London House, Hampstead Road, London NW1

© Orbis Book Publishing Corporation Limited 1986

Printed in Italy by Arnoldo Mondadori, Vicenza

INTRODUCTION

MODERN armies need to respond to a wide range of potential threats. At a purely conventional level, they must be capable of defending the state or its overseas interests against open attack, taking on the enemy army in full-scale battle, using all the latest technology and weapons. At the same time, however, they must be aware of and prepared to counter the less obvious (but no less dangerous) internal assaults carried out by guerrilla or terrorist groups intent on the overthrow of the existing political system: for this they need to be well versed in the arts of intelligence gathering, 'hearts and minds' (winning the support of the local people) and hard-hitting military tactics appropriate to small units. It is a complex mix of capabilities, requiring soldiers of courage, flexibility and dedication if the state is to remain secure.

Not all armies prove able to cope with such complexity, but those that do have come to depend more and more upon 'elite' or specialised units to answer their various needs. In general terms, and for the purposes of this book, the concept of an elite may be taken to denote those military (land force) units that are trained and deployed to carry out specialised tasks in both conventional and sub-conventional operations, although from the information provided, it may be possible to divide them further into three broad categories. None is necessarily exclusive – quite often a unit will be expected to carry out roles in more than one area of operations – but all contribute to the overall concept of 'elite'.

The most obvious category, especially among the older-established armies of the world, is that based upon tradition and fighting reputation. However, it is interesting to note that even in armies of more modern origin, certain units with a reputation for toughness and professionalism may also be included: in Israel, the paras, armoured corps and specifically the Golani Infantry Brigade all spring to mind, while in Britain, France, the United States and the Soviet Union, the relatively recent creation of airborne forces fits the bill.

That takes us on to the second category – that of precise specialisation – for there can be no doubt that any unit raised and trained to carry out a specific, often dangerous task in war will assume (and in most cases richly deserve) the status of elite. Many of the units in this category date back to World War II, when 'special forces', designed to conduct behind-the-lines raiding or swift, surprise assaults on key enemy locations, were present in abundance. Since 1945 their numbers may have declined but their roles have remained valid, particularly in such areas as seaborne landings and quick-reaction airborne operations. At the same time, new techniques have been absorbed – most notably in the use of the helicopter – and all such forces have been expected, in addition, to fight as extra-tough ground troops.

The third category is arguably the most important in the modern age, for elite units have emerged to satisfy the needs of counter-insurgency and counter-terrorism. In this the British have enjoyed some success, using existing elites such as the SAS and SBS to operate at appropriately low levels against the guerrilla or terrorist, but other states, especially those of the West, have been forced to follow suit. In Vietnam, for example, the Americans raised and deployed a whole range of units geared to the specific needs of the war. Other armies have done the same elsewhere: in South Africa and (before 1980) in Rhodesia special units were created to operate at the level of the guerrilla.

Many of these techniques proved equally useful in the process of counter-terrorism, but with the growth of 'international' attacks, often resulting in hijacks or prolonged sieges, the emphasis has shifted towards the provision of ruthless reactive forces. Some armies have merely refined the training of existing elites – in Britain, for example, the development of the Counter Revolutionary Warfare Group of 22 SAS produced siege-breakers of exceptional ability – but elsewhere such forces have often had to be specially raised.

Such a combination of different roles – as extra-tough fighters, specialist soldiers and counter-terror experts – means that the men involved in modern elite units have to be carefully chosen and superbly trained. It is their story that the present book examines, concentrating on the processes of selection and training as well as the myriad of operations carried out by elites worldwide since 1960, and there can be no doubt that, in a complex international and domestic framework, these units have made a major contribution to the maintenance of state security.

1·FORCES IN THE UNITED KINGDOM

THE British Army has a long and glorious history. For more than 300 years, red-coated or khaki-clad regiments have helped to defend the state and its overseas interests against a wide range of internal and external enemies. Although victory in battle has not always been achieved, the overall record of success is undeniably impressive and the British Army has constantly shown an ability to adapt to the ever-changing circumstances of war.

Part of this process has been a willingness to raise, sustain and use elite formations, geared to a specific tactical need. In some cases, this has merely reflected a requirement for soldiers whose extra discipline, toughness and professional skills will increase the chances of success in battle. The oldest and most famous such units are the Guards, recruited as an elite to protect the ruling monarch.

Other types of elite formations are based upon a need for specialist skills. Since 1945 the Royal Marines have perpetuated the skills of seaborne landing developed by the wartime Commandos and added an expertise in arctic warfare, while The Parachute Regiment has maintained a basic airlanding capability. Even more specialised are the units dedicated to covert observation, intelligence-gathering and raiding – the Special Air Service and Special Boat Squadron – for which men of exceptional self-discipline and bravery are required.

Nor have these units been kept idle, for all have played their part in the campaigns of the post-war period, particularly those involving counter-insurgency (COIN) or counter-terrorist activity. The British Army rarely creates new units for such tasks, preferring to exploit and

develop existing skills, and for this reason elite forces have found their responsibilities growing in proportion to the threat.

This is only one side of Britain's elite forces, however, for all retain conventional warfare capabilities which are constantly refined and occasionally tested, most recently in the Falklands. Here the elite forces, acting as the spearhead of British military response, proved beyond doubt that Britain has access to some of the best trained and most effective regiments in the modern world.

THE SAS

The 22nd Special Air Service Regiment

History and role of the SAS

In mid-1941, David Stirling, a Scots Guards subaltern serving in North Africa with a commando brigade known as Layforce, received permission to recruit a small unit for raids deep behind enemy lines. Under the rather odd title of 'L' Detachment of a non-existent Special Air Service Brigade, Stirling's force, operating closely with the Long Range Desert Group, soon gained a reputation for daring and tactical skill. In January 1943, after considerable expansion, the unit was renamed 1st Special Air Service Regiment (1 SAS), and in April of the same year it was joined by 2 SAS, commanded by Stirling's brother, William. These regiments fought with distinction in Sicily, Italy and northwest Europe, but were disbanded in 1945.

The name reappeared two years later, when 21 SAS – part of the Territorial Army and successor to the Artists' Rifles – was formed. In 1950, a unit called the Malayan Scouts (SAS) also appeared, tasked with taking the war against communist guerrillas into the Malayan jungle; men from 21 SAS were attached to B Squadron and in 1952 the Scouts formally became 22 SAS, which has remained a Regular Army regiment ever since. From the start, its main task was one of counter-insurgency, gathering intelligence, conducting 'hearts and minds' campaigns among tribesmen in guerrilla-affected areas and mounting offensive patrols at the level and in the environment of the enemy. By the end of the Malayan Emergency in 1960, the SAS had gained a well-deserved reputation for toughness and professional skill, and had carved itself a role as an indispensable element in the distinctively-British pattern of counter-insurgency. It was a pattern that was to be repeated and refined in Borneo (1963–66), Dhofar (1970–76) and Northern Ireland (since 1969, but specifically in South Armagh since 1976), and one that was to ensure the regiment's constant employment.

There is more to the SAS than that, however, for as the terrorist threat to Britain emerged in the 1970s, both at home and abroad, the regiment provided an ideal base from which to develop counter-terrorist techniques. By 1975 a special Counter Revolutionary Warfare (CRW) Group had been set up within 22 SAS, dedicated to providing a trained, ruthless and effective instrument to British and allied governments caught in the nightmare of hijacks, hostage sieges and urban bombing campaigns. In May 1977, elements of the CRW Group offered advice to Dutch Marines and police coping with a train-load of hostages hijacked by South Moluccan terrorists, and five months later a two-man SAS team took part in the West German GSG9 rescue mission in Mogadishu. At home, the Group kept a low profile until May 1980, when it successfully ended the Iranian embassy siege in London.

Finally, the SAS continues to train for more conventional military operations, acting as the 'eyes and ears' of the land-force commander while retaining its traditional role of behind-the-lines raiding – tasks that were carried out with courage and success in the Falklands War of 1982. Such capabilities make the SAS a remarkably well-rounded force, and for this it has to thank its notoriously tough selection and training procedures. Drawing its recruits from the mainstream of the army, the regiment emphasises physical fitness, endurance, self-discipline and weapons skill, refining and developing such attributes over a two-year period to produce soldiers who are close to professional perfection. Capable of operating with initiative beyond the support of the main force, they enjoy a degree of military freedom that can only be given to the most disciplined of soldiers.

Left: Members of the SAS training on the Brecon Beacons, South Wales. The man in the foreground is armed with a self-loading rifle.

WHEN elements of 22 SAS were first deployed to Borneo in January 1963, as part of Britain's response to growing Indonesian cross-border pressure, their orders were to act as a defensive intelligence network. It was potentially a daunting task. One squadron, totalling less than 100 men, was all that was available at any one time, and it was being expected to keep watch along a jungle frontier almost 1600km long – a frontier so wild that in some places it had not even been mapped. In addition, the Indonesian-backed infiltrators held some important trump cards: they had intimate local knowledge, knew how to live off the land, and used the native tribesmen as informants and providers of food.

Fortunately, the SAS had extraordinary qualities. More so than any other British regiment, they possessed the ability to operate in inhospitable terrain for long periods, often without resupply, and, having taken part in the Malayan Emergency of 1948–60, were well-versed in the twin techniques of jungle patrolling and 'hearts and minds' (winning the support of the local people). Indeed, it soon became clear that the only effective means of controlling the border was to enlist the support of the local tribes, particularly along likely infiltration routes from Indonesian Kalimantan into Sarawak or Sabah, and for this reason, during the early stages of the 'Confrontation' it was hearts and minds that took precedence. Organised into basic four-man teams, usually comprising a signaller, a medic, a linguist and a weapons expert, the SAS men went into the native settlements, made contact

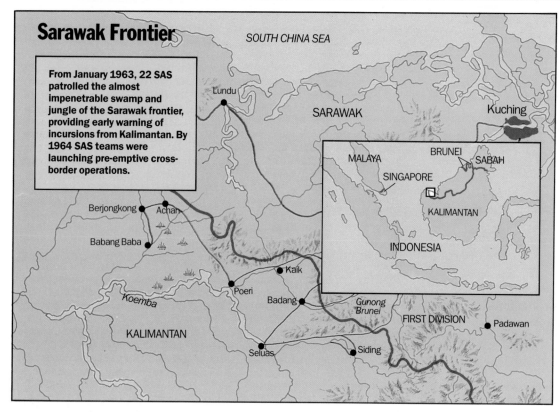

Sarawak Frontier

From January 1963, 22 SAS patrolled the almost impenetrable swamp and jungle of the Sarawak frontier, providing early warning of incursions from Kalimantan. By 1964 SAS teams were launching pre-emptive cross-border operations.

SOUTH CHINA SEA

Lundu

SARAWAK

Kuching

MALAYA

SINGAPORE

BRUNEI

SABAH

KALIMANTAN

INDONESIA

Berjongkong   Achan

Babang Baba

Kaik

Poeri

Badang

Koemba

Gunong
Brunei

FIRST DIVISION

Padawan

KALIMANTAN

Seluas

Siding

Right: An SAS radio operator makes contact from a forward operations base in Borneo.

Below: Surrounded by dense jungle in Borneo, an SAS detachment launches a riverboat containing weapons and kit at the start of a patrol. Craft of this type provided perhaps the best means of transport through the often impenetrable rain forest.

with the headman, set up a rudimentary clinic and generally discovered the needs of the tribesmen. By satisfying these, a degree of confidence would be gained, enabling the SAS teams to live in the local area for weeks or even months, helping with the planting, harvesting and weeding of crops, giving medical assistance and at all times respecting the local customs and traditions. In return, the natives would provide news of any useful findings, such as spoors or bootmarks left by the Indonesians.

Such information was relayed back to squadron HQ on high-frequency radios and was supplemented by further intelligence, gathered by the SAS patrols mounted from the village bases. So successful were these activities that by the time the Indonesians began their cross-border incursions in earnest in April 1963, the SAS had already won over many of the tribes and had provided the security forces, commanded by Major-General Walter Walker, with 'eyes and ears' of inestimable value. It was a role that was to continue for many months, aided by the formation, under SAS leadership, of a force of native irregulars known as the Border Scouts. By the end of 1963, large areas of the border had been effectively sealed, and

any Indonesian incursions that did take place were often monitored by the border units, enabling Walker to hold back his main-force battalions until precise targets had been defined.

As the Indonesians stepped up their attacks, however, the role of the SAS had to be modified. By early 1964 they were not only detecting incursions but were also helping heliborne infantry to intercept the infiltrators, guiding ambush parties or deploying their own 'killer groups' over the border into Kalimantan to hit the enemy before he could penetrate Malaysian territory.

These offensive forays – ultra-secret operations codenamed 'Claret' – called for the utmost skill and care. Because Britain was not at war with Indonesia and needed to avoid any accusation that she was escalating the conflict, such missions were subject to definite limitations and could only be undertaken by experienced jungle troops, guided by SAS or Border Scouts. They were also limited in terms of depth of penetration – initially 2700m and then, when an Indonesian build-up of troops was monitored in December 1964, up to 9100m inside enemy territory. The overall intention was to deny the Indonesians the military initiative.

At first, during December 1964 and the early months of 1965, Claret teams were ordered to concentrate on reconnaissance, with SAS patrols crossing the border to identify Indonesian bases, infiltration routes and lines of communication by land and water. Inevitably, such patrols found targets that were too tempting to ignore and by early May 1965 Major-General George Lea, Walker's successor in overall command, permitted an extension of Claret operations to include the mounting of selected ambushes in Indonesian territory. The SAS were in the ideal position to carry these out.

One of the objectives chosen was a major supply route, the Koemba river near Poeri, just across the border from Sarawak. A four-man team of SAS troopers led by Don Large was directed to investigate river traffic and, if possible,

Below: This SAS corporal's tropical kit in Borneo comprises olive-green trousers, shirt of uncertain origin and jungle hat worn over a cloth-scarf sweat band. On his belt he carries two ammunition pouches, compass pouch and water-bottle carrier. Armament is an AR-15 assault rifle, fitted here with twin magazines.

To their amazement, the team suddenly found a way through, climbing onto dry land which rose some 9m above the swamp before entering a narrow belt of jungle. Once through that, they saw the Koemba river, fast-flowing and about 40m wide, before them. Large immediately set up an observation post on a 3m-high bank with a ditch on the near side. During the afternoon he noted movements on the river and planned his ambush, deploying his three team-mates – Troopers Walsh, Millikin and Scholey – into positions overlooking the river bend. As soon as a suitable target presented itself, they would rake the boat from stem to stern before melting back into the jungle fringe.

After spending a day monitoring traffic, Large radioed for permission to mount his attack. For five hours the team lay in their ambush positions, watching small boats pass before them, but as the sun became obscured and rain began to fall, it seemed as if they had missed their chance. Just then, however, another launch, about 12m long, with sentries astern and other soldiers on board, came into view. As it passed by, less than 45m away, Large gave the order to fire. Within half a minute, over 60 rounds of smallarms ammunition had been unleashed, killing the sentries and holing the boat. As smoke belched out, soldiers jumped for their lives, just in time before the vessel burst into flames. The SAS team hastily collected their gear and withdrew, eventually calling for helicopter lift-out when they were well away from the ambush site. It was a significant blow to the Indonesians, forcing them to divert troops to protect supply routes and to take much greater care in the build-up of infiltration units.

Other cross-border raids took place during the succeeding months up to the end of the Confrontation in mid-1966, and although none of these involved the SAS alone (they acted as guides rather than sole participants), this did not matter. They had done their bit in ensuring the containment of Indonesian pressure, adding to their reputation and expertise in the process. It was a pattern of operations that was to be repeated with equal success elsewhere, particularly in the Omani province of Dhofar in the early 1970s.

Above: Armed with an American Armalite assault rifle, an SAS trooper carefully negotiates a bamboo bridge.

to engage suitable targets. It was a tall order, particularly as six previous attempts to reach this sector of the Koemba had been foiled by heavy going across swamps, but Large felt confident when he set out on 10 May 1965. At first his optimism seemed misplaced – within 48 hours the team had been forced to make a detour to avoid enemy soldiers and had entered an apparently impenetrable jungle. Worse was to follow, as the jungle gave way to swampland, and Large had to make the difficult decision to backtrack, hoping to reach the river further downstream.

Dhofar

At 0530 hours on 19 July 1972, Captain Mike Kealy, commanding an eight-man SAS detachment in the small remote town of Mirbat in the Omani province of Dhofar, was woken by the sounds of battle. Struggling to grab his rifle and equipment, he hauled himself onto the roof of the building that was his team's HQ. In the cold light of dawn, with low cloud and a steady drizzle hampering visibility, he tried to make out what was happening, little realising that he was about to take part in an epic action that would further demonstrate the fighting ability of the SAS. Without the courage, weapons skill and tactical acumen of all the SAS men involved, Mirbat would surely have fallen to a numerically superior enemy force.

The SAS had arrived in Dhofar in mid-1970, in response to a request for British aid against Marxist guerrillas of the PFLOAG (Popular Front for the Liberation of the Occupied Arabian Gulf) made by Sultan Qaboos bin Said

immediately after he had deposed his repressive father in a near-bloodless coup. SAS men were no strangers to the area, having been deployed to northern Oman in 1958–59 to counter a revolt on the Jebel Akhdar (Green Mountain) and, as recently as 1969, to the strategically vital but inhospitable Musandam peninsula, overlooking the Strait of Hormuz, to guard against possible guerrilla attack. Indeed, despite an official lack of British involvement in Dhofar before 1970, seconded officers, including members of the SAS, had advised the old sultan as the PFLOAG threat emerged, and were well aware of the need for a properly organised counter-insurgency campaign. In April 1970 the commander of 22 SAS, Lieutenant-Colonel John Watts, had even paid an 'unofficial' visit to the province, where he had been shocked by the failure of the sultan's policies. His report, suggesting new approaches, acted as a basis for action once permission was granted for elements of the regiment to be committed.

Watts had stressed the overriding need for an 'information service', designed to disseminate pro-government propaganda to the peoples of the rebel-affected mountains (the jebel) of Dhofar, and the first SAS men to arrive concentrated on such things as distributing leaflets and setting up a radio station, Radio Dhofar. Other men followed, organised into BATTs (British Army Training Teams), and they used many of the techniques familiar from the Borneo experience, making contact with the jebali tribesmen, offering medical aid and rudimentary military training. By early 1971 the first of a number of local defence units – *firqat* – had been raised, using SEPs (surrendered enemy personnel) and, under SAS leadership, these were used to spearhead assaults on the rebel-controlled mountains by units of the British-officered SAF (Sultan's Armed Forces). All this took time, however, and by 1972 Kealy's SAS team at Mirbat was still vulnerable to attack, even though the town was on the coastal plain and contained a *firqa* group. If they had been wiped out, it would have been a major blow to the sultan's campaign.

The attack on Mirbat was well planned. A force of 250 rebels, backed by

Below: *Firqat* troops patrol open country in Dhofar. These groups were often made up of former rebels, or otherwise comprised local inhabitants who had joined the government forces.

mortars, heavy machine guns, 75mm recoilless rifles and at least one 84mm rocket launcher, aimed to surround the town on a day during the monsoon period, when low cloud would hamper observation and seriously affect the use of airpower, a key advantage enjoyed by the SAF. At first, all went according to plan, but as the rebels crept forward before dawn on 19 July, they stumbled across an outpost at Jebel Ali, about 800m north of the town. Manned by a patrol of the paramilitary Oman Gendarmerie, the post was destroyed, but only at the cost of losing surprise. It was the sound of this firefight that alerted Kealy.

When he reached the roof of the 'Batthouse' (headquarters), all seemed confusion, but the calm attitude of Corporal Bob Bradshaw soon made things clearer. Looking round, the two men assessed the situation. About 100m to the northwest, near the sea, was the Wali Fort, held by about 30 tribesmen who were now returning enemy fire; about 700m to the northeast lay a larger fort held by 25 men of the Gendarmerie, and they too were beginning to fight. In a gun-pit beside the fort was a single 25-pounder field gun, manned by an Omani gunner, and Trooper Labalaba, a Fijian serving with the SAS, was already at his side. Around Kealy on the roof and under heavy fire, Lance-Corporal Pete Wignall and Corporal Roger Chapman were firing two heavy machine guns, while Lance-Corporal Harris was operating a mortar from a pit below. Kealy quickly realised that the key to his defences lay in the Gendarmerie fort and its gun-pit, so he concentrated his attention there, hoping to gain time for support units to reach Mirbat from elsewhere.

The weapons skill of the SAS was now tested, for the rebels mounted a sustained assault on the Gendarmerie fort, trying to overwhelm it by sheer weight of numbers. Wignall and Chapman laid down a murderous pattern of long-range fire, while another Fijian member of the BATT, Trooper Savesaki, sprinted some 700m over open, bullet-swept ground to reinforce the already-wounded Labalaba in the gun-pit. The rebels kept advancing, despite heavy casualties, but barbed-wire entanglements slowed them down: by 0700 it was clear

that the first crisis had passed. Kealy took the opportunity to report by radio to his HQ in Salalah, requesting air support. Unfortunately, the cloud was still too low.

At this point, the gun-pit fell ominously quiet and Kealy, together with Trooper Tobin, raced forward to investigate. Tobin reached the pit safely, while Kealy took refuge in a nearby ammunition bay, only to discover that all three men serving the 25-pounder, despite having been wounded, were still holding out. Suddenly, there was an enormous explosion, heralding another rebel attack. Labalaba, ignoring his wound, continued to man the gun, firing one round and reaching down for another, only to be shot dead before he could load it into the breech. At the same time, Kealy's position also came under fire and, as he fought rebel attackers at point-blank range, he was relieved to see Tobin step forward to load the 25-pounder. However, he too fell to an enemy bullet.

Kealy radioed back to the Batthouse for Bradshaw to concentrate the mortar and machine-gun fire on the approaches to the gun-pit, receiving in reply the welcome news that Strikemaster jets were on their way. Moments later, they screamed down, cannons blazing and, as both Kealy and Bradshaw guided them onto key targets, the rebels began to falter. A second airstrike at 0915 was followed by the sound of helicopters, bringing 23 members of the newly-arrived G Squadron, 22 SAS, well-armed with machine guns and rifles. As they deployed around the town, the rebels melted away, leaving more than 30 bodies on the battlefield. By comparison, Kealy's team had lost two dead – Troopers Labalaba and Tobin – and two badly wounded, but had broken the back of what turned out to be the last full-scale attack by the PFLOAG during the Dhofar War. It would take nearly four years for the SAF to clear the jebel for civil development, and the SAS still had an important role to play in basic counter-insurgency, but the tide had turned. Kealy, awarded the DSO for his leadership in the action, tragically died on exercise in the Brecon Beacons in 1979, but his example remains an inspiration to future SAS men.

Above: Captain Mike Kealy, 23-year-old commanding officer of the SAS detachment at Mirbat.

Winning the Dhofar War
22 SAS in Oman, 1970-1976

The Battle of Mirbat
19 July 1972

Dhofar Gendarmerie outpost on Jebel Ali (800m north of perimeter).

Fort
Dhofar Gendarmerie

25-pdr gun-howitzer

Wali's Fort
North Omani *askars*

Market

MIRBAT BAY

Batt House
SAS

Wadi

Mirbat

Key
- –x–x– Barbed-wire perimeter
- ➔ Adoo assault groups
- – – ➔ Route to fort followed by Labalaba, and later by Savesaki.
- ➔ Route to fort followed by Trooper Tobin and Captain Kealy.

N

0   100m

Onto the Jebel

March — May 1971 SAS troops first move onto the guerrilla-held *jebel* (plateau) in March 1971, engaging insurgents near Tawi Atair. In May they attack a heavily defended artillery emplacement near Aram that has been shelling Taqa, forcing the rebels to withdraw after a fierce battle.

Operation Jaguar

October — December 1971 A large SAS-led force lands by air near Jibjat and mounts a surprise attack from the north. The first permanent base on the *jebel* is established near Medinat al Haq and held despite determined counter-attacks. SAS troops mount further raids harassing insurgent communications along the escarpment.

Key
Defensive line

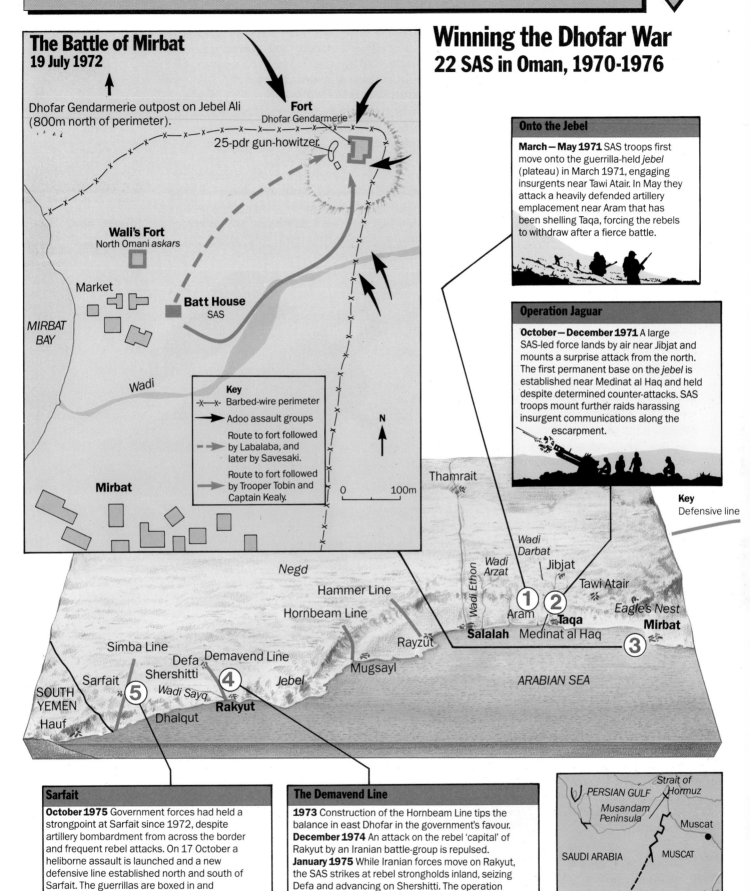

Thamrait

Negd

Hammer Line

Hornbeam Line

Rayzut

Simba Line

Defa
Shershitti

Demavend Line

Sarfait

Wadi Sayq

Jebel

Mugsayl

Rakyut

SOUTH YEMEN

Hauf

Dhalqut

Wadi Ethon

Wadi Arzat

Wadi Darbat

Jibjat

Tawi Atair

Aram ① ②

Taqa

Medinat al Haq

Salalah

Eagle's Nest

Mirbat ③

④

⑤

ARABIAN SEA

Sarfait

October 1975 Government forces had held a strongpoint at Sarfait since 1972, despite artillery bombardment from across the border and frequent rebel attacks. On 17 October a heliborne assault is launched and a new defensive line established north and south of Sarfait. The guerrillas are boxed in and resistance collapses; isolated insurgents in the rest of Dhofar are soon mopped up by SAS teams and the Sultan's armed forces.

The Demavend Line

1973 Construction of the Hornbeam Line tips the balance in east Dhofar in the government's favour.
December 1974 An attack on the rebel 'capital' of Rakyut by an Iranian battle-group is repulsed.
January 1975 While Iranian forces move on Rakyut, the SAS strikes at rebel strongholds inland, seizing Defa and advancing on Shershitti. The operation draws enemy troops from the defence of Rakyut, enabling the Iranians to take it. Construction of the Demavend Line begins.

Strait of Hormuz

PERSIAN GULF

Musandam Peninsula

Muscat

SAUDI ARABIA

MUSCAT

OMAN

DHOFAR

Salalah

SOUTH YEMEN

Mirbat

ARABIAN SEA

Iranian Embassy

With sirens blaring and lights flashing, police units raced to the Iranian embassy at No 16 Princes Gate, in the heart of London's fashionable SW7. It was a little after 1130 hours on Wednesday, 30 April 1980, and they were responding to an emergency signal from PC Trevor Lock, a member of Scotland Yard's Diplomatic Protection Group. Minutes earlier he had witnessed an armed attack on the embassy as a group of unidentified gunmen burst through the front doors and rounded up the terrified occupants, including Lock and six other non-Iranians. Altogether 26 hostages were seized and held at gunpoint, although for the moment no clear indication of motive could be gained.

The police quickly assumed a familiar pattern of siege, deploying their own specialist units to seal off the embassy building and begin the delicate business of negotiation. As 'Blue Beret' marksmen of Scotland Yard's D11 took up positions in doorways and on rooftops overlooking the embassy, members of C13 – the anti-terrorist squad – set up a control HQ, while C7 – the Yard's Technical Support Branch and specialists in the art of electronic surveillance – approached the building with microphones and 'bugging' devices. At first nothing was known of the gunmen, but they soon made their demands. Representing the 'oppressed people' of Khuzestan, an oil-rich area of southwestern Iran inhabited by Arabs, they threatened to shoot their hostages unless 91 Arab prisoners in Iran were released. Their deadline was noon the following day – 1 May.

Although this gave the police some idea of who they were up against, it did not solve a number of other problems: it was not clear, for example, how many gunmen were involved, nor where the

Above: 1250 hours on Friday 2 May 1980. One of the Iranian gunmen is glimpsed briefly as he picks up a package of food at the front door of the embassy.

Left: The SAS assault begins. Armed with a 'Hockler', the Heckler and Koch MP5A3 sub-machine gun, an SAS man moves into position to enter the embassy.

Right: Having blown in the embassy windows, the SAS frontal-assault team wait for the smoke to clear.

Right: Flames shoot out of the front windows as the furnishings catch fire following the explosions of the frame charges and the stun grenade.

hostages were being held in the five-storey embassy. Thus, although the usual 'softly-softly' approach was adopted – talking to the gunmen and allowing food, cigarettes and medical supplies to be delivered in exchange for the release of selected hostages or just to gain time – it soon became obvious that more help was needed. Within hours of the beginning of the siege, plain-clothes SAS men joined the police in Princes Gate, intent on planning a rescue mission should that be deemed necessary.

They were well suited to the task, for while SAS teams had been gaining experience in counter-insurgency in Dhofar and Northern Ireland in the early 1970s, their colleagues back at the regiment's HQ in Hereford had been perfecting anti-terrorist techniques. They recognised the need for some sort of crack force which would avoid the nightmare experienced by the West Germans at Munich in September 1972, when a police attempt to rescue Israeli hostages from the hands of Palestinian terrorists had led to a massacre. Since then all SAS troopers, as part of their training, had received detailed instruction in the difficult art of using smallarms in enclosed spaces, particularly in the specially-built CQB (close-quarter battle) house at Hereford. In addition, new techniques and equipment had been introduced, including abseiling down the outside of buildings and the use of 'frame charges' (large rectangles of plastic explosive to blow in windows) and stun grenades to effect an entry. By the beginning of 1980 the SAS was well prepared and raring to go.

However, before the team could mount their assault on the Iranian embassy (Operation Nimrod), much more information was needed and all alternative responses had to have been tried. Scotland Yard's C7 had installed a number of microphones and surveillance devices in the chimneys and walls of buildings adjoining the embassy, covering the sound of their work with a barrage of road drills in nearby Ennismore Gardens, so a picture of terrorist deployment was beginning to emerge. At the same time, a section of wall between the embassy and the house next door had been carefully removed, leaving only a thin sheet of plaster for an assault team to kick their

way through. Such contingencies would only be used if the negotiations broke down entirely and the hostages were consequently at risk, and on Monday, 5 May, that suddenly appeared to be the case.

Despite having secured the release of several hostages in exchange for food, the police were in no position to offer the gunmen safe conduct out of Britain – even when the demand for the release of the Arab prisoners was dropped. Inside the embassy, tempers were frayed, especially when demands for media broadcast of the terrorists' aims did not seem to have been met, and at 1140 on 5 May PC Lock, leaning out of a window, let it be known that hostages would soon begin to die. Two hours later, shots were heard from inside the building and, at 1850, the body of the embassy press officer was pushed out of the door. The police responded at once, pretending to give in to the gunmen's demands. In reality, the SAS was about to go in.

At 1923, in full view of television cameras, the black-clad assault team crashed into the embassy. Their faces masked with respirators, the SAS men stormed the building from three sides. The initial assault came from the rear. Abseiling down ropes from the roof, the

first pair of troopers reached a terrace at the back of the embassy, but were unable to detonate their frame charges because of a colleague entangled in a rope above them. A second pair dropped to the first floor back balcony and both teams were forced to hack their way in through bullet-proof glass. A stun grenade was lobbed in and the SAS made for the telex room on the second floor where they knew, from C7 surveillance, that a number of hostages were being held.

On the first-floor landing, the terrorist leader was with PC Lock, and as an SAS man appeared at the window, the Iranian raised his gun to fire. Lock hurled himself at the gunman and grappled with him until the SAS man could climb in and kill him. Meanwhile, at the front of the building, the SAS blasted through the first-floor windows, and out of the thick smoke came the first of the hostages, a BBC sound recordist, Sim Harris, to be helped to safety by a waiting SAS trooper. A third team stormed through the thin sheet of plaster where the bricks had been removed.

Racing through the burning building, the SAS converged on the telex room. Hearing the assault, the gunman guarding the hostages opened fire, killing one and wounding three others. When the SAS burst in, the gunman and two of his colleagues tried to hide among the surviving hostages, but were soon pointed out to the rescuers, who promptly shot them down.

The sequence of events in the telex room has never been fully established, but the SAS men, trained to kill amidst the smoke and confusion of an assault, carried out their duty swiftly and effectively. In the wake of the attack, the bodies of five of the six gunmen were carried out of the embassy: two had been killed in the telex room, one in the office at the back, one in the embassy hallway near the front door and the fifth on the first floor. All had died from firearm wounds to the head or chest. As for the SAS, they suffered no casualties and left the area in two Avis vans. It had been a brilliant rescue mission, for although one of the hostages had died in the final shoot-out, the siege had been ended in a surgical operation lasting less than 17 minutes. As a counter-terrorist force, the SAS was second to none.

Above: The strain of the siege shows on Lebanese journalist Mustapha Karkouti as he and PC Trevor Lock — two of the hostages — relay the demands of the gunmen, who spoke little English, to the police waiting below.

Assault on the Iranian embassy

Microphones and surveillance devices are lowered down the chimney to monitor the movements of the terrorists and hostages inside the embassy.

①

telex room

Members of the frontal-assault group blast their way through the first-floor windows with 'frame charges' and lob in a 'stun' grenade. Reaching the telex room, the SAS burst in and shoot two terrorists dead.

③

first-flo landing

front hallway

South Atlantic War

When the Argentinians invaded the Falklands in early April 1982, it was only natural that the SAS should have an integral part to play in Britain's military response. As a notoriously tough and superbly trained elite, they could be used to carry out a host of difficult and dangerous tasks, ranging from the setting-up of observation posts inside enemy-held territory to the mounting of hit-and-run raids in the best Stirling tradition. It was a unique opportunity to test the skills of the SAS in conventional war in the modern age.

The first official indication of SAS involvement came in late April, when the Mountain and Boat Troops of D Squadron, 22 SAS, played a crucial part in the recapture of South Georgia. At first their role was one of observation, landing by helicopter on the formidable Fortuna Glacier overlooking the enemy garrison at Leith, but this proved to be something of a nightmare. On 21 April, 15 men under Captain John Hamilton were dropped at the chosen spot, only to experience some of the harshest winter conditions known to man: that night the barometer fell, the wind gusted up to 130km/h and the troopers had to endure temperatures equivalent to 55°C of frost. To cap it all, their tents had blown away in the blizzard. The fact that they survived the night is a tribute to their physical toughness, but worse was to follow. When Hamilton requested evacuation on the morning of the 22nd, two of the three Wessex helicopters sent to pick him up crashed in the appalling conditions, and it was only through the bravery of the third pilot, Lieutenant-Commander Ian Stanley, that the patrol was saved. Even so, within 72 hours Hamilton's men were fit for further action, and on 25 April, having advanced straight through an unmarked minefield, it was they who took the surrender of the enemy garrison at Grytviken.

Hamilton was in the thick of the fighting again on the night of 14/15 May, when he led D Squadron on a daring raid on Pebble Island, off the north coast of West Falkland. The aim was to destroy enemy airfield facilities and aircraft

An SAS assault force abseils down from the roof in pairs. On the way down a flailing boot breaks a back window and the element of surprise is almost lost. One of the team becomes entangled in a descent rope and the SAS are unable to use 'frame charges'. They hack their way in through the strengthened-glass windows on the first and ground floors and toss in a 'stun' grenade. Entering the building, they shoot a gunman in the front hallway and race towards the telex room.

Right: Armed with an M16 assault rifle, a lone SAS man presses on in the vicinity of Goat Ridge, west of Port Stanley, on East Falkland.

Below: This SAS trooper of the South Atlantic War wears a basic uniform of SAS smock and Royal Marine issue DPM (disruptive pattern material) trousers. The black wool balaclava helmet is widely used by the SAS when operating behind enemy lines. Worn on the belt are two US M16 ammunition pouches and two water-bottle carriers. Armament is a US-built 5.56mm Colt 'Commando' XM177, a cut-down version of the M16 assault rifle. Painted in camouflage colours, it has a spare magazine taped to the rifle's 20-round magazine.

which might be used to disrupt the projected British landing at Port San Carlos, and it was a brilliant success. Landing by Sea King helicopter after dark on 14 May, the SAS men, weighed down with extra weapons and explosives, marched across difficult terrain towards their objective. A few hours later, under cover of an accurate and devastating naval bombardment, a selected group of men crept silently forward, placed charges on a total of 11 enemy aircraft and destroyed them all. It was the first of a series of such raids on outlying Argentinian posts, each one of which kept the enemy guessing and diverted his attention from the intended landing site.

Meanwhile, other elements of the SAS had been deployed onto East Falkland to set up covert observation posts. Their reports of enemy dispositions and force levels were of inestimable value to the Task Force planners, who then altered the emphasis of SAS operations to include diversionary attacks while the landing took place. On 21 May, for example, a group of 40 troopers, well armed and eager for a fight, tied down a numerically superior Argentinian garrison at Darwin, to the south of San Carlos, to prevent any interference with the landing force, while other SAS men seized the summit of Mount Kent, overlooking Port Stanley. Initially undisturbed, the latter held on to their positions until relieved, under fire, by forward elements of 42 Commando, Royal Marines, 10 days later.

During the subsequent battles to contain and destroy the main Argentinian force around Port Stanley, the SAS continued to gather intelligence, reconnoitre ground and act as guides to the paras and Marines of the main force. Simultaneously, they monitored troop movements elsewhere, principally on West Falkland, and it was during this phase of the campaign that John Hamilton was killed. Detected while observing enemy units around Port Howard, he sacrificed his life so that his signaller might escape – an action which prompted an Argentinian colonel to describe Hamilton as 'the most courageous man I have ever seen'. There can be no more fitting tribute both to Hamilton and the SAS.

THE SBS

The Special Boat Squadron, Royal Marines

ON the bitterly cold evening of 22 April 1982, 2 Section SBS was flown by Wessex helicopter from the frigate HMS *Antrim* to a remote corner of South Georgia, an island some 1300km southeast of the Falklands. Their mission was to establish 'hides' (observation posts) on a headland jutting out into Cumberland Bay and report on enemy dispositions at Grytviken, the island's main settlement, situated on the rugged north coast.

After a difficult landing in the Sörling Valley, at a point about 200m above the icy waters of Hound Bay, the men, weighed down by equipment, began humping the 180kg bags containing their Gemini inflatable boats towards Cumberland Bay, 5km away. The journey took eight hours, and when the team members tried to launch their craft, a gale-force wind threatened to capsize them. Despite the obvious dangers, the section set out, paddling into a northwesterly wind which whipped up

Left: Well-equipped for action in the South Atlantic War, this SBS Marine wears an arctic windproof smock in DPM, and DPM trousers. Special features include a woollen cap, and civilian boots and gaiters. Field dressings are taped to his belt and to the foreguard of his 5.56mm AR-15 assault rifle. Across his chest he wears an SBS five-pocket magazine waistcoat.

Previous page: Swimmer-canoeists on a training exercise paddle their lightweight, collapsible Klepper canoe towards the shore.

jagged pieces of glacier ice. The boats' skins were soon punctured and the section was forced to withdraw, calling for a helicopter evacuation. It was a frustrating start to the Falklands campaign.

The men involved in this incident were highly-trained specialists, who had undergone a demanding and rigorous period of instruction before qualifying as swimmer-canoeists, grade 3 (SC3). Although many potential recruits come forward from the Royal Marine Commandos every year, very few are selected even for the initial training course. All have to be of above-average intelligence, since much of the unit's wartime work is likely to involve the use of complex electronic equipment and the compilation of detailed and accurate reports in a factual, no-nonsense way. Intellectual skills are also crucial to high quality and effective beach reconnaissance. During such operations, teams would be expected to identify suitable landing points for larger forces, take beach samples to test the load-bearing characteristics of the sand, and measure the beach profile. All of these activities have to be carried out right under the noses of the enemy, with no trace of the visit left behind. It takes a rare mix of intelligence, ability and courage to join the SBS.

Once accepted for training, the potential swimmer-canoeist is made to feel at home both on and under the water, which reflects the fact that much of his wartime work will involve

Left: An SBS team on a training exercise take up position to monitor movements of enemy troops and equipment.

Right: Armed with an L34A1 sub-machine gun, the silenced version of the 9mm L2A3 Sterling, an SBS man moves stealthily ashore from his Klepper canoe on an intelligence-gathering mission.

and to operate under water for considerable periods of time. Underwater swimming also allows SBS teams to engage in sabotage operations and recruits are shown how to attach limpet mines to the hulls of enemy ships and set the fuzes so that the explosions occur when they are safely out of range.

Weapons proficiency is highly prized in the SBS, and although most recruits are usually skilled in the use of standard-issue smallarms when they arrive, they will have to learn the finer points of the US Ingram and West German Heckler and Koch MP5 sub-machine guns, among other items of 'unusual' kit. Particular attention is paid to the development of sniping skills. Finally, men are also taught how to rendezvous with submarines at sea. After slipping free of his parachute harness a few metres above the water, the recruit will wait for the submarine to home in on him, usually by means of the 'bongle'. This is a sealed 15cm-long tube containing a large ball-bearing which, if turned over, makes a distinctive underwater echo that can be detected by the submarine's sonar.

Having qualified, the SC3 will serve with the squadron for a number of years, after which he will return to his Commando unit, acting as a useful reserve should the SBS need to be expanded quickly. Many qualified men return to the squadron for refresher courses and some go on to gain further qualifications – SC2 and SC1 – each

clandestine journeys deep into enemy territory. Teams are inserted by a number of methods: on the surface the Gemini inflatable boat or the Klepper two-man canoe is used, although SBS teams are equally capable of deploying from helicopters or submarines, or of making 'wet' jumps with parachutes. Recruits must be able to handle all craft in the most hazardous conditions and be able to paddle their boats over long distances.

Another essential proficiency is free-diving. In their first exercises, recruits train with compressed air and then progress to oxygen which requires the use of bulky tanks. Divers are taught to get in and out of a submerged submarine

History of the SBS

The present-day Special Boat Squadron (SBS) is a direct descendant of the plethora of seaborne raiding forces formed in World War II. Most of these were disbanded in 1945, but elements of three – the Royal Marine Boom Patrol Detachment (RMBPD), the Royal Navy's Combined Assault Pilotage Parties (COPPs) and the Marines' School of Combined Operations Beach and Boat Section (SCOBBS) – continued in service.

In autumn 1947, the RMBPD was transferred from its wartime base at Appledore in Devon to the Amphibious

School at Eastney in Hampshire. The RMBPD had already been joined by members of COPPs, and at Eastney it received recruits from SCOBBS. COPPs had been formed in September 1942 from Royal Navy and Royal Engineer officers training for reconnaissance missions along the North African coast. Most of the men left at the end of the war, but one detachment joined the RMBPD in 1946. The other unit to arrive at Eastney was SCOBBS, which had been formed at the School of Combined Operations at Instow in Devon in summer 1946 from 'Detachment 385' of the Royal Marines, and men from COPPs who had not been demobilised. The assembled forces were then forged into a single command known either as the Small Raids Wing (SRW) or the Small Boat Wing. Immediate control over the unit rested with the Royal Marines.

The SRW was reorganised in 1957, with its headquarters, training cadre and Special Boat Sections becoming the Special Boat Unit. A year later the Unit was retitled the Special Boat Company. This survived until 1975, when it was renamed the Special Boat Squadron.

Details of SBS operations are, of necessity, shrouded in secrecy: since the main task of the unit is to gather and report covert intelligence, particularly in advance of an amphibious landing, many of the techniques are not discussed in public. It is known, however, that a wealth of practical experience has been gained in places as far apart as Malaya, Borneo and Oman. As with so many of Britain's 'special forces', the SBS came into its own in the Falklands, where all the hard training and expertise of the 'swimmer-canoeists' made a significant contribution to success.

progressively more difficult than the last.

The full range of such skills was utilised to the full in the Falklands and, despite the problems on South Georgia on 22/23 April, the SBS went on to play a key part in preparations for the San Carlos landings on 21 May. Three weeks before the main invasion force arrived, the first SBS teams, usually consisting of four men each, were landed on East Falkland to carry out intelligence-gathering missions, reporting on Argentinian defences, identifying suitable landing sites and finding a base for the Brigade Maintenance Area (forward supply base).

One team established a hide overlooking the Mutton Factory at Ajax Bay, where 3 Commando Brigade intended to come ashore. The team confirmed that no Argentinians occupied the factory and reported that the site would be an ideal landing point. However, another team, operating a little way across the entrance to San Carlos Water, reported that Fanning Head was held by an enemy observation post; clearly, this would have to be eliminated.

On the evening of 20 May, as the invasion fleet approached the landing site, SBS teams were inserted by helicopter onto high ground above Port San Carlos, and they set off to cover the 10km of rough moorland towards Fanning Head. When the force was less than 600m from its objective, a Spanish-speaking Marine went forward to demand surrender. There was no reply, so fire-support was requested from HMS *Antrim*. As the first shells landed, the Argentinians opened fire on the SBS. Moments later, under a barrage of naval and smallarms ordnance, the Argentinians gave in, having lost several men killed and three wounded. The SBS team, pausing only to disarm their enemy, raced back eastwards to Port San Carlos to set up the landing lights for the fleet. In the rush of events, buildings could not be searched. If they had been, the SBS would have found the best part of an enemy company that later in the day would shoot down two British helicopters. Nevertheless, everything else went according to plan and, at dawn on 21 May, 3 Commando Brigade came ashore virtually unmolested. The SBS had earned their pay.

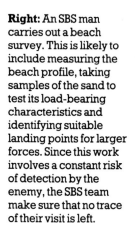

Right: An SBS man carries out a beach survey. This is likely to include measuring the beach profile, taking samples of the sand to test its load-bearing characteristics and identifying suitable landing points for larger forces. Since this work involves a constant risk of detection by the enemy, the SBS team make sure that no trace of their visit is left.

Right: A detachment of SBS swimmers stows gear under cover at the rear of a beach before moving inland on a reconnaissance mission.

THE PARAS

The Parachute Regiment

THE right to wear the famous red beret of The Parachute Regiment is not easily earned, and the man who wears it has proved himself through hard training to be a tough, professional soldier. The regiment requires three main qualities in its recruits – determination, physical ability and initiative – and the 22-week training course is designed to bring them out to the full in those who manage to complete the course.

The initial selection of recruits takes place at Sutton Coldfield, where would-be paras undergo tests to evaluate their physical and mental qualities. If successful, they move on to Aldershot where, after a thorough medical examination, the real training begins. The first two weeks at Browning Barracks, the Parachute Depot, are spent on course familiarisation, during which kit is issued, instructors are introduced and the traumatic transition from civilian to military life takes place, with first experience of the sort of rigid discipline designed to ensure that orders are obeyed quickly and without question. In weeks three and four the pace hots up with a taste of living in the field, constructing basic shelters and learning the rudiments of map-reading, fieldcraft, patrolling and camouflage. Drill comes next, the aim being to make the recruits adept in the basic marching manoeuvres.

Training goes up another gear in weeks five and six, with even greater emphasis on strength and stamina, culminating in the first real hurdle, known as 'Basic Wales'. This takes place in week seven at Sennybridge in the Brecon Beacons, a week of tough physical exercises in which recruits learn section tactics and assaults, patrolling skills and defensive deployments. The exercise ends with a 22km speed march over the highest point of the Beacons carrying full combat gear. Anyone not making the

grade at this point is relocated, back-squadded or discharged.

Recruits then spend weeks eight to eleven acquiring all-arms proficiency in a period of concentrated skill-at-arms training, supplemented by cross-country

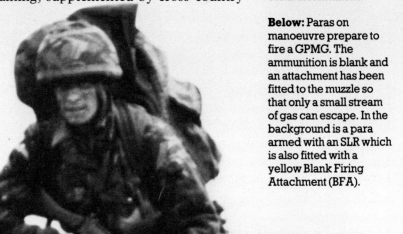

Previous page: Armed with SLRs, a para instructor leads a file of recruits on a training exercise to develop stamina and teach combat formations.

Below: Paras on manoeuvre prepare to fire a GPMG. The ammunition is blank and an attachment has been fitted to the muzzle so that only a small stream of gas can escape. In the background is a para armed with an SLR which is also fitted with a yellow Blank Firing Attachment (BFA).

History of the Paras

The history of British airborne forces begins in June 1940, when Prime Minister Winston Churchill requested the formation of a parachute corps. The first contingent to begin training was drawn from the newly-formed No 2 Commando, and on 13 July the men made their first jump.

On 21 November 1940 the force was renamed No 11 Special Air Service Battalion. It first saw action in February 1941, when 31 men parachuted deep into Italy and destroyed the Tragino aqueduct. Expansion followed, and in September 1941 the 1st Parachute Brigade was formed under Lieutenant-Colonel Richard Gale, part of which successfully raided Bruneval radar station in February 1942. By then an entire airborne division had been put together. Later expanded to two divisions (the 1st and 6th), the airborne forces went on to carry out a host of key actions in the latter part of World War II, most notably in Normandy as part of the D-Day landings, at Arnhem and in the crossing of the Rhine.

Once the war was over, The Parachute Regiment (officially formed on 1 August 1942) was drastically reduced in size, from 17 to only three battalions, eventually numbered 1, 2 and 3 Para. But opportunities for airborne operations were few, and although 3 Para was to jump into Port Said as part of the Suez campaign in 1956, the paras soon came to be regarded as extra-tough line infantry. As such, they certainly earned their reputation, serving in Palestine (1945–48), Malaya (1955–57), Cyprus (1956), Jordan (1958) and the Gulf (1961–67) – the specialised training of the paras, with its emphasis on determination, courage and endurance, making them well-suited to a wide variety of tasks. This has been shown more recently by their success in operations from the mountains of Radfan (1964) and the jungles of Borneo (1965) to the streets of Northern Ireland (since 1969) and the freezing conditions of the Falklands (1982). Indeed, so successful were they in the last-named campaign, that a restoration of the airborne role was ordered: the formation of 5 Airborne Brigade in 1983 ensures the continuation of a proud tradition.

and road runs to improve stamina. Weapons that are dealt with at this stage include the SLR (self-loading rifle), SMG (sub-machine gun) and GPMG (general-purpose machine gun), as well as heavier support weapons such as the 2in mortar, 66mm LAW (light anti-tank weapon) and 84mm MAW (medium anti-tank weapon). As week 12 approaches, recruits are introduced to the 'trainasium', a system of aerial walkways designed to prepare them for their toughest obstacle – 'P Company'.

P Company is used to test courage, military aptitude and endurance, often under stress. Tests include two battle marches over 16km and 24km, carrying loaded bergens (rucksacks) and weapons, to be completed in one hour and 45 minutes and two hours and 15 minutes respectively. There is also a log-race, a stretcher-race, a steeplechase and an assault course, ending up on the trainasium, where nerves are fully tested preparatory to jump training. Those who pass go on to an exercise known as 'Advanced Wales', in which the aim is to weld all the training together to produce a proficient combat unit. This takes until week 15.

After completing Advanced Wales, the trainee paras begin their run-up to parachute jumping, spending weeks 16 to 19 at Brize Norton Parachute School in Oxfordshire. Simulators are used to teach correct jump and landing techniques, after which the recruits make simulated jumps from the Tower (a huge, crane-like structure) and practise rapid descents along a cable system known as the Exit Trainer. Then comes the moment of truth when jumps are made from a balloon car moored at a height of 244m. Once completed – and a refusal to jump means instant dismissal from the regiment – the recruits go on to make eight jumps from aircraft, one at night, before receiving the coveted wings of The Parachute Regiment. After a return to military training at Aldershot and Salisbury Plain, the paras are then ready, in week 22, to join one of the three battalions. Only about 45 per cent actually make it that far, but those who do are already tough, determined and superbly fit young soldiers, ready for anything.

Right: A testing moment for a trainee para as he prepares to jump. Eight jumps have to be made in all – one of them at night, and the last from 800ft when weapons are carried – before the trainee receives the prized wings of The Parachute Regiment.

The Radfan and Aden

The Radfan is a wild, mountainous region, scored by deep ravines, situated some 110km from the town of Aden at the southwestern tip of the Arabian peninsula. It is inhabited by the Quteibi, Ibdali and Bakri tribes, fierce and hardy people who have traditionally supplemented their meagre income with raids on travellers on the Dhala road, which connects Aden with the interior. In the early 1960s the British protectorate of Aden and the small independent states surrounding it were becoming increasingly influenced by Arab nationalist movements. The Radfan peoples, already incensed by the imposition of a customs authority which denied them their income from the road, rose in revolt, backed by the Yemenis. A punitive action by the Federal government of Aden in January 1964 enjoyed only limited success, and by April control of the Radfan was effectively lost. The British Army was called on to restore order.

Initially, the intention was to use men of B Company, 3 Para, to drop onto a rebel stronghold on the key feature known as 'Cap Badge', acting as an anvil against which the hammer of 45 Commando, Royal Marines, would strike as they swept in from the west, but a troop of 22 SAS, sent to secure the DZ (dropping zone), became embroiled in a firefight and was withdrawn. On 29 April, therefore, the decision was made to go in on foot. It was an exceptionally difficult night march and, as the officers struggled to navigate over unfamiliar terrain, the schedule of the attack gradually slipped. When dawn broke on the 30th, the paras were still far short of their objective.

The company commander, Major Peter Walter, managed to avoid an encounter by skirting crests and resting in shadows, but the element of surprise was lost when, 1km from the village and its distinctive stone watch-towers, rebel marksmen opened fire. Walter, realising the danger of inaction, ordered his men forward and, using rocks and small

Cap Badge and Bakri Ridge
3 Para, May 1964

The mountains of the Radfan, in the north of the Federation of South Arabia, were the scene of a Yemen-backed revolt in the early 1960s. In January 1964 a joint British/Federal Government operation was launched in the Radfan to restore order, and late in the following April a force of marines and paras moved into the Radfan and commenced operations in the Bakri Ridge area. On 5 May, the Cap Badge feature was seized, and on 26 May 3 Para began their sweep along the Bakri Ridge.

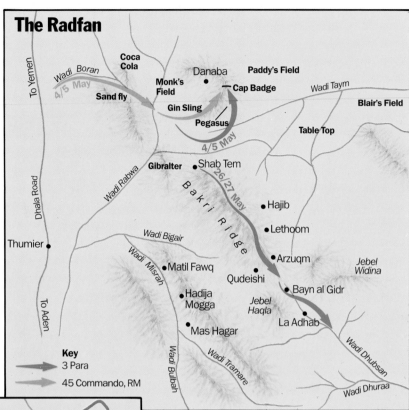

The Radfan

Key
→ 3 Para
→ 45 Commando, RM

Top: A radio operator, his Sterling SMG close to hand, reports back to para HQ from his vantage point in the Radfan.

ravines as cover, they succeeded in clearing positions around the central towers, even catching a rebel force in the open and destroying it. The firing soon attracted other rebels, however, and a prolonged struggle ensued in which the fighting was intense. Short of mortar ammunition and outside the range of artillery at the Thumier fort on the Dhala road, the paras clung on until RAF Hawker Hunters flew in to strafe enemy positions. This caused the rebels to falter, then to pull back, and their firing gradually subsided, particularly as 45 Commando arrived to clear the heights of snipers. Fighting patrols were then sent out to consolidate the paras' hold over the area and, by 5 May, all was quiet.

Fierce though this action was, however, it did not destroy the power of the tribesmen, so a larger expedition was planned, under the command of

Brigadier C. H. Blacker, newly-arrived from Northern Ireland. As part of his force, the rest of 3 Para, commanded by Lieutenant-Colonel A. H. Farrar-Hockley, was brought to Aden from the Persian Gulf, while B Company travelled in the opposite direction to relieve them. Farrar-Hockley was joined by 1 Parachute Light Battery, Royal Horse Artillery (equipped with four 105mm pack howitzers), para-affiliated Royal Engineer Troop, transport and medical elements, and his orders were to clear the central Bakri ridge before turning south to penetrate Wadi Dhubsan, a known rebel stronghold.

On the night of 16/17 May, Farrar-Hockley advanced the anti-tank platoon to the deserted village of Shab Tem, and from here three forward patrol missions probed a route along the Wadi Rabwa towards the Bakri ridge. No rebels were encountered, so the next night the main column set off, with A Company in the lead, supported by the machine-gun and mortar platoons. C Company and the Royal Engineers were used as porters, each man carrying about 80kg as well as a personal weapon. It was extremely hot and progress was slow, only about 1km/h, up and down precipitous slopes. Just before dawn on the 18th, Farrar-Hockley

Above: Lieutenant-Colonel Anthony Farrar-Hockley, commanding officer of 3 Para in the Radfan.

called a halt, ordered A and C Companies to swap roles and concentrated on bringing up supplies. That night a fighting patrol from C Company pushed on to secure the Hajib escarpment, ideally placed to threaten Wadi Dhubsan.

The rebels were unsure what to do in the face of such relentless determination, and it was not until A Company began to advance once more, into the rebel stronghold, that fighting commenced. C Company rushed forward as reinforcement, and the artillery, firing at extreme range, dropped shells onto reported enemy positions, but once again it was the arrival of Hunter jets that turned the tide. Farrar-Hockley was just about to pursue the demoralised rebels when a violent rainstorm imposed an unexpected delay.

There were two tracks into Wadi Dhubsan, one fair and one poor, but Farrar-Hockley, acutely aware of the dangers of ambush, chose to ignore them both. Instead, he sent his men to abseil down a 9m rock-face before advancing silently along a dry stream-bed and taking the village of Bayn al Gidr. Surprise was complete, forcing the enemy garrison to pull back and leaving the British in control by 0600 hours on 26 May. X Company of 45 Commando, under temporary command of Farrar-Hockley, maintained the momentum, advancing down the right side of the wadi while A Company, 3 Para, took the heights to the left.

A firefight ensured, pinning down the paras and Marines in exposed positions, and it was while on an aerial reconnaissance over enemy lines to pinpoint snipers that Farrar-Hockley's Scout helicopter was hit by smallarms fire. Struggling back to British lines, the helicopter landed safely, but immediately became a focus of rebel attention. This enabled C Company, moving east from Jebel Haqla, to outflank the enemy, who withdrew to regroup. 3 Para set up a defensive ring around the crippled Scout while fitters from the Royal Electrical and Mechanical Engineers toiled to repair the damage. The next morning – 27 May – the paras started to burn the grain stores found in Wadi Dhubsan and, as the Scout took to the air again amid cheers from the men on the ground, the operation was deemed a success.

Later that day the paras and Marines climbed back up the escarpment and were airlifted out to Aden; with the exception of a reconnaissance patrol down the Shaab Lashab by D Company in mid-June, 3 Para's involvement in the Radfan was over and they returned to the Gulf. At a cost of one man killed and seven wounded, over 500 square kilometres of rebel territory had been secured and a major stronghold penetrated. Unfortunately, as British troops faced growing unrest in Aden itself, this success could not be consolidated – the Radfani tribes were to continue to plague the British until the final withdrawal from Aden in 1967 – but no one could doubt that the paras were capable of tough action in extremely inhospitable terrain.

The paras were not to be involved in Aden until 1967 when, during the run-up to withdrawal, 1 Para was deployed to police the districts of Al Mansura and Sheik Othman. They were to remain until November, during which time they faced the full range of problems associated with an urban revolt. In early June their observation posts in Sheik Othman came under sustained and co-ordinated smallarms fire which only

South Atlantic War

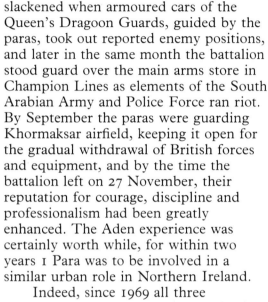

Above: Paras use medium artillery pieces to bombard rebel positions. British patrols pursuing tribesmen into the mountains found that they could easily be pinned down without artillery support.

Below: A machine gunner takes a break in a sheltered spot and waits for the order to advance.

slackened when armoured cars of the Queen's Dragoon Guards, guided by the paras, took out reported enemy positions, and later in the same month the battalion stood guard over the main arms store in Champion Lines as elements of the South Arabian Army and Police Force ran riot. By September the paras were guarding Khormaksar airfield, keeping it open for the gradual withdrawal of British forces and equipment, and by the time the battalion left on 27 November, their reputation for courage, discipline and professionalism had been greatly enhanced. The Aden experience was certainly worth while, for within two years 1 Para was to be involved in a similar urban role in Northern Ireland.

Indeed, since 1969 all three battalions have seen extensive service in the province, experiencing all the problems of peacekeeping and counter-insurgency in both urban and rural areas. During their frequent 'tours' – with nine under its belt, 2 Para currently holds the record for the entire British Army – their reputation for toughness and military skill has been enhanced, putting fear into the hearts of extremists, Loyalist as well as Republican, and absorbing the shocks of counter-action. In February 1972, for example, less than a month after the incident in Londonderry known as 'Bloody Sunday', in which 13 male civilians were shot dead by 1 Para during a riot, the Officers' Mess at Aldershot was bombed by the IRA, killing six people, and in August 1979 2 Para was caught in an horrific ambush at Warrenpoint, losing a company commander and 15 soldiers. As in so many other cases, however, the paras displayed both discipline and resolution – attributes that were to be brought out to the full in the Falklands War of 1982.

At the beginning of April 1982, all three regular battalions of The Parachute Regiment were in the United Kingdom. 1 Para, recently returned from yet another tour of Northern Ireland, was on public duties in Edinburgh, 2 Para was on block leave prior to deployment to Belize and 3 Para had just assumed the Spearhead (standby) role. None was expecting active service, so when, in response to the Argentinian invasion of the Falklands, 2 and 3 Para were ordered to join the Task Force as part of a reinforced 3 Commando Brigade, it came as something of a surprise. After hasty preparations, 3 Para left the UK aboard the liner *Canberra* on 9 April, to be followed by 2 Para on the less glamorous ferry *Norland* 17 days later.

Both battalions took part in the landing at San Carlos on East Falkland on 21 May, 3 Para on the left around Port San Carlos and 2 Para on the right, towards the Sussex mountains. Digging in on exposed ground, the paras had a grandstand view of the air battles over San Carlos Water and it was not until late on 26 May that orders were received to begin the breakout. In the initial stage 2 Para, with Lieutenant-Colonel H. Jones as commanding officer (CO), was to advance south to take the twin settlements of Darwin and Goose Green, capturing the airfield and destroying an Argentinian garrison estimated to comprise no more than a battalion of men. The paras, only lightly equipped and denied armour support, began their approach on 27 May, little realising that they were, in fact, heavily outnumbered.

The attack began at 0635 hours on 28 May, with A Company under Major Dair Farrar-Hockley taking out Burntside House on the left of the axis of advance. As soon as this had been achieved, using 84mm anti-tank weapons and white phosphorus grenades, B Company under Major John Crosland pushed forward on the right, destroying the first of the enemy trenches and making quite rapid progress. In the centre, however, Major Phil Neame's D Company, together with Battalion Tactical HQ, found the going hard across difficult terrain and, when ordered to press forward, came under heavy enemy fire which forced the men to go to ground. Argentinian artillery fire now rained down with considerable accuracy, and although the soft peaty ground absorbed the impact of the shells, keeping casualties to a minimum, progress was slowed. D Company, pressing home its attack with great determination, lost three men killed, but it was not until 0900 hours that A Company could be ordered to pass through towards Darwin, over a kilometre further on. Artillery fire continued to cause problems.

Over to the right, B Company advanced down the side of a shallow valley towards a line of gorse below the ruins of Boca House. As they moved forward at 1030, they came under heavy fire which pinned them down, and when the same happened to A Company as they approached Darwin Hill, it began to seem as if the whole attack had stalled. Argentinian machine guns in prepared positions had effectively contained the advance, and the situation was not helped by the fact that 2 Para was running low on ammunition, artillery support had virtually ceased and bad weather at sea was preventing either naval or air operations. It was a crucial point in the battle.

Colonel Jones and his Tac HQ inched forward under heavy fire to A Company's position, arriving at about 1125. The CO knew that the momentum of the attack had to be restored, but another attempt on the hill cost the lives of two officers and a corporal; under a storm of bullets, A Company was forced back to the shelter of its protective gulley. It was during this attack that Colonel Jones and his party moved round to the right. While the enemy was engaging A Company, he led his own assault at 1330, only to be shot down and mortally wounded. Far from lowering the paras' morale, however, Jones's sacrifice (for which he was later to be awarded a Victoria Cross) gave his men new determination: grimly A Company attacked again and this time found a way through the Argentinian lines, capturing the entire position.

When Jones was killed, the second-in-command, Major Chris Keeble, took over. After consultation with Major

Above: Lieutenant-Colonel H. Jones, commanding officer of 2 Para.

Goose Green
East Falkland, 28 May 1982

Goose Green settlement

1600 C and D Coys advance down the slope from the gorse line and attack Goose Green airstrip and the Schoolhouse. B Coy performs a flanking manoeuvre, approaching Goose Green from the southwest.
1840 B Coy moves into position south of Goose Green.
1900 Schoolhouse taken after heavy fighting.
1925 Harrier strike on Goose Green Point.
29 May
1450 Argentinians surrender.

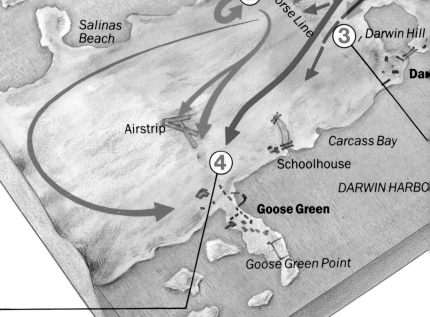

BRENTON LOCH

Boca House

Salinas Beach

Gorse Line

Darwin Hill

Da

Airstrip

Carcass Bay

Schoolhouse

DARWIN HARBO

Goose Green

Goose Green Point

Boca House

1030 B Coy crosses the gorse line near Boca House and comes under heavy fire.
1400 D Coy advances to the west of Boca House. Support Coy brings Milan into action against enemy bunkers.
1530 D Coy moves up the slope from the beach behind Boca House. The Argentinians surrender.

Right: In a sheep-shearing shed at Fitzroy a para prepares a meal with his standard-issue solid-fuel stove.

Burntside House

0200 2 Para 'tabs off' from Camilla Creek.
0630 A and B Coys cross the start line near Burntside House.
0635 A Coy attacks the forward platoon of Argentinians in Burntside House, overwhelming them with superior firepower.

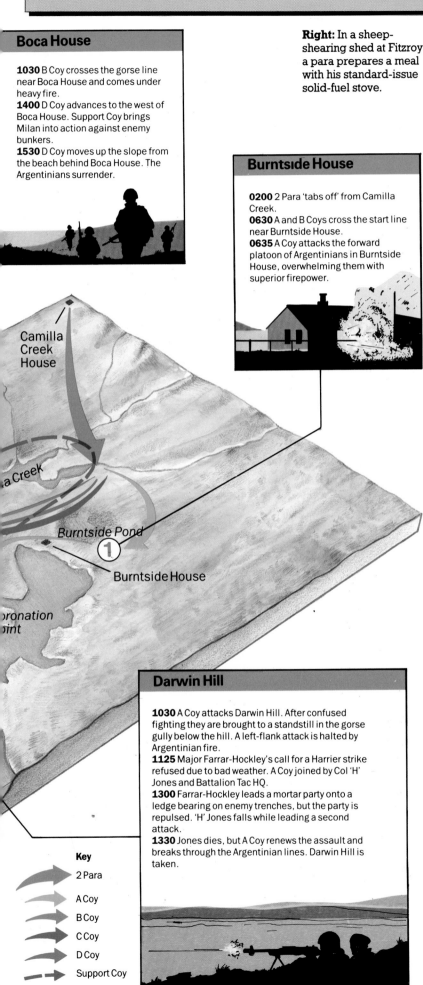

Camilla Creek House

a Creek

Burntside Pond

①

Burntside House

ronation
oint

Darwin Hill

1030 A Coy attacks Darwin Hill. After confused fighting they are brought to a standstill in the gorse gully below the hill. A left-flank attack is halted by Argentinian fire.
1125 Major Farrar-Hockley's call for a Harrier strike refused due to bad weather. A Coy joined by Col 'H' Jones and Battalion Tac HQ.
1300 Farrar-Hockley leads a mortar party onto a ledge bearing on enemy trenches, but the party is repulsed. 'H' Jones falls while leading a second attack.
1330 Jones dies, but A Coy renews the assault and breaks through the Argentinian lines. Darwin Hill is taken.

Key

→ 2 Para

→ A Coy

→ B Coy

→ C Coy

→ D Coy

---→ Support Coy

Neame, Keeble ordered D Company to push forward along the shoreline by Boca House, outflanking enemy positions and breaking the deadlock in front of B Company. The plan worked: at 1400 hours D Company advanced to the west of Boca House, while B Company and Support Company (the latter equipped with Milan anti-tank missiles) engaged the Argentinian positions. The enemy soon decided they had seen enough and at 1530 white flags began to appear. D Company immediately pushed on towards the Goose Green schoolhouse while B Company set off in a wide sweep southwards which would take them to the right of the airfield and then on for some distance before swinging left across the isthmus. The intention was to surround Goose Green, and it worked. After clearing Darwin settlement, A Company and C Company advanced down a long gentle gradient to approach the airfield from the north. Despite coming under fire from 20mm anti-aircraft guns and experiencing a stiff fight around the schoolhouse, 2 Para could afford to relax a little, particularly as the weather cleared and Harrier jets swept in to provide fire support.

Keeble decided to leave the Argentinians, by now bottled up, to think about their plight, sending them a carefully-worded ultimatum of surrender with directions that it was to be answered by 0830 on 29 May. After a cold night on the battlefield, the paras were pleased to see white flags appear at 0825 and more than surprised when a total of 1300 Argentinians emerged to lay down their arms. It was a remarkable victory: for a loss of 15 men killed and 30 wounded, 2 Para had defeated an enemy force twice its size and imposed a moral ascendancy over the Argentinians which the British were not to lose.

While this battle was going on, 3 Para under Lieutenant-Colonel Hew Pike had made its contribution to the breakout, pushing forward from Port San Carlos towards Teal Inlet. Setting out on 27 May, the battalion 'tabbed' (marched) all the way, across difficult terrain, arriving at the objective on the night of the 28th. The next step was to flush out the 300 enemy said to be at Estancia House to the east, but fortunately the Argentinians had pulled back, so no fighting took place. By now the paras

were desperately tired after the days of marching and nights without sleep. From Estancia they took up positions opposite Mount Longdon, a key feature in the ring of enemy defences around Port Stanley, and prepared for action against it, scheduled for the night of 11/12 June. It was to prove a harrowing night of the most intense close-quarters fighting.

The plan was for B Company, commanded by Major Mike Argue, to tackle the Longdon summit (composed of two features codenamed Fly Half and Full Back), while A Company under Major David Collett seized a ridge immediately to the northeast (Wing Forward). C Company under Major Martin Osborne was to hold back, out of contact, as a reserve and the Fire Support

Above: Lieutenant-Colonel Hew Pike, commanding officer of 3 Para during the South Atlantic War.

Mount Longdon
3 Para, 11 - 12 June 1982

The battle for Mount Longdon was the climax of 3 Para's three-week-long campaign, a campaign that began with the battalion's landing at Green Beach near Port San Carlos on 21 May. After consolidating its bridgehead 3 Para 'tabbed' across East Falkland, retaking the settlements at Teal Inlet and Estancia House, and pushing the enemy back towards Stanley. By 3 June fighting patrols were being conducted in the area of Mount Longdon and on the night of 11/12 June the battalion moved off from its start line west of the mountain to attack one of the most important Argentinian defensive positions around Stanley.

Key
→ A Coy
→ B Coy and CO's Tac HQ
— 3 Para start line
OOO Minefields

Drunken Rock Pass

Murrell River

Furze Bush Pass

Wing Forward

Fly Half

4 Pltn

①

A Coy

C Coy
(reserve)

B Coy

Free Kick

5 Pltn

6 Pltn

②

Mount Longdon

Full Back

③

Moody Brook

Two Sisters

Full Back
A Coy is ordered to move off Wing Forward and join the assault on Full Back. Despite tough enemy resistance, A Coy pushes across to Full Back, engaging the enemy with rifle and bayonet. By daybreak the mountain is in British hands.

Fly Half
As A Coy moves on Wing Forward, B Coy goes into the attack on the slopes of Mount Longdon itself. Coming under heavy machine-gun fire, 4, 5 and 6 Platoons of B Coy fan out and work their way towards the summit bunker by bunker. After securing Fly Half B Coy comes under attack from the rear before being pinned down by fire from Full Back. B Coy assaults are beaten off.

Wing Forward
11 June A, B and C Coys move on Mount Longdon.
2100 With C Coy held in reserve west of the battalion start line, A and B Coys cross the stream running north to the Murrell River. A Coy launches its assault on Wing Forward, north of the main feature. The company reaches its objective but is pinned down by Argentinian cross-fire.

Above: This soldier of 3 Para in the Falklands campaign wears the red beret of The Parachute Regiment, windproof trousers and combat jacket in DPM, short khaki puttees and direct moulded sole boots. He is armed with a 9mm L2A3 Sterling sub-machine gun (stock folded).

Teams (equipped with Milan and extra GPMGs) were to go to a point west of the mountain (Free Kick) for subsequent redeployment as required. A battery of 105mm Light Guns and the 4.5in gun of the frigate HMS *Avenger* were available for support.

Both assaulting companies crossed the stream running south from Furze Bush Pass just as the moon rose to silhouette the dominant, craggy outline of the mountain. They advanced steadily over open moorland, hoping to reach enemy positions with the full benefit of surprise, but this was lost when one of the section commanders in B Company stepped on a mine. The Argentinians opened up on both companies with heavy machine-gun fire, mortars and artillery; the only way forward was by combining intensive support fire with an immediate follow-up by the rifle sections, using rifles, GPMGs, 66mm LAWs and grenades. The nature of the battle was quickly revealed: a rush forward, a pause, some creeping, a few isolated shots here and there, some artillery and mortar fire, more creeping, another pause, dead silence, quick orders, more firing, great concentrations of fire followed by a concerted rush. Then the whole process would start again. It was a pattern which demanded great leadership and bravery, particularly from the junior officers and NCOs.

In B Company, 5 and 6 Platoons were the first to come under fire when surprise was lost, fighting from rock to rock to carve out a foothold on the southern side of Fly Half. But the advance soon stalled as, in the freezing rain and sleet, enemy bunkers were missed and fire began to come from behind. 6 Platoon was particularly bogged down, with casualties lying among rocks covered by enemy fire, and it looked as if the attack had been contained. Meanwhile, on the northern side of Fly Half, 4 Platoon, coming up on the left of 5 Platoon, also came under heavy fire. The platoon commander, Lieutenant Andrew Bickerdike, was shot through the thigh and, although he continued to fire his weapon, he was effectively out of action. Sergeant Ian McKay took over command, gathering a number of men for an assault on a heavy machine gun that formed the core of the

enemy position. This HMG was situated in a well-built sangar (shelter) and protected by several riflemen who covered all approaches. Sergeant McKay led the charge, continuing alone when the two men with him were hit. On reaching the sangar, he threw grenades to destroy the machine gun, only to be killed at the moment of victory. He was later awarded a richly-deserved Victoria Cross.

But McKay's sacrifice, although an inspiration to 4 Platoon, did not break the enemy's resistance and, as Argentinian soldiers continued to lay down a withering fire, the battle degenerated into a slogging match in which all the reserves of discipline and training of the paras had to be brought to bear. They had secured a hold on the objective but enemy fire, particularly from Full Back, was effectively pinning down both A and B Companies. Colonel Pike, moving forward to see for himself, ordered A Company to fight through to Full Back as a priority. They fought a slow, systematic battle, well supported by GPMGs and artillery in the face of very heavy and accurate machine-gun fire from rocks above the grassy saddle between Fly Half and Full Back. The impact of artillery, mortars and machine guns, and the stunning effect of Milan, Carl Gustav anti-tank weapons and 66mm LAWs at short range – exploited with grim, dogged courage by small groups of soldiers using rifles, grenades and bayonets at close quarters – proved too much for the Argentinians, although it was already daylight before Full Back was finally secure.

The scene at dawn on 12 June was a memorable one. Groups of young paras, grim-faced, shocked but determined, moved through the mist with their bayonets fixed to check the enemy dead. The debris of battle was scattered along the length of the mountain; the sour and distinctive odour of death lingered in the nostrils. As temporary graves were dug for the enemy dead, 3 Para began to realise the full implications of their victory: the battle, although costly (23 men killed and 47 wounded), had cracked open the outer ring of defences around Port Stanley, leaving the way clear for the second phase of the assault, against Wireless Ridge, Mount Tumbledown and Mount William.

This was by no means a walkover, however, and the fighting on 13/14 June was to be as hard as any so far encountered. 2 Para, the only Falklands battalion to be committed to battle twice, was ordered to attack Wireless Ridge, having recovered from its experience at Goose Green. Under a replacement CO, Lieutenant-Colonel David Chaundler, the battalion had been flown forward from Goose Green to Bluff Cove and Fitzroy on the southern coast of East Falkland as soon as elements of 5 Infantry Brigade arrived to relieve them on 3 June. Three days later they were relieved again, this time by the Scots Guards, and on the 11th were flown north to prepare for their assault on Port Stanley. Advancing towards Wireless Ridge during the night of 11/12 June, they witnessed 3 Para's fight for Mount Longdon and, at first light, were given details of their own objective. Initially planned for the night of 12/13 June, the attack was postponed to allow existing gains to be consolidated and artillery stockpiles renewed.

Colonel Chaundler therefore enjoyed time to prepare his attack in detail. Liaising with Colonel Pike and aware of the problems experienced by his own battalion at Goose Green, he decided to

Left: A wounded para is brought in for casualty evacuation during the fighting on Mount Longdon.

Below: 2 Para advanced from Moody Brook on 14 June and were the first British unit to enter Port Stanley after the surrender of the Argentinians.

avoid a silent approach, preferring to utilise all available fire support – two batteries of 105mm artillery, the frigate HMS *Ambuscade*, the mortars of 3 Para and the Scorpion and Scimitar light tanks of The Blues and Royals – to create a noisy, awe-inspiring shock effect. Thus, when the paras moved forward to their FUPs (forming-up positions) at last light on 13 June, they did so behind a fierce preliminary bombardment which kept the enemy's heads down and the opposing fire remarkably light. At 0045 on the 14th, D Company opened the assault, advancing towards Hill X to the north of the main ridge-line, and the objective was

quickly overrun. This allowed Chaundler to shift his firepower to support A and B Companies as they pushed south from the Lower Pass towards the north spur of Wireless Ridge. Argentinian artillery zeroed in on the advancing companies, inflicting some casualties, but when the paras rushed forward, they found the enemy sangars unmanned.

There was now a pause in the battle as 2 Para prepared for its next move. This began at 0245 when C Company moved east to take out reported positions on the Murrell river, but once again the weight of fire support had proved too much and the company, led by Major Roger Jenner (who had been wounded at Goose Green but had refused to be evacuated), soon gained ground. Meanwhile D Company, in a wide outflanking march, had approached the ridge from the direction of Hill X, gaining a foothold preparatory to a sweep east along the summit to roll up the enemy positions, liberally supported by artillery and mortars. Indeed, back on the mortar line, the paras' mortar crews were making herculean efforts to keep their weapons in action on soft ground: so as not to let their comrades down, they had to stand on the baseplates while the mortars were fired and four men suffered broken ankles. But it was all worth while for, despite some problems with British artillery shells dropping short, D Company quickly rolled up the enemy line, fighting off a half-hearted Argentinian counter-attack (the only one of the entire war) as the first streaks of dawn lit the sky. By then Wireless Ridge was firmly in British hands, at a cost of three paras killed and 11 wounded.

As dawn broke, the paras were witness to a spectacular sight – the bulk of the Argentinian army, broken by battle, was streaming back in disorder towards Port Stanley. Chaundler received permission to order pursuit and, in an impromptu gesture, helmets were discarded and crumpled red berets proudly put on. With the light tanks of the Blues and Royals in attendance, 2 Para marched down towards the Falklands capital. Fittingly, they were the first to arrive. It was a memorable end to a remarkable campaign in which the paras, once again, had displayed all the attributes of a great fighting force.

THE ROYAL MARINES

The Royal Marine Corps

AS with any elite fighting force, the Royal Marine Commandos have to attract a special type of man – self-disciplined, tough, adaptable and adventurous – but it is the training process that moulds him into a fighting Marine. Before 1970 the initial selection of recruits took place at the Royal Marine Depot at Deal in Kent, where the men were put through a series of preliminary physical and mental tests to gauge their

suitability, but since then the whole process of training has occurred at the Commando Training Centre at Lympstone in Devon.

The training at recruit stage is divided into two parts. Part One, the basic training, is a 12-week course designed to teach rudimentary infantry skills, weapons-handling and how to operate with helicopters and Gemini raiding craft; Part Two, the advanced

History of the Royal Marines

Although members of the present-day Royal Marine Commandos can trace their unit's history back to 1664, when the Duke of York and Albany's Maritime Regiment of Foot was formed to serve aboard Royal Navy ships, the corps did not receive its 'Royal' title until 1802, and was not deployed in the commando role until World War II.

Since 1945 the corps has undergone several reorganisations and has seen extensive service in the infantry role, but it has retained a specialisation in amphibious operations, based upon the original commando idea of seaborne raiding. By the 1960s, with the deployment of special Commando Carriers such as HMS *Albion* and *Bulwark*, each capable of transporting and sustaining a self-contained Commando Group, this idea had been well developed, although in more recent years, reflecting Britain's diminishing global responsibilities and continuing economic problems, it has been gradually undermined. By June 1981, with the government's decision to mothball the landing ships HMS *Fearless* and *Intrepid* and to sell the carrier HMS *Hermes*, many people feared that the flexibility of the commandos had been destroyed, but the success of the Royal Marines in the South Atlantic in 1982 ensured a reprieve.

The Royal Marines are currently organised into 3 Commando Brigade, containing 40, 42 and 45 Commando. Each Commando has a strength of approximately 650 men, and is divided into three rifle companies (each of three troops), a support company and headquarters. The rifle companies are equipped as normal infantry, while support company has mortars, extra machine guns and Milan anti-tank missiles. The brigade is supported by 29 Commando Regiment, Royal Artillery, with 18 105mm Light Guns, 59 Independent Commando Squadron, Royal Engineers, the Commando Logistic Regiment, an air squadron of 18 helicopters and a Blowpipe-equipped air defence troop. More specialist units, attached to the brigade and trained principally for the NATO role, include the Special Boat Squadron, the Mountain and Arctic Warfare Cadre, and the Raiding Squadron. Separate from the brigade is the Comacchio Group, responsible for protecting Britain's North Sea oilrigs against enemy sabotage attacks.

Whatever his unit, however, the individual Marine remains one of the best trained and most professional fighting men in the modern world. With a record of almost continuous active service since 1945 – in Malaya (1948–60), Cyprus (1955–59), Suez (1956), Brunei and Borneo (1962–66), Radfan and Aden (1964–67), Northern Ireland (since 1969) and, of course, the Falklands (1982) – the commandos also enjoy a richly-deserved reputation as an effective instrument of war.

Left: The face of the Royal Marines today – confident and immaculately turned out.

Right: The 81mm L16A1 mortar is a vital component of weaponry currently used by the Royal Marines.

training, lasts a further 10 weeks, during which the weapons instruction becomes more sophisticated and such techniques as amphibious assault, seamanship and cliff-climbing are covered. The training comes to a head in a final exercise which aims to test the skills so far acquired in situations of great personal hardship and stress. Those who complete both parts of the course earn the right to wear the distinctive green beret, after which they will be posted, as riflemen, to an appropriate Commando. Further specialisation – whether as a signaller, sniper, logistician or mountaineer – usually comes after the Marine has seen more basic service and gained invaluable experience.

Throughout the training period the emphasis is upon physical fitness – so much so, that recruits come to fear their instructors and their ceaseless demands for extra effort. During a work-out, an instructor can reduce his squad almost to nervous wrecks as he puts them through their paces, moving from outdoor exercises to the gymnasium and then on to the assault course. The latter consists of obstacles designed for leaping across,

climbing over, crawling under and swinging along, and includes water troughs, brick walls, parallel bars, ropes, nets and concrete tunnels. The aim is to get each recruit to complete a circuit in a given time, eventually in full combat kit and carrying a rifle. As an added refinement the 'Tarzan Course' is also used, involving an 18m slide down a specially-constructed ropeway which tests personal courage as well as stamina and physical fitness.

Nor does the punishment end there, for the recruits then progress to endurance runs, each of 9½km against the clock in full combat gear, at the end of which the would-be commando is expected to fire his rifle accurately at a chosen target. Experience is also gained of 'living rough', spending chilly nights in small tents or specially-constructed bivouacs, and learning the basics of fieldcraft and camouflage. It is an exhausting course, and anyone not up to the required standard will soon find himself homeward bound.

By this stage, the recruits will have been introduced to the standard infantry weapon of the British forces, the 7·62mm SLR (self-loading rifle), and will have fired both the 9mm Sterling SMG (sub-machine gun) and the 7.62mm GPMG (general-purpose machine gun). Once aware of their capabilities, the recruits

next hear and see these weapons fired 'in anger', when they crawl close to the ground as their instructors aim live rounds above their heads: an exercise designed not just to test nerves but also to familiarise the men with the sounds of battle. Instruction is then given in unarmed combat, more advanced fieldcraft and basic tactical skills, and it will be appreciated that a commando is now beginning to emerge. A final exercise to bring these skills together is followed by the proud moment when each recruit receives his own coveted green beret.

However, the training does not end there. Even if the Marine chooses not to specialise, much of his time when not on active service will be spent preparing for or participating in exercises designed to hone his skills to perfection. Since 1970 much of the time has been spent in northern Norway – 42 and 45 Commando, with their support units, exercise there for at least three months every year – gaining experience of living, moving and fighting in the most trying conditions of cold. Here, instructors from the Mountain and Arctic Warfare Cadre come into their own, teaching Marines how to ski, climb and survive in a hostile environment. Other exercise areas have been used – in Sardinia, Greece, Turkey, Canada and Holland – giving the commandos a unique capability over a wide range of geographical conditions. It has not been wasted.

Left: Tackling the assault course and carrying out isometric exercises are instrumental in building up recruits' stamina. The assault course consists of a collection of obstacles which provide experience of climbing over, leaping across, swinging along and crawling under, and include ropes, nets, parallel bars, water troughs and brick walls.

Left: Having led the way through a flooded tunnel, an assault-course instructor grabs a recruit and pulls him into the fresh air.

Brunei and Borneo

It was a beautifully clear, tropical day. At 0600 hours on 11 December 1962, as the early morning sun rose over Brunei airport, Brigadier 'Pat' Patterson, commander of 99 Gurkha Infantry Brigade, greeted Captain Jeremy Moore and the advance party of L Company, 42 Commando, Royal Marines. Perched on the bonnet of his Land Rover, Patterson, head of operations against the North Kalimantan National Army (TNKU) in Brunei, issued clear, precise orders:

'Your company will rescue the hostages in Limbang'.

Situated just across the border in Sarawak, Limbang was a small community 20km up-river from Brunei Town. On 8 December, as part of a co-ordinated attempt to seize political power, the TNKU had moved into Limbang, Seria, Miri and other towns, taking pro-British hostages. A small contingent of Gurkhas had been hurriedly deployed from Singapore; they had managed to fight through to Seria and to secure Brunei Town, but Moore's company – initially no more than 56 men, backed by medium machine guns – was expected to do far more. Speed and surprise were essential, together with

Limbang raid
L Company, 42 Commando, RM
13 December 1962

On 8 December 1962, Indonesian rebels launched a revolt in Brunei aimed ultimately at the creation of a Borneo confederation dominated by neighbouring Indonesia. The rebels moved on key positions in Brunei and in neighbouring parts of Sarawak and North Borneo. In Limbang and Seria the insurgents seized British hostages. Seria was retaken on 10 December — and the stage was set for L Company's daring raid on Limbang.

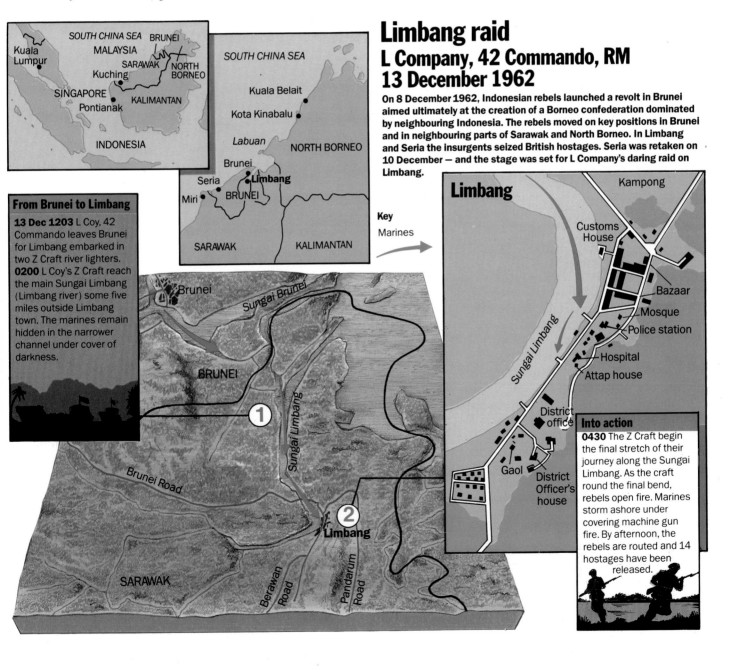

From Brunei to Limbang

13 Dec 1203 L Coy, 42 Commando leaves Brunei for Limbang embarked in two Z Craft river lighters.
0200 L Coy's Z Craft reach the main Sungai Limbang (Limbang river) some five miles outside Limbang town. The marines remain hidden in the narrower channel under cover of darkness.

Key
Marines →

Limbang

Kampong
Customs House
Bazaar
Mosque
Police station
Hospital
Attap house
District office
Gaol
District Officer's house

Into action

0430 The Z Craft begin the final stretch of their journey along the Sungai Limbang. As the craft round the final bend, rebels open fire. Marines storm ashore under covering machine gun fire. By afternoon, the rebels are routed and 14 hostages have been released.

L2A3 Sterling SMG

fore sight assembly

barrel casing

barrel

34-round box magazine

chambered round (fired)

magazine release

cocking handle

sear

bolt

magazine housing

trigger

guard

trigger mechanism

information about the enemy and the provision of suitable river craft. Within less than three hours, preparations were under way for an assault on Limbang at dawn the following day.

Two coastal minesweepers, HMS *Fiskerton* and *Chawton*, sailed in to Brunei later on 11 December, and officers from these ships took charge of two old lighters, or Z Craft, discovered in the harbour. By late afternoon both craft had been overhauled and given rudimentary sandbag protection. Meanwhile Moore was collecting what intelligence he could, but it was sparse. Information on the strength of the enemy in Limbang was virtually non-existent (estimates varied from 30 men to over 100), and no one knew how well-armed they were nor how they were deployed. The only assumption that could be safely made was that the rebels would find it hard to stand against the tough, disciplined Marines of L Company in a close-quarters fight.

In fact, Moore hoped that it would not come to that. He thought he might be able to bluff the rebels into surrendering by a show of force, so avoiding any action that might jeopardise the lives of the hostages. Their rescue was always the first priority, although no one had a clear idea where they were being held in Limbang. Several locations were possible – the police station, the hospital, the

administrative offices or the British Residency – but all were separated by at least 300m, giving ample time for executions to begin if the Marines attacked the wrong place. In the event, Moore decided quite logically that the police station would have been commandeered as the rebel HQ, and he planned to knock that out first. Each Marine was under strict instructions to hold his fire until the rebels opened up.

In order to be off Limbang at dawn, it was necessary to sail at midnight from Brunei Town, giving plenty of time for the assault craft, with their Marine passengers, to negotiate the narrow, complicated channels as far as the Limbang river. At 0003 hours on 12 December, therefore, Lieutenant David Willis, *Chawton*'s first lieutenant, slowly and silently led the way in his Z Craft. By now L Company had been reinforced to about 100 men.

The craft reached the Limbang river at 0200, well ahead of schedule, and rested up until 0430. When they set off again, last-minute preparations were hastily made as the lights of the town hove rapidly into view. Moving forward as quietly as possible, the Marines got to within 300m of the town before it suddenly exploded like a disturbed ants' nest as the rebels woke up. Full-ahead was ordered and the leading craft surged towards the bank, a loud-hailer calling

Above: Captain Jeremy Moore, MC, was the commanding officer of L Company on the Limbang raid. In 1982 he commanded British land forces during the South Atlantic War.

Right: A Marine of 42 Commando at Brunei in 1962. He is wearing the green beret of the Royal Marines and the standard jungle-green uniform issued to men serving in the Far East. Woollen puttees are worn over leather boots with rubber soles. Armament is the British 7.62mm L1A1 rifle with a curved magazine, and the bayonet is worn on his left side.

rear sight assembly

return spring

back cap

safety cam

grip

folding stock

Calibre 9mm
Length (stock extended) 69cm
Weight (loaded) 3.47kg
System of operation blowback
Rate of fire (cyclic) 550rpm
Muzzle velocity 390mps
Range 200m

Above: The L2A3 Sterling sub-machine gun was introduced in 1954 and was accepted by the British Army as a worthy replacement of the trusty Sten. The Sterling has minimal recoil and can be fired either from the shoulder with the stock extended, or from a crouching position with the folded stock resting in the pit of the stomach. The weapon is generally preferred only for close-quarter fighting over a range of 30m, beyond which the stopping power is uncertain.

for surrender. At this, a storm of fire came down, to be answered by an immediate response from the Marines. By the time the leading craft had beached about 30m from the police station some 20 seconds later, it was clear that L Company had the fire advantage, especially when they used the Vickers medium machine guns.

Two Marines from the leading section were killed and a number wounded, even before they reached dry land, but No 5 Troop stormed ashore, clearing the approaches to the police station in its stride. Corporal Bill Lester took his section across the road, mopping up and providing a cut-off to the rear. Meanwhile, its coxswain wounded, the leading Z Craft had drifted off the bank, and although Lieutenant Willis immediately took the wheel, by the time he had righted the situation, he was 150m further downstream. Moore had no choice but to commit his reserve section to take attention away from the now-isolated men around the police station, and they moved steadily north, denying the enemy use of the jungle fringe. The reserve section reached the hospital, only to encounter a group of determined rebels, who opened up, killing the troop sergeant and two Marines. This hardened the hearts of the survivors, who swept through the area with force, eliminating the rebel group. Through the sounds of

Above: Marines of 42 Commando check their kit and prepare themselves for battle.

battle came English voices, singing unharmoniously: the main party of hostages had been found.

During all this, the second Z Craft had been manoeuvring in the fast-flowing river to give supporting fire. It now came ashore to land its Marine sections, before resuming its former station. Moore, with most of his company available, concentrated on clearing the town entirely. A number of rebels were routed by 5 Troop around Attap House, while 6 Troop cleared the police station building and 4 Troop moved north into the bazaar. Rebel defences collapsed, and although sniping was to continue, the battle was effectively over. As the Marines consolidated their gains, the town was thoroughly searched until a total of 14 hostages had been found. They, together with the wounded, were hurriedly put on board the Z Craft and the Marines re-embarked. Returning at speed to Brunei Town, Moore assessed

the operation: at a cost of five Marines killed and five wounded, the hostages had been saved and a substantial enemy force (estimated later to comprise 350 men) defeated. It was a classic rescue mission.

Although actions such as this broke the back of the rebellion in Brunei, this proved to be merely a precursor to a more general threat to British interests in Borneo as a whole, initiated by Indonesia. Between 1963 and 1966, as Indonesian troops and their local supporters attacked British outposts on the borders of Sabah and Sarawak, the Royal Marines were inevitably drawn in. Both 40 and 42 Commando saw extensive service during the 'Confrontation', mounting long, exhausting patrols through mangrove swamps, thick jungle and rugged mountains in search of the enemy. Some remarkable successes were achieved: in February 1964, for example, L Company of 42 Commando, the victors of Limbang, joined B Company of the 1st Battalion, 2nd Goorkha Rifles, in an extensive search mission (Operation Dragon's Teeth) against an Indonesian incursion in the Lundu district of Borneo, killing five of the enemy and capturing a further four. Even as late as March 1966, within months of the end of the Confrontation, actions were still being fought, giving the Royal Marines a continuity of jungle and riverine experience that was unmatched elsewhere in the British forces.

Jungle fighting, however, is only one of the skills of the modern Marine that has been proved in battle. In April and May 1964, 45 Commando operated alongside 3 Para in the unforgiving terrain of the Radfan, remaining in the area long after the paras had gone; both 42 and 45 Commando served in the rabbit-warren of Aden Town in 1967; and since 1969 all Marine units have seen action in Northern Ireland. Add to this the role of the Marines in UN peacekeeping operations in Cyprus and the constant training in arctic warfare that has taken place since 1970, and some idea of the very wide range of Commando activities may be gauged. It was all brought together in 1982 in the Falklands, where 3 Commando Brigade proved its worth as a highly-trained, infinitely adaptable and extremely tough fighting force.

South Atlantic War

The Royal Marines were the first British troops to be involved in the Falklands War when, on 2 April 1982, Naval Party 8901 – 67 Marines responsible for garrisoning the islands – faced the full force of an Argentinian invasion. Commanded by Major Mike Norman, they fought a gallant but hopeless battle around Government House, being forced to accept the humiliation of surrender when it was obvious they were overwhelmingly outnumbered. Twenty-four hours later, Lieutenant Keith Mills and a detachment of 22 Marines displayed similar resolve on the island of South Georgia, giving up only after downing a Puma helicopter, damaging an Alouette and even engaging an enemy frigate, all with little more than smallarms fire.

Britain's response was immediate. Within hours of the news of the invasion, a special Task Force was formed, the military element of which was 3 Commando Brigade, commanded by Brigadier Julian Thompson and comprising 40, 42 and 45 Commando, Royal Marines, their support services – 29 Commando Regiment, Royal Artillery; 59 Independent Commando Squadron, Royal Engineers; the Commando Logistic Regiment, Royal Marines; 3 Commando Brigade Air Squadron, RM: Raiding Squadron, RM; Air Defence Troop; and Assault Squadrons, RM – and, as a temporary reinforcement, 2 and 3 Para. All set sail from British ports in early April. The only exception was M Company, 42 Commando, flown straight down to Ascension Island to join a naval task group charged with the recapture of South Georgia. Spearheaded by 2 SBS and D Squadron, 22 SAS, M Company went ashore by helicopter on 25 April, seizing Grytviken and Leith from an Argentinian garrison shocked by the crippling of the submarine *Santa Fe* by missile-armed helicopters. Despite a host of practical problems and appalling weather conditions, the liberation of the island was a morale-boosting success, serving notice that the Marines, Arctic-trained, superbly fit and eager for a fight, had arrived.

All other elements of 3 Commando Brigade went ashore at San Carlos on East Falkland on 21 May, carving out a beach-head which proved that the Marines had lost none of their amphibious-warfare skills. They then had to endure the frustrating business of digging in and watching the Argentinian air attacks on shipping in San Carlos Water, but plans for a breakout were being made. On 26 May Lieutenant-Colonel Andrew Whitehead, commanding 45 Commando, was ordered to gather his men for an advance on foot to Douglas Settlement and Teal Inlet on the northeast coast, in conjunction with 3 Para. As the paras 'tabbed', so the Marines 'yomped' the 35km to their objective over waterlogged, broken ground, carrying everything on their backs. With reconnaissance teams in front and to the flanks, the Commando was spread out by companies over a distance of nearly 3km, but the move was a major success. At 0200 on 28 May, Whitehead paused to regroup at New

Above: Major Guy Sheridan, second-in-command of 42 Commando during the South Atlantic War. He commanded the landing forces that took back South Georgia from the Argentinian invaders.

Below: After the landing on South Georgia, a Marine takes a break in the vicinity of Grytviken.

House, before pushing on to enter Douglas Settlement at 1600. The Argentinians had already left, enabling the Marines to advance across rivers and inlets to Teal, where they arrived shortly after midnight on 30/31 May. There they dug in, patrolled forward and waited for further orders. By then, 42 Commando, under Lieutenant-Colonel Nick Vaux, had been flown from San Carlos to seize the summit of Mount Kent, from where the lights of Port Stanley could be clearly seen. 40 Commando, much to its chagrin, was left behind to protect San Carlos.

While this was going on, the Royal Marines Mountain and Arctic Warfare Cadre, a small group of specialists under Captain Rod Boswell, had been scouting forward, conducting covert observation of enemy positions. By 30 May they had been on the go for nearly 10 days and were desperately tired, when Boswell suddenly received a radio report that one of his patrols – four men under Lieutenant Frazer Haddow – had spotted 16 men of the Argentinian Special Forces (602 Company) making their way to a deserted farm building called Top Malo House. Boswell's first thought was an airstrike, but no Harriers were available, so he turned instead to his own resources.

Gathering a total of 19 of his men together, he gained the use of a single Sea King helicopter, which dropped the group some distance away from Top Malo at 1230 on 31 May. Moving silently forward, the Marines – divided into a fire group and an assault group – achieved complete surprise. The assault was short and sharp, and although three Marines were wounded, the enemy force was destroyed, losing five men killed and the

Above: Marines of Naval Party 8901 – the original Falklands garrison, which had to face the Argentinian invasion – prepare to raise the flag of the Governor of the Falkland Islands after the Argentinians had surrendered.

remainder captured, many with gunshot wounds. As the only occasion during the war that special forces from both sides clashed, it was a sign for all to see that the Marines had the edge as fighting men.

On 3 June, 45 Commando moved forward again, this time to occupy positions on the western slopes of Mount Kent, supporting 42 Commando which was still on the summit, with companies further out on neighbouring Mount Challenger. The two Commandos, together with 3 Para, were charged with mounting attacks on the outer ring of Argentinian defences around Port Stanley, scheduled for the night of 11/12 June. As 42 Commando assaulted Mount Harriet, 45 Commando advanced on Two Sisters and 3 Para attacked Mount Longdon, it was hoped that the enemy would be dealt a concerted blow from which he would not recover.

Colonel Vaux had been told that his objective was Mount Harriet while 42 Commando was enduring the bitter cold on top of Mounts Kent and Challenger in early June, and he was well aware of the difficulties of terrain. Mount Harriet rose approximately 300m above the plateau skirting Harriet Sound. Along its base

ran the track between Port Stanley and Goose Green, and the mountain itself was divided from Challenger by a rocky chasm, across which enemy troops could be seen from observation posts on a jumble of crags called Wall Mountain. The main problem was that enemy minefields had been strewn liberally along the likely approaches to Mount Harriet and heavy machine guns were known to be covering the forward slopes; at the same time, ground to the south was ominously open, while the area to the north, close to Two Sisters, was too near to 45 Commando's area of operations. In such circumstances, Vaux decided on an unorthodox approach from the rear along a route laboriously recced by Sergeant Collins of K Company. That still left the problem of protection, particularly if the night was clear, and 42 Commando worked out an elaborate fireplan, whereby major firefights would be simulated to force the enemy to reveal his positions, upon which illuminants would bathe the area and allow Milan operators to locate appropriate targets for their missiles.

On the afternoon of 11 June Vaux gave his final orders and his companies, guided by men of the Reconnaissance

Below: Royal Marines of 42 Commando during the famous 'yomp' over the barren landscape of East Falkland, heading for Port Stanley.

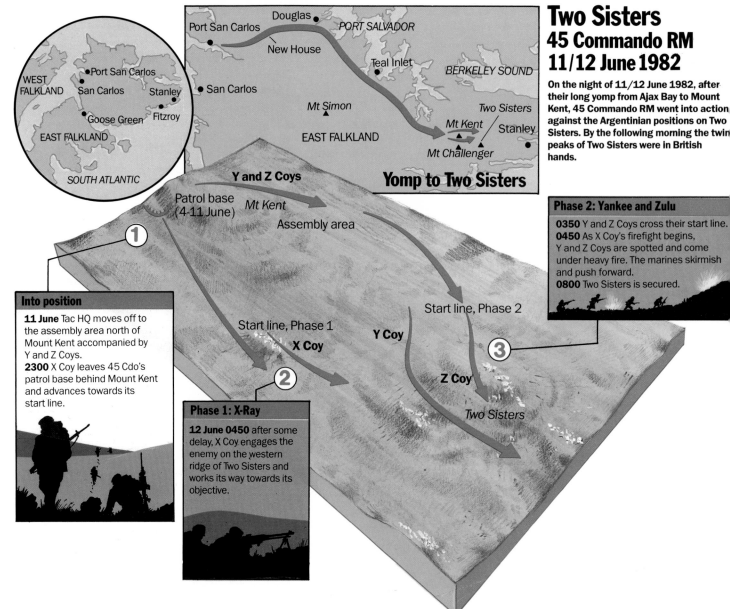

Port San Carlos
Douglas
PORT SALVADOR
New House
Teal Inlet
BERKELEY SOUND
San Carlos
Mt Simon
Two Sisters
Mt Kent
Stanley
EAST FALKLAND
Mt Challenger

Yomp to Two Sisters

WEST FALKLAND
Port San Carlos
San Carlos
Stanley
Goose Green
Fitzroy
EAST FALKLAND
SOUTH ATLANTIC

Two Sisters
45 Commando RM
11/12 June 1982

On the night of 11/12 June 1982, after their long yomp from Ajax Bay to Mount Kent, 45 Commando RM went into action against the Argentinian positions on Two Sisters. By the following morning the twin peaks of Two Sisters were in British hands.

Y and Z Coys
Patrol base (4-11 June)
Mt Kent
Assembly area

①

Phase 2: Yankee and Zulu

0350 Y and Z Coys cross their start line.
0450 As X Coy's firefight begins, Y and Z Coys are spotted and come under heavy fire. The marines skirmish and push forward.
0800 Two Sisters is secured.

Into position

11 June Tac HQ moves off to the assembly area north of Mount Kent accompanied by Y and Z Coys.
2300 X Coy leaves 45 Cdo's patrol base behind Mount Kent and advances towards its start line.

Start line, Phase 1
X Coy

Y Coy

Start line, Phase 2

③

Z Coy

Two Sisters

②

Phase 1: X-Ray

12 June 0450 after some delay, X Coy engages the enemy on the western ridge of Two Sisters and works its way towards its objective.

Troop and accompanied by engineers, artillery observers, snipers, medics and signallers, filed out, menacingly silhouetted in the waning light. Each man was camouflaged, blacked up, bowed down with ammunition and equipment, and festooned with deadly weapons. Several hours later they stood shivering at the FUP (forming-up point), waiting to follow the route mapped out by Collins. By 0200 on the 12th they were ready. K Company under Captain Peter Babbington led the way and, as the planned diversions attracted enemy attention, they advanced undetected towards their objectives on the Stanley side of Mount Harriet. Babbington's leading troop pushed forward about 700m before making contact, and by then

his men were almost on top of the bewildered Argentinians, who were quickly overwhelmed. As the defences began to crumble, the Marines leapfrogged in groups along the spine of the ridge, using 66mm light or 84mm medium anti-tank weapons with fearful effects among the rocks. L Company followed up on the western side of Mount Harriet, but soon came under heavy fire which caused a number of casualties. For a while the enemy seemed to rally, only to wilt again in the face of superior courage and resolution by the Marines.

As reports came in of success elsewhere – by 45 Commando on Two Sisters and 3 Para on Mount Longdon – Vaux ordered his men to dig in and

Above: Lieutenant-Colonel Andrew Whitehead, commanding officer of 45 Commando, Royal Marines, during the South Atlantic War.

Below: Argentinian prisoners, under the watchful eye of Marine guards, sit and await repatriation in Port Stanley. The sun may be shining in a clear sky here but the cold winds blowing from the Antarctic kept the temperatures well down.

prepare for possible counterattack. None materialised: instead, as Vaux took his Tac HQ to the summit, he passed dazed groups of prisoners, walking wounded and all the grim testimony of the recent fighting. Even so, the attack had not been costly: for the loss of one man killed and 13 wounded, a key feature had been taken, together with nearly 300 prisoners.

In the meantime, 45 Commando had achieved a similar victory on Two Sisters, which had been assigned as their objective on 7 June. During much of the next four nights, patrols went out to probe at enemy defences and to build up a picture of what to expect. Some of these patrols were spectacularly successful, catching the Argentinians by surprise and inflicting a number of casualties before fighting their way off the position, sometimes in broad daylight. By 10 June, 45 had the moral ascendancy and Colonel Whitehead had finalised his plan of attack.

Orders were given out on the morning of 11 June and by late afternoon Tac HQ, plus Y and Z Companies, were moving around the north side of Mount Kent to an assembly area from which a two-phase attack would take place that night. X Company remained where it was, since it was to carry out the first of these phases – attacking due east onto the nearer of the two peaks. As the companies formed up, the battery commander of 7 (Sphinx) Battery, 29 Commando Regiment, prepared his fireplan, mortars were moved to bring them within range of the objective and engineer reconnaissance parties searched for mines. The team of 45 Commando Group was working well.

The plan was simple. X Company would attack the western 'Sister' at 0100 on 12 June from the west, followed two hours later by Y and Z Companies from the northwest onto the eastern peak. The attack was to be a silent one, with guns and mortars being used only if surprise was lost. Radio silence was imposed and, as it grew dark, the Marines of Y and Z Companies, accompanied by the Reconnaissance Troop, began the 5km approach march. They moved out at 2300 on the 11th, pushing their way carefully over rocky terrain, and arrived at their FUP at 0255, having heard nothing of X Company's attack. Fortunately X

Company's commander ignored the orders about radio silence to inform Colonel Whitehead that he had been unduly delayed by the terrain. Y and Z Companies had to wait.

By 0350, however, Whitehead could afford to delay no longer. He ordered his assault to go in and, to his amazement, the Marines were able to get within 450m of the enemy without being spotted. At this point, two things happened simultaneously: away to the left, X Company became engaged in a sharp firefight, while on the eastern Sister, Y and Z Companies came under fire from mortars, 0·5in machine guns and smallarms. The battle had begun.

For 15–20 minutes it was a ding-dong firefight, until the Marines of Z Company began to gather momentum, skirmishing forward in textbook fashion. Y Company on the right came driving in, swinging east and moving to the extreme end of the feature, clearing the enemy as they went. X Company, supported by Milan missiles, reached the summit of the western Sister, finishing off an Argentinian machine gun that had been causing problems. By first light the feature was in British hands. Prisoners were being rounded up, ammunition redistributed and casualty reports made. It could have been worse: for the loss of four dead and 10 wounded, 45 Commando had made a major contribution to eventual victory.

Neither Commando saw action again before the Argentinian surrender on 14 June, but it was already clear that as a fighting force they were virtually unstoppable. From the initial, unequal, fight in early April, through the recapture of South Georgia, the amphibious landing at San Carlos, the move eastwards and the battles around Port Stanley, the green beret had been to the fore, proving the worth of all the training, specialist skills and co-operation involved in the Commando concept. The fact that in the aftermath of the war 3 Commando Brigade was retained with all its support services – something that had seemed threatened since the Defence Review of June 1981 – showed that, as an out-of-area force as well as a NATO force, the Royal Marines were still an integral and important part of Britain's defences.

THE GUARDS

The Household Cavalry and the Guards Division

IT was a bright moonlit night, with a deep frost, as the Scimitar light tank moved forward into battle. The atmosphere was quite eerie, with the intermittent chatter of distant machine guns and the sudden flashes of bursting illuminants. The only movement came from little groups of stretcher-bearers, dark figures against the white carpet of frost, carrying their sad loads. It was more like a scene from World War I than the Falklands campaign of the 1980s.

History of the Guards

The Household Cavalry and the Guards are among the oldest regiments in the British Army, most of them tracing their origins back to the mid-17th century, before the establishment of a regular, standing force. They have always constituted an elite, having as their main task the protection of the ruling monarch and the Royal Family.

By the time of the Restoration in 1660, King Charles II had at his disposal troops of Horse and Horse Grenadier Guards (amalgamated in 1788 to form The Life Guards) and two regiments of Foot Guards – the 1st (later the Grenadier) Guards and the 2nd or Coldstream Guards. A Scottish Regiment of Foot Guards was added in 1666, and at the beginning of the 19th century the Royal Horse Guards (The Blues) officially joined the Household Cavalry, having existed as a separate entity for over 100 years. In 1900 a regiment of Irish Guards was added to the list, and the Foot Guards were completed 15 years later with the raising of the Welsh Guards. In 1969 the Royal Horse Guards were amalgamated with the 1st or Royal Dragoons to form The Blues and Royals, and they, together with The Life Guards, now constitute the Household Cavalry, being trained and equipped primarily as armoured regiments.

Most people associate the Guards, cavalry as well as infantry, with ceremonial duties in London, little realising that they are, first and foremost, fighting soldiers with a tradition that is second to none. Throughout the history of the British Army, the Guards have played a crucial role: at Waterloo in 1815, for example, it was the Foot Guards who held the key position of Hougoumont farmhouse against repeated French attacks, while the Life Guards, Royal Horse Guards and Royal Dragoons all took part in charges which helped to break Napoleon's resolve. In the Crimean War (1854–56), Foot Guard battalions saw hard service, and the same was true of all Guards units in both world wars of the present century. Nor has the Guards' experience been restricted to major battles: since 1945 units have regularly served in a variety of trouble-spots – in Malaya (1948–60), in the Middle East and, more recently and much nearer home, in Northern Ireland since 1969. Thus, when the Falklands War occurred in 1982, it was only natural that the Guards should be called upon to take part, represented by two troops of Blues and Royals (as part of 3 Commando Brigade) and both the 2nd Battalion Scots and 1st Battalion Welsh Guards (as part of 5 Infantry Brigade). Their record of bravery, fortitude and fighting skill showed that the traditions were still intact.

Left: A trooper of the Blues and Royals in ceremonial dress.

As part of 3 Troop, Blues and Royals, the Scimitar was providing vital fire support for 2 Para's assault on Wireless Ridge during the push to recapture Port Stanley on the night of 13/14 June 1982. The Blues and Royals had been involved in the campaign from the start; in early April, when news of the Argentinian invasion first broke, the regiment had been ordered to provide two 14-man reconnaissance troops for deployment with the Task Force. Under temporary command of 3 Commando Brigade, 3 and 4 Troops of B Squadron, each with two Scorpions (armed with 76mm anti-tank guns) and two Scimitars (with 30mm Rarden cannon), supported by a single Samson recovery vehicle, travelled to the South Atlantic and went ashore at San Carlos on East Falkland with the first wave of liberating forces on 21 May.

At first there seemed little to do – senior commanders clearly doubted the ability of the tracked vehicles to cope with the bogs, marshes and rocky terrain of the island – but during the breakout from the beach-head in late May the Blues and Royals soon proved their value. The relative ease with which Lieutenant Mark Coreth's 4 Troop supported 3 Para on the march to Teal Inlet, reinforced by Lieutenant Lord Robin Innes-Ker's 3 Troop escorting Brigade HQ along the same difficult route, dispelled any remaining doubts. Indeed, when elements of the newly-arrived 5 Infantry Brigade began to push forward along the southern coast in early June, it was decided to order both troops to cross the central range of hills on East Falkland to link up with them at Bluff Cove. On the map, the going looked almost impossible and the light tanks were given two days to complete the journey. They actually made it in just six hours, much to the relief of the commander of 5 Infantry Brigade, who described their arrival:

'I never expected to see them make it so quickly. . . . I looked up and saw them winding down the side of the mountain towards us, their leading vehicles mud-spattered and rain-soaked and their commanders half-frozen in their turrets. It was one of those moments I am not likely to forget.'

The Blues and Royals were now operating with fellow guardsmen of the

2nd Battalion, Scots Guards, and 1st Battalion, Welsh Guards, some of whom were still being ferried round by sea from San Carlos. The process had begun on the night of 5/6 June, when 600 Scots Guards had left San Carlos aboard the assault ship HMS *Fearless*, but it was not going smoothly. Appalling weather conditions, coupled with the need to withdraw *Fearless* as soon as it became light, had forced the guardsmen to endure seven hours in open LCUs (Landing Craft, Utility) before reaching Bluff Cove, and the arrival of the main body of the Welsh Guards was delayed by the need to divert shipping elsewhere. On 7 June the Blues and Royals supported the Scots Guards as they set up a forward patrol base at Port Harriet House, returning to Fitzroy in time to witness the horrifying Argentinian air attack on the logistic landing ships *Sir Galahad* and *Sir Tristram* on the 8th. By the end of the day, in a cruel baptism of fire, the Welsh Guards had lost 33 men killed and, to all intents and purposes, were temporarily out of action.

This left the Scots Guards and Blues and Royals to carry out the southern part of the plan to close in on Port Stanley, although in the event the latter were split up, with 3 Troop moving back to the north to support 2 Para in the assault on Wireless Ridge. The Scots Guards retained 4 Troop for their attack on the difficult and well-defended Mount Tumbledown. Both attacks were

scheduled for the night of 12/13 June, only to be postponed for 24 hours because of a shortage of helicopters. The CO of the Scots Guards, Lieutenant-Colonel Mike Scott, was quite relieved; the original plan had been for an assault at first light against the mountain's southern slopes, and it was obvious that well-sited machine guns in that area would wreak havoc on the advancing guardsmen. Using the delay to persuade his superiors to authorise a night assault from the west, covered by a diversionary attack from the south, Colonel Scott briefed his officers in detail and prepared for a difficult battle.

Above: Spattered with mud, a Scorpion light tank of the Blues and Royals moves towards Moody Brook, just 3km west of Port Stanley.

Final orders were issued at 1400 hours on 13 June. All three companies of the battalion were to advance down Goat Ridge while a special assault force, spearheaded by the Reconnaissance Platoon and commanded by Major Nicholas Bethell (just back from a tour with the SAS), tied down the Argentinians in the south. They would then be withdrawn, leaving G Company to consolidate positions in the western sector of Tumbledown, with Left Flank Company moving through against the main part of the mountain and Right Flank Company finishing the job against the southern defences. The Blues and Royals would concentrate initially on supporting Major Bethell, then be available for general back-up as the battle demanded.

The attack was to begin at 2100 hours, preceded by Major Bethell's diversionary assault. This began at 2030, with the guardsmen advancing through a hail of machine-gun and artillery fire towards the Argentinian defensive positions. The going was poor and, with two men killed and 10 wounded during a two-hour engagement, the cost was high, but the enemy's attention had been diverted at a crucial time.

This enabled G Company to move forward at 2100 against fairly light opposition to seize their objectives without loss. Ninety minutes later, Left Flank under Major John Kiszely passed through and the battle began in earnest. As the two lead platoons advanced, they came under increasingly heavy and accurate fire from enemy sangars (shelters) well-sited among the rocks of Tumbledown and manned by members of the crack 5th Marines. Despite using 66mm and 84mm rocket launchers as well as M79 grenade launchers, the Scots Guards soon ground to a halt, pinned down in exposed positions. All they could do was to wait for artillery support.

When this materialised at 0230 on the 14th, Kiszely ordered Lieutenant Mitchell's platoon to attack the first ridge. With fixed bayonets, the guardsmen charged up the slope, closely followed by Kiszely and company headquarters. They made it to the ridge and then began a confused series of small fights from crag to crag. Determined to maintain the momentum, Kiszely led the attack on the next ridge, surprising the Argentinians with a superb display of courage backed by rifles, grenades and bayonets. As the assault continued, the need to clear enemy bunkers and guard an increasing number of prisoners depleted Left Flank's strength so that when Kiszely finally reached the summit of Tumbledown he had only six men still with him, three of whom were wounded almost immediately by long-range machine-gun fire. The rest only just managed to keep hold of the ridge until reinforcements arrived in the form of Right Flank under Major Simon Price. They pushed forward onto the southern slopes, fighting a fragmented battle with Argentinians still prepared to hold on, and it was not until 0815 that all objectives had been seized. The Scots Guards had lost nine men dead and 41 wounded, but were rewarded with the unforgettable sight of the enemy streaming back towards Port Stanley in obvious disorder.

Tumbledown was a soldier's battle, fought hand-to-hand in difficult terrain, and once it began, the Blues and Royals had not been able to offer direct support. The same was not true further north, where 3 Troop had advanced with 2 Para onto Wireless Ridge for a night battle characterised by its heavy weight of supporting fire. Lieutenant Innes-Ker conducted a forward recce on foot late on 13 June, locating good fire positions for his light tanks less than 300m from the enemy, and throughout the night he had been able to 'zap' Argentinian defences using passive night-sights on his cannon. By first light on the 14th, the Blues and Royals too were relieved to see the enemy in full flight and, with paras in attendance, the men of 3 Troop were the first to re-enter Port Stanley. The campaign was over and, as so often in history, the Guards had played an integral part in achieving a memorable

victory, in this case providing a combination of mobility, firepower and professional fighting skills in some of the toughest battles of the war. Casualties had not been light (particularly among the Welsh Guards, who advanced onto Mount William on 14 June without meeting any opposition from the enemy, who had pulled back to Port Stanley), but no one could doubt that the Guards were still a formidable fighting force.

Above: This man of the Scots Guards wears a variety of winter clothes in standard British Army DPM for service in the Falklands. He is dressed in cold-weather overtrousers and over his parka is a nylon waterproof jacket with characteristic bright colouring. Fixed to his 7.62mm SLR is the Individual Weapon Sight Type SS20, used for intensifying images in low-light conditions and thereby sighting targets up to a range of 700m.

THE GURKHAS

The Brigade of Gurkhas

ON 21 November 1965, C Company and elements of Support Company of the 2nd Battalion, 10th Gurkha Rifles, moved silently along a knife-edged ridge towards an Indonesian outpost on top of a high hill near Serikan on the Sarawak–Kalimantan border in Borneo. By superb fieldcraft, the leading section reached a point barely 20m from the enemy when, suddenly, a machine gun opened up, wounding one of the leading group. The

section commander, Lance-Corporal Rambahadur Limbu, rushed forward and killed the Indonesian machine gunner, only to attract heavy fire from elsewhere. Two of his men were hit, going down in exposed positions. Having led the other men to a position of relative safety, Rambahadur concentrated on the rescue of his fallen comrades. His first attempt to crawl forward was met by heavy and accurate fire, so he decided that speed was his only chance. In a series of short dashes, he reached one of the wounded riflemen; covered by fire from his section, the young NCO carried him to safety.

The Indonesians were ready for his second rescue bid, but Rambahadur did not hesitate. After one short sprint he was pinned down for some minutes by intense fire, but once again he dashed forward before hurling himself down by the side of the second wounded man. Picking him up, he ran back through a hail of enemy bullets and by some miracle arrived unscathed. For his selfless gallantry, Rambahadur was awarded the Victoria Cross. It was an action in the best Gurkha tradition.

Gurkhas had been deployed to Borneo three years earlier when, on 8 December 1962, 4000 men of the North Kalimantan National Army (TNKU) in Brunei rose in rebellion against the proposed inclusion of their small state in the British-sponsored Federation of Malaysia. Hostages were taken and the rule of the Sultan threatened, but swift action by men of the 1st Battalion, 2nd Goorkha Rifles, dispatched from Singapore, had saved the day. Arriving in small parties by air, HQ, C Company and two platoons of D Company took the initiative without delay, shooting their way towards Seria through patches of dense jungle to relieve a number of embattled police posts. They then retired to secure Brunei Town and await reinforcements. By the end of the month, the revolt was effectively over.

History of the Gurkhas

Between 1814 and 1816, troops of the British East India Company fought a bitter war in the mountains of Nepal, on the northern borders of India. Their enemies were Gurkhas – small, tough hillmen, adept at fighting in difficult terrain – and, despite the fact that they were eventually defeated by the British, the latter were so impressed that they immediately raised four battalions of Gurkhas to serve the Company. The first Gurkha force to fight for Britain was the Sirmoor Battalion, in the Mahratta War of 1817, and throughout the 19th century the Gurkhas, conventionally equipped except for their distinctive kukri or curved fighting knife, helped to defend British interests throughout India.

In 1903 all the regiments of the 'Gurkha Brigade' were named 'Rifles' and numbered one to ten. During World War I over 200,000 recruits were raised in Nepal, seeing service in all theatres, and in World War II the pattern was much the same, with a total of 40 battalions made available. The cost was high – in the two wars together, more than 45,000 casualties were sustained – but the fighting spirit and courage of the Gurkhas was widely recognised, not least by the award of 12 Victoria Crosses.

When India and Pakistan gained their independence in 1947, the Gurkhas faced the prospect of either continuing to serve Britain or becoming part of the new Indian Army. In the event, six of the ten regiments joined the Indian Army, leaving Britain with a brigade of four, soon to be supported by its own engineers, signals and service personnel. For a time, a Gurkha Independent Parachute Company and a contingent of Gurkha Military Police also existed. After service in the Malayan Emergency (1948–60), the Brunei Revolt (1962) and the Borneo Confrontation (1963–66), the brigade was retitled a 'field force' in 1975 and given specific responsibility for Hong Kong, with single battalions detached to Brunei and the United Kingdom. In 1982, it was the battalion stationed in the United Kingdom which sailed down to the South Atlantic and fought in the Falklands War. In 1986, over 8000 Gurkhas were in British service, comprising six infantry battalions – 1st and 2nd Battalions, 2nd King Edward VII's Own Goorkhas (The Sirmoor Rifles), 1st Battalion, 6th Queen Elizabeth's Own Gurkha Rifles, 1st and 2nd Battalions, 7th Duke of Edinburgh's Own Gurkha Rifles, and 1st Battalion, 10th Princess Mary's Own Gurkha Rifles – backed by a Gurkha Engineer Field Regiment, a Gurkha Signals Regiment and a Gurkha Transport Regiment. All are commanded by British officers, although quite a number of Gurkhalis now receive commissions.

Recruits are raised in Nepal, principally by retired Gurkha officers known as Assistant Recruiting Officers, and competition for places is high, with many families maintaining strong traditions of British service. Once accepted, the recruits are flown to Hong Kong for training, with emphasis on the sort of fighting likely to be experienced in southeast Asia, and the Gurkhas remain the foremost exponents of jungle warfare in the British Army. They enjoy an awesome reputation as men of bravery and fighting skill, so much so that it is not unknown for their enemies to flee rather than face them in battle.

This proved to be just a beginning, however. The idea of a Federation, comprising Malaya, Singapore and three states under British protection in Borneo – Sabah (British North Borneo), Sarawak and Brunei – was bitterly opposed by President Sukarno of Indonesia, who believed that all of Borneo should be under his rule. Taking full advantage of local dissidents, he sent forces into Indonesian-controlled Kalimantan, intent on mounting guerrilla-style raids all along the 1600km border which would wear down British resolve and prepare the way for Indonesian takeover. Setting up bases just inside Kalimantan, often no more than a kilometre from the border, Sukarno's soldiers were ideally placed to exert maximum pressure through rugged and seemingly inaccessible terrain. Within Sabah and Sarawak, the only means of travel was by jungle tracks and rivers, while on the border itself the mountains rose rapidly to 900m, culminating in peaks of about 2400m. It was tough, uncompromising country that was to test the stamina of any soldier who was sent there, but the Gurkhas proved well able to adapt, drawing on their experience of jungle fighting gained in the Malayan Emergency. Indeed, in the early stages of the 'Confrontation', individual Gurkhas were sent in to train Iban tribesmen to act as 'eyes and ears' astride likely incursion routes.

During this early phase, Gurkha tactics were to 'clear, hold and dominate' ground. Each of the battalions deployed – and all saw service at one time or another during the four years of crisis – knew that the enemy could only be defeated by forces ready and willing to live in the jungle for long periods, gaining local support and exploiting all available intelligence information. Deep in the rainforests, the Gurkha became a self-sufficient fighter, carrying his base on his back, wrapped in a plastic sheet. With a sockful of rice and a pocket full of ammunition, he could stay in the jungle for days, even weeks, on end, matching

Above: A passing-out parade, marking the start of a Gurkha's service with the British Army.

Right: A rifleman of The Duke of Edinburgh's Own Gurkha Rifles on active service in Borneo in 1966. He wears jungle-green trousers and shirt, and a jungle hat with a cloth company sign at the front and rear as a recognition sign intended to prevent riflemen from shooting each other while patrolling in thick jungle. The anti-mosquito face veil is worn as a neck-scarf and a pair of British rubber and canvas jungle boots complete his tropical dress. Armament is the lightweight US 5.56mm M16 assault rifle.

Previous page: A Gurkha of The 7th Duke of Edinburgh's Own Gurkha Rifles en route to the Falklands in 1982.

his enemy at every turn.

However, Sukarno's men continued to enjoy the initiative, choosing the time and place for their incursions, and it was not until political clearance had been given, late in 1963, that cross-border pre-emptive strikes could be made by the Gurkhas. At first these were restricted to penetrations of no more than 2700m, but as Sukarno escalated the conflict by mounting attacks on Malaya, this was gradually extended. The Gurkha raids imposed a great mental and physical strain on the troops involved. Courage and resolution were required to overcome the tensions of operating well behind enemy lines and the problems were accentuated by the rigid political restrictions imposed on the officers and men who took part. A typical raid will illustrate the point.

Deployed in Sarawak, C Company of the 1st Battalion, 2nd Goorkha Rifles, had a base at Ba Kelalan which guarded the approaches across the border. The inhabitants of the valley all belonged to the same tribe, the Muruts, and from time immemorial they had crossed and recrossed the border to carry on trading. Then, in late 1964, from their base at Long Medan, the Indonesians forbade any more cross-border trade. The Muruts suffered hardship which eventually led them to ask the officer in command of the Gurkha company to take action. Reconnaissance patrols were duly carried out and political permission for a raid was granted.

C Company was to move by night to cover a distance of 12km without being detected. Each of the 150 Gurkha soldiers had to carry two mortar bombs in addition to his own weapon and kit. They were to follow a circuitous route that would enable them to dump the bombs near the mortar positions that would give covering fire. To complicate matters further, strict instructions were laid down that the attack was to take only an hour, to prevent C Company from becoming embroiled with enemy reinforcements.

The night of 29 January 1965 was chosen for the attack and the company, after marching all night, was tired when it reached the jump-off position close to Long Medan in the early hours of the 30th. Everything went as planned until an Indonesian soldier suddenly walked towards one of the Gurkha platoons. The platoon commander did not hesitate: he gave the order to fire and four rockets slammed down on the enemy bunkers. At the same time the company commander gave the order to charge, and under close covering fire his party fought through the position from bunker to bunker using rifles and grenades. The camp was taken, but from across the river an Indonesian 12·7mm heavy machine gun opened up, to be joined by a 60mm mortar and medium machine guns. There were several Gurkha casualties and the situation was only saved by the prompt

action of the mortar fire controller, a corporal who was to be awarded the Military Medal, who stood in full view of the enemy to direct very accurate fire onto their positions, destroying the 60mm mortar before turning his attention to the machine guns.

The 12·7mm remained in action, though, pinning down the forward Gurkha section and threatening to inflict more casualties. In response, a corporal and two riflemen were sent in. After crawling with a rocket launcher across a paddy-field, they stealthily approached the gun position while the rest of the platoon kept up noisy diversionary fire. A few minutes later the corporal opened up and the first rocket hit the gun-pit, killing its occupants. The battle came to an abrupt end.

By late afternoon, using a more direct route, the raiding force was back across the border, carrying their wounded and the body of a dead rifleman. A few days later it was confirmed that 50 per cent of the Indonesian strength at Long Medan had been killed and that the camp had been abandoned. It was not to be occupied again and no more attacks were to be made by the Indonesians into the Ba Kelalan area during the Confrontation. The conflict was to continue elsewhere along the border for another 18 months, but in the end the Indonesians, confronted by the fortitude, endurance and sheer fighting qualities of the men from Nepal, had to admit defeat.

Above: Armed with an M16 assault rifle, a Gurkha rifleman patrols warily in Malayan jungle.

South Atlantic War

Right: Although the Gurkhas travelled southwards to the Falklands in style aboard the *Queen Elizabeth 2*, they trained hard during the voyage to be ready for combat.

Below: A Gurkha turns a grinding wheel so that his companion can keep his kukri – a distinctively curved knife – in razor-sharp condition. The kukri is Nepal's national weapon and is used for many purposes, ranging from hacking through dense undergrowth to being a much feared and highly effective combat weapon.

In early 1982, the 1st Battalion, 7th Gurkha Rifles, was stationed at Church Crookham in Hampshire as part of 5 Infantry Brigade. The officers and men were understandably disappointed when, in response to the Argentinian invasion of the Falklands in April, the other two units in the brigade – 2 and 3 Para – were sent to the South Atlantic. For a while they wondered if they were being kept back for political reasons, but they need not have worried. When reinforcements for the Falklands were organised in early May, the 1/7th was placed on 24-hour alert. As Baliprasad Rai, a member of the unit's Pipes and Drums, recalled:

'Now there was a different atmosphere in camp, electric you might say. . . . For everyone, there was a hectic time and especially the harassed quartermaster because extra equipment had to be issued in a hurry: snow boots, foam mattresses, parkas and huge, heavy rucksacks to carry them all in. These rucksacks, when packed, looked even larger than some of us.'

Amid a frenzy of publicity, the Gurkhas boarded the liner *Queen Elizabeth 2* at Southampton, departing for the South Atlantic on 12 May. Under the energetic leadership of Lieutenant-Colonel David Morgan, the battalion used every available moment on the giant liner to train, to keep fit and to prepare themselves for the prospect of battle. Even so, as the Atlantic weather deteriorated, the majority of the men became seasick, and this was not eased when they transferred from the *Queen Elizabeth 2* to the less luxurious ferry *Norland* off Grytviken in South Georgia. Baliprasad described how the Gurkhas felt:

'We swayed, shook and rolled towards, as we were told, the East Falklands. It was only about 800 miles [1300km] away, they said, but to me it seemed to be a 1000 miles [1600km] as my bowels remained in a constant state of turmoil and no amount of sea-sick tablets could settle them. We were bounced and buffetted like rag dolls.'

The Gurkhas were therefore more than happy to reach firm ground when,

on the morning of 1 June, they landed at San Carlos. D Company immediately moved on foot to take over a position in the Sussex mountains, while the remainder of the battalion flew to Darwin and Goose Green to relieve 2 Para. During the next week, patrols were sent out on foot and in Scout helicopters from Goose Green to scour East Falkland for Argentinian soldiers left behind in the retreat to Port Stanley. On 7 June a small party of Gurkhas, under a young subaltern from the Reconnaissance Platoon, captured seven of the enemy and, after setting up an ambush overnight, secured another three – all without firing a shot.

By now the weather had deteriorated, with high winds and fierce driving rain. Lieutenant-Colonel Morgan noted in his diary, 'everybody very, very wet' and his feelings were echoed by Baliprasad:

'All our clothing and kit was soaked, and remained soaked, and the icy winds of the Antarctic would chill us to the bone, no matter how many woollies we wore. It was colder and wetter than 10 English winters combined, and they said this was just the starters.'

Despite such conditions, the 1/7th continued to push forward. On 9 June, leaving C Company and the Assault Pioneers to guard Goose Green, the remainder of the battalion flew, or went by sea, to the Fitzroy/Bluff Cove area. They did not remain there long: next

Below: Flanked by cases containing 81mm mortar shells, Gurkhas wait for the order to take Mount William.

day, B Company – to whom Baliprasad was attached as a machine gunner – was embarked on a ferry which then steamed about 16km before being ordered back to Goose Green. But this was only a temporary move: 24 hours later, the Gurkhas were transported forward again by helicopter to Bluff Cove, from where they moved on foot towards enemy positions on Mount Harriet. During this advance the battalion came under shell-fire for the first time in the campaign; four men (including Baliprasad) were wounded and the rest given their baptism of fire. It was a frightening experience.

On 12 June, HQ 5 Infantry Brigade issued orders for an attack against Mount Tumbledown and Mount William, to the southwest of Port Stanley. During the daylight hours of 12/13 June, reconnaissance patrols were sent out to probe the enemy positions, before the two assaulting units – the 2nd Battalion, Scots Guards, and the Gurkhas – moved forward to their assembly areas on the

13th. The plan was for the Scots Guards to take Tumbledown, whereupon, in their wake, the Gurkhas were to capture Mount William. The Guards were due to open the assault at 0100 hours on 14 June, and their subsequent progress was to determine the speed of the Gurkhas' advance. However, the Guards soon met fierce enemy resistance in extremely difficult terrain; as a consequence, the Gurkhas' assault time, originally planned for 0200, had to be put back to 0430. Once under way, the men were only able to move forward slowly, in single file, towards the northern ridge of Tumbledown, keeping a sharp lookout for mines. In the event, none was found, but heavy enemy artillery and mortar fire wounded eight men.

During this period, Lieutenant-Colonel Morgan faced a dilemma: although he had to keep the momentum of the advance going, he could not allow his men to overtake the Scots Guards, who had to capture their objective first. In the confusion, C Company got into an accidental firefight with the Guards, during which another Gurkha was wounded. Eventually, D Company reached its objective, the highest peak on the eastern end of Tumbledown, and this enabled the other Gurkha companies to attack Mount William, only to find that the Argentinians had fled, leaving three prisoners and a host of dead around their shattered trenches. In Lieutenant-Colonel Morgan's words:

'It was most frustrating but I am absolutely certain that they knew, first they were outflanked when they saw this line of men coming towards them, and they couldn't do anything about it. And second, they also knew that they'd not yet come up against the Gurkhas! A prisoner told us that they were dreadfully . . . scared of meeting us.'

By dawn, the Argentinians were streaming back towards Port Stanley, where a surrender was negotiated. While the Gurkhas were waiting for transport back to the United Kingdom, they suffered their only fatality of the campaign. While helping to clear up the debris of war, Lance-Corporal Buddhaparasad Limbu was killed by a booby-trap. He was buried in Darwin Civil Cemetery with full military honours.

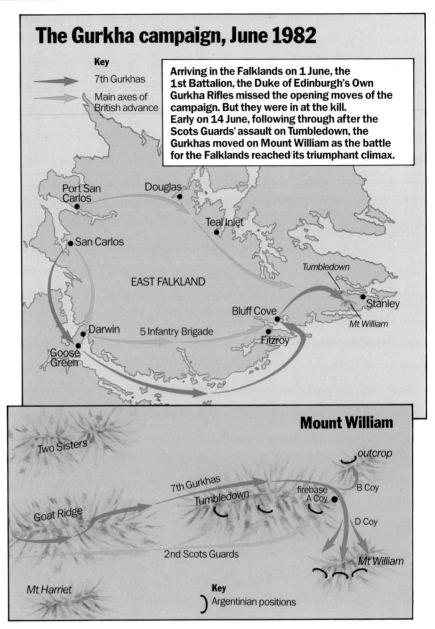

The Gurkha campaign, June 1982

The rest of the battalion sailed for England aboard the *Uganda* and, to the surprise of the soldiers, they received a tumultuous welcome both at Southampton and at Fleet, near their camp at Church Crookham. Many of them were deeply frustrated by the fact that they had not been given the chance to prove their prowess in battle, but there can be no doubt that their very presence in the Falklands had helped to bring the campaign to a speedy conclusion. Their reputation as fighting troops had preceded them to the South Atlantic and in many cases the enemy simply surrendered without waiting to see if it was justified. There can be no higher accolade for professional soldiers.

2·FORCES IN THE UNITED STATES

WITH the exception of the US Marine Corps, which has been in existence since 1798, most modern US elite units are products of World War II experience. It was the need for specialist troops to mount raids on Nazi-occupied Europe that produced the 1st Special Service Force, forerunners of the Special Forces, in 1942. In the same year, the problems of establishing bridgeheads during large amphibious operations saw the creation of the first of six US Army Ranger Battalions. Similarly, the value of airborne troops, as demonstrated by the German forces in 1940 and 1941, resulted in the creation of the US 82nd and 101st Airborne Divisions. The Special Service Force and the Ranger Battalions were all disbanded by the end of 1945 but the airborne formations survived World War II and, in 1952, the US Army Special Forces revived the concept of irregular forces within the US military establishment.

However, the existence of the Special Forces or 'Green Berets' was only guaranteed by the widening global commitment to resisting communist insurgency, associated with the administration of President John F. Kennedy. Kennedy increased the numbers of US advisers in South Vietnam, and these numbers escalated under his successor, Lyndon B. Johnson. And, of course, the Vietnam War was to produce new specialist units as responses to particular problems. Thus the Marines and Special Forces, who added to their achievements in Vietnam, were joined by units such as the US Navy SEALs, the 1st Air Cavalry and the 'Tunnel Rats' of the 1st Engineer Battalion. As specialist units, some did not survive disengagement from Vietnam in 1973 but the SEALs and Air Cavalry did so. Indeed, the United States still deployed more elite units than any other country.

The large number of elite units derives in part from the sheer size of the US armed forces and the rivalries that have emerged between them, which in the past gave rise to problems of co-ordination. The US Marine Corps, for example, which enjoys an entirely separate status from the other armed forces, did not fall under the control of the commander of the US Military Assistance Command, Vietnam during the war there.

In order to provide co-ordination a Joint Special Operations Command was established in 1980 embracing Special Forces, Rangers, a psychological warfare group and a civil affairs battalion. This can be expected to avoid the duplication of the past and ensure greater success than has sometimes accompanied US elite units. The performance of elite units, however creditable, did not bring victory in Vietnam, where the armed forces as a whole failed to come to terms with the problems of waging warfare against an unconventional

opponent. Elite operations have also been marred by intelligence lapses such as that involved in the Special Forces' assault on an empty prison compound at Son Tay in North Vietnam in 1970. In a similar operation, the US Marines had 77 casualties in an assault on Koh Tang island in the Gulf of Thailand on 15 May 1975, where it was mistakenly thought that the crew of the US freighter *Mayaguez* were being held by Khmer Rouge forces – the crew turned up offshore in a fishing boat after the main assault had begun.

Nevertheless, the Joint Special Operations Command has already proved an outstanding success and, under its auspices, SEALs, Rangers, Marines and the 82nd Airborne all participated with undoubted expertise in the US intervention in Grenada in October 1983. Their performance as professionals and the success of the operation resulted, in turn, in a new Joint Special Operations Agency being established on 1 January 1984 and, during 1984, increases were authorised in the establishment of both Rangers and Special Forces.

THE MARINES
The United States Marine Corps

History of the US Marines

Formally established in 1798, the United States Marine Corps has had a long and distinguished history as one of the world's premier fighting forces. For most of the 19th century, the US Marines were a small force deployed mainly as guards aboard ship or at the gates of naval stations, although they formed provisional units whenever necessary for such campaigns as the Seminole War in the 1830s and the Mexican War in 1846. The role changed, however, during the Spanish-American War of 1898. The US Navy suddenly found itself having to provide not only the defence forces for overseas bases but also the ground troops necessary to attack and secure the bases of enemy powers. These roles naturally fell to the Navy's own ground forces, the Marine Corps.

In December 1913 an Advance Base Force was established as a combat-ready combined arms force of brigade size. During World War I, the Marines gained prominence attacking Belleau Wood on the Western Front in June 1918 and, of course, won particular fame during World War II when they spearheaded the American campaign in the Pacific. Such actions as Guadalcanal, Tarawa, Iwo Jima and Okinawa saw the size of the Marine Corps expanded to just under half a million men, complete with armoured, naval and air-support units. In the process the Marines earned themselves a 'gung-ho' reputation for combat eagerness.

Since 1945 the prime role of the Marines has been to act as an amphibious 'rapid deployment force' ready to be sent into action at a moment's notice, and in 1951 their separate identity within the US military establishment was enshrined in a law passed by Congress. In both the Lebanon in 1958 and the Dominican Republic in 1965, US Marines were active in coming to the aid of pro-Western governments faced by internal instability. But there have also been major conflicts. In the Korean War, Marines were among the first to enter the fray and, when the Chinese came to the assistance of their North Korean allies in the winter of 1950, the 1st Marine Division conducted an epic withdrawal from the Chosin reservoir to the sea.

In 1965 elements of the 3rd Marine Division were the first US ground forces sent to South Vietnam and, during the major communist offensive in 1968, Marines again distinguished themselves in the defence of Hue and Khe Sanh. Disengagement from Vietnam led to a reduction in numbers to some 194,000 men but the Marines have continued to prove their worth – most recently as part of the peacekeeping Multi-National Force in Beirut in 1982 and during the US intervention in Grenada in 1983.

ASK any United States Marine what makes his Corps so special and he will probably answer 'boot camp'. For the demanding, rugged, searing experience of Marine recruit training is the price of entry into that elite fraternity. This training is carried out at two bases – Parris Island, South Carolina, which was established in 1915 and is actually only slightly higher ground surrounded by humid salt-marshes, and San Diego in California, which was opened in 1923.

As soon as a new recruit arrives, his whole civilian frame of reference is shattered under the concerted onslaught of the drill instructors (always known as 'DIs'), whose purpose is to strip away civilian attitudes and reduce all recruits to the same level as quickly as possible. DIs ceaselessly stalk around the recruits (known as 'boots'), their anger ready to boil over at any moment. They shout or scream in unfamiliar ways, using words most of the young 'boots' have never heard before – and certainly not at such close quarters, for DIs deliberately establish their domination by engaging literally in face-to-face and even nose-to-nose confrontation. A visit to the barber is early on the agenda and little attention is paid to preferences in style; there is only one. The repetition of basic military movements in the first phase of the long-standing training programme continues

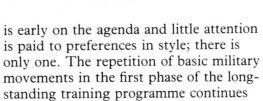

Above: The haircut and 'war faces' of Marines in training.

Left: A US Marine in ceremonial uniform.

M16A1

rear sight adjustor

charging handle

foreward bolt assist

buffer tube

gas tube

bolt assem

hammer firing pin

auto sear

selector cam

disconnect

grip

trigger

magazine release spindle

magazine

sling swivel

stock

until the recruit gets them right. Lessons go on until lights-out but, even in sleep, some will be unable to escape their new environment and will wake with muscle cramps from sleeping rigidly to attention. Many young men are sent into a terrified, bewildered state close to shock. But, as recruits progress through the second phase of marksmanship training to the last phase of 'polishing' basic skills, DIs encourage both intense competition and also identification with the spirit of the Corps. After the last major hurdle of the Final Field Inspection, an elaborate graduation ceremony adds significance to the formal bestowing of the title of 'Marine'.

Although often seeming petty, the unique brand of discipline might well save a recruit's life in combat where automatic response and obedience to orders is an essential quality. Similarly the procedures drilled into the men during marksmanship training could literally mean the difference between life and death if they saved precious seconds otherwise wasted fumbling with a jammed rifle mechanism. But, above all, the development of an *esprit de corps* through a demanding initiation rite is the fundamental reason for the Marines to

keep their recruit training so intense. The basics could be taught in a far more benign atmosphere but boot camp gives all Marines a common background with which they cannot help identifying. A man will never be the same again after boot camp and, throughout his life, he will know he is a member of an elite body of fighting men.

Above left: Recruit private R.A. Keller as he appeared at the Receiving Barracks, and (above), three months later, on graduation from recruit training.

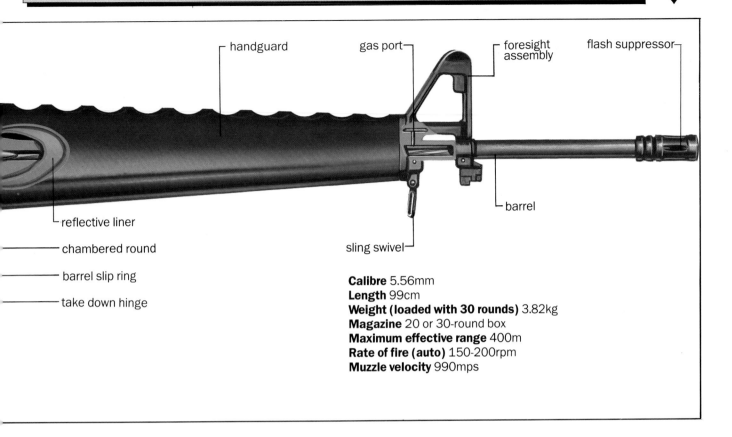

handguard gas port foresight assembly flash suppressor

reflective liner

chambered round

barrel slip ring

take down hinge

sling swivel

barrel

Calibre 5.56mm
Length 99cm
Weight (loaded with 30 rounds) 3.82kg
Magazine 20 or 30-round box
Maximum effective range 400m
Rate of fire (auto) 150-200rpm
Muzzle velocity 990mps

Above: This model of the US M16A1 rifle is fitted with the current-issue curved 30-round box magazine and closed flash suppressor. Made of aluminium alloy and lightweight plastic, the rifle is easy to handle and its short length, together with its rapid rate of fire, make it an ideal weapon for close-quarter combat.

Vietnam

The worth of the Marines' rigorous training was proved emphatically by the performance of the Corps in Vietnam. Between 1954, when the US had begun to support the government of South Vietnam, and 1965 the Marines provided only a small advisory group to work with the South Vietnamese. However, following President Johnson's decision to commit US ground forces to help defend South Vietnam, elements of the 3rd Marine Division were landed at Da Nang in March 1965. By January 1966 the 1st Marine Division was also deployed and, by the end of 1967, 21 battalions from the 1st, 3rd and 5th Marine Divisions were operational in South Vietnam.

Of these battalions, the 26th Marine Regiment of 5th Division formed the core of a 6000-strong garrison of Khe Sanh, a remote combat base in the northwest of the country, some 23km south of the Demilitarized Zone with North Vietnam and 10km east of the border with Laos. The base was designed to cut the infiltration of troops and supplies into South Vietnam and to block any incursions along the strategically important Route 9. To the east, the 1st and 5th Marine Regiments of 1st Marine Division formed a 4000-strong Task Force X-Ray at Phu Bai combat base, tasked with screening the western approaches to the important former Imperial capital of Hue and with the maintenance of traffic along Route 1 – the key link between north and south.

Both Khe Sanh and Hue were to become focal points in the Tet (Lunar New Year) offensive, planned by the NVA (North Vietnamese Army) and VC (Viet Cong) to coincide with the celebration of Tet in South Vietnam, when it was hoped that the South Vietnamese might be caught off guard and the Americans' ability to use airpower might be restricted by bad weather. If a popular rising could be encouraged in South Vietnam through the communist action, then the government in Saigon might collapse and the military and political standing of the Americans would then be seriously undermined. In all, 84,000 NVA and VC troops would be hurled at five cities, 36 provincial capitals and 64 district capitals. The offensive was not unexpected but the scale and intensity did surprise the United States and the South Vietnamese. Moreover, the opening of the NVA offensive against Khe Sanh on 22 January 1968 served to divert attention in the northern provinces prior to the opening of the main communist effort, which struck Hue and other centres on 31 January.

Few units of the ARVN (Army of the Republic of (South) Vietnam) were stationed in Hue when the early morning of 31 January opened to the crump of mortars and the roar of rockets. NVA units took up blocking positions north and south of the city and the VC flag soon fluttered over the old Imperial Palace. During the morning, as reports began to reach the commander of Task Force X-Ray, Brigadier-General Foster Lahue, Company A of the 1st Battalion, 1st Marines, was sent towards Hue to investigate. The Marines had barely covered half the distance to Hue when they became pinned down by heavy fire. Lieutenant-Colonel Marcus Gravel was then sent with the command group of 1st Battalion and Company G of 2nd Battalion, 5th Marines, to support Company A. Gravel was able to force his way across the Nguyen Hoang bridge into the Old City, but tanks could not follow because of their vulnerability in street fighting, and he was forced to withdraw. Gravel tried again on the following morning to reach ARVN units still holding out in the Old City but could not make progress.

By 4 February Colonel Stanley Hughes, regimental commander of the 1st Marines, had arrived to take charge of the units already committed under Gravel and three rifle companies of the 5th Marines under the command of a World War II veteran, Lieutenant-Colonel Ernest Cheatham. The battle that followed to clear the Old City was in many ways more like the gruelling episodes of the war in the Pacific than anything previously experienced in Vietnam. Most of the Marines were short-term enlistees who had expected to fight in the countryside with enormous resources of fire support at their disposal. Now, however, they faced close-quarters combat, with movement restricted to swift dashes across fire-swept streets.

Blanket shelling was of little assistance since it only created more rubble for the defenders to shelter behind. The attacking Marines therefore had to put up their own covering fire and discovered that the M16 assault rifle, which many had criticised prior to its arrival in South Vietnam, could produce a powerful burst in its fully automatic mode, which kept the defenders under pressure. There was no front line as such and, soon after the Marines moved into the New City, saboteurs blew up the bridge over the Phu Cam canal, which meant that all supplies had to be brought in by helicopter or up river. The problems of moving supplies into Hue were mirrored by the difficulties of shifting the wounded out. Five landing craft brought supplies in until the canal was rebridged on 12 February, but not without cost. One unit – Major Robert Thompson's 1st Battalion, 5th Marines – was deployed into the Old City to support ARVN troops operating there; and this battalion had an even more difficult task than those south of the Perfume river, for the greater density of buildings and even greater determination of the NVA and VC made fighting here a grim struggle indeed. But for all the Marines at Hue the fighting under leaden skies in the period of the northeast monsoon assumed almost a kind of routine. By day they would force their way forward to prise the communists out of concealed defences, bringing up what support weapons they could and then hope to catch a hot meal at night. But during the night the VC would launch local counter-attacks and set booby traps.

In the New City the US forces began to assert control within a week and, by 9 February, all organised resistance south of the Perfume river had been crushed. However, it was not until 22 February that the final series of attacks carried the Old City, a rare break in the monsoon enabling Marine aircraft to deliver a devastating weight of 115kg 'Snakeye' bombs and 225kg napalm canisters. Hue had seen some of the bitterest fighting of the Vietnam War with the Marines suffering 142 dead and just under 1000 wounded. Elsewhere in South Vietnam other attacks had been repulsed and massive casualties inflicted on the NVA and especially the VC but, even as the communist effort slackened, fighting continued at Khe Sanh. Indeed,

Above: US Marines at Hue regroup during the fighting for the Citadel. By 1968 the Marines were armed with the M16 rifle, which proved superior to its predecessor – the M14 – in close combat. Besides their M16s, these Marines were well equipped with a variety of infantry-support weapons, including machine guns, mortars and grenades and it was the grenades which were particularly effective in the house-to-house fighting that characterised the battle for Hue.

the day that marked the end of communist resistance at Hue was only the 32nd of a 77-day 'siege' of the Khe Sanh base.

The defenders of Khe Sanh who endured the 77-day 'siege' comprised the three battalions of the 26th Marine Regiment and the artillerymen of the 1st Battalion, 13th Marines. The garrison was later augmented by the 1st Battalion, 9th Marines and the ARVN 37th Rangers. The Marines had made a detailed study of the battle for Dien Bien Phu, where French forces had suffered a devastating defeat in 1954 at the hands of the Viet Minh. The French had made the grave mistake of allowing the Viet Minh to bring up massive quantities of heavy artillery that wreaked havoc on the French positions. The Marines therefore recognised that the denial of the hills surrounding Khe Sanh to the enemy was crucial to the successful defence of a base as low-lying as that of the French at Dien Bien Phu. Not all the surrounding hills offered defensible terrain but there were sufficient to enable the Marines to engage the enemy and to provide observation over likely approach routes.

No hill was more crucial, nor more exposed, than Hill 881S, a steep-sided hill rising 500m from its surrounding

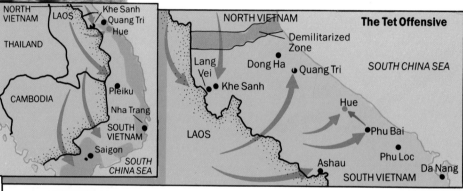

Hue
US Marines
January - February 1968

In January 1968 towns and military installations throughout South Vietnam were attacked by communist forces. The old imperial city of Hue was the scene of some of the bitterest and most prolonged fighting.

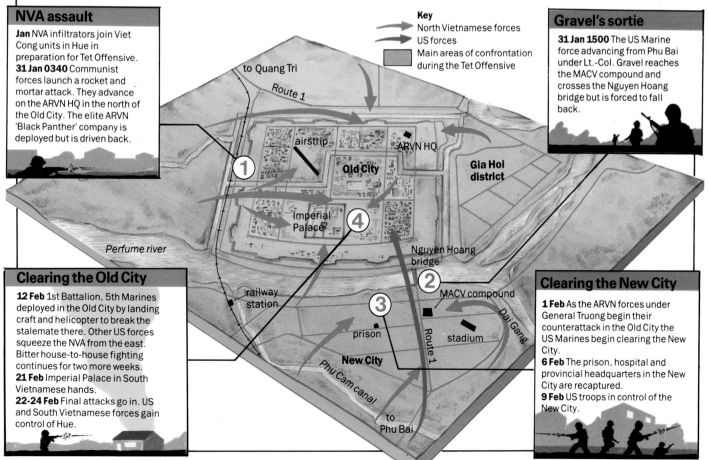

Key
→ North Vietnamese forces
→ US forces
■ Main areas of confrontation during the Tet Offensive

NVA assault

Jan NVA infiltrators join Viet Cong units in Hue in preparation for Tet Offensive.
31 Jan 0340 Communist forces launch a rocket and mortar attack. They advance on the ARVN HQ in the north of the Old City. The elite ARVN 'Black Panther' company is deployed but is driven back.

Gravel's sortie

31 Jan 1500 The US Marine force advancing from Phu Bai under Lt.-Col. Gravel reaches the MACV compound and crosses the Nguyen Hoang bridge but is forced to fall back.

Clearing the Old City

12 Feb 1st Battalion, 5th Marines deployed in the Old City by landing craft and helicopter to break the stalemate there. Other US forces squeeze the NVA from the east. Bitter house-to-house fighting continues for two more weeks.
21 Feb Imperial Palace in South Vietnamese hands.
22-24 Feb Final attacks go in. US and South Vietnamese forces gain control of Hue.

Clearing the New City

1 Feb As the ARVN forces under General Truong begin their counterattack in the Old City the US Marines begin clearing the New City.
6 Feb The prison, hospital and provincial headquarters in the New City are recaptured.
9 Feb US troops in control of the New City.

valleys some 8km west of the base. It had only been seized with difficulty from the NVA in the preceding year. Like most of the other advanced Marine positions, it could only be served by helicopter and constant resupply was necessary; only the crest was held and there was no access to fresh water. To send a water party down

the slope was to invite a major skirmish and was too much of a risk to contemplate. In any case, it was not tactically sensible to engage in firefights lower down the slopes since the Marines' main advantage lay in occupying fixed positions with everything around being a 'free-fire zone'. The simple, and ultimately successful, tactic was to hold the hills and direct massive fire from virtually unlimited artillery and air support on to every possible observed or expected enemy position.

Hill 881S was the responsibility of Company I of the 3rd Battalion, 26th Marines, together with elements of Company M, a section of 81mm mortars and 106mm recoilless rifles, and a detachment of 105mm howitzers. Totalling some 400 men, the whole was under the command of Company I's Captain William H. Dabney. Aware of intelligence predictions and of skirmishes fought by his patrols in preceding days, Dabney took all of Company I on a reconnaissance in force before dawn on 20 January 1968. Barely 500m from their start positions, his two lead platoons came under fire and a medevac helicopter was also forced down in a nearby gully. Marines from Lieutenant Michael Thomas' reserve platoon jumped unordered from their positions and dashed 200m down the hill to the crash site. Their charge was so unexpected that they scattered a group of startled North Vietnamese, who fled without firing a shot. While Thomas' men were rescuing the injured crew, the other lead platoon under the command of Lieutenant Thomas Brindley called in artillery fire on NVA positions some 200m away on a commanding knoll. The platoon then launched into a classic infantry assault to carry the knoll but Brindley was killed and his platoon was left holding the high ground with depleted ammunition and only a lance-corporal in command. A counter-attack was only repulsed by a napalm drop so close to the Marines' lines that several soldiers had their eyebrows singed. Dabney led Thomas' platoon to rescue the survivors of Brindley's command but Thomas was killed trying to extricate one of Brindley's reconnaissance teams that had got detached. Heavy fire was now being brought to bear on the communist

Left: This Private 1st Class of the US Marines is pictured at the time of the Tet offensive in January 1968. Particular features of his uniform include foliage slots in the camouflage helmet cover (and a bottle of insect repellent in the helmet band), a flak vest with a fighting knife suspended, and nylon and leather tropical-patterned boots. Like many Vietnam combat soldiers this Marine carries a profusion of water bottles (in this case, three).

Armament is the 7.62mm M60, the standard general-purpose machine gun used in Vietnam.

mortars on 881S, using white phosphorus shells, of the surrounding known enemy anti-aircraft positions. Within seconds, a flight of four Marine A-4 Skyhawks systematically attacked the emplacements marked by the shells. As further flights saturated the hill with napalm and canisters of delayed-fuse bomblets and the mortars fired further shells to blind whatever anti-aircraft positions had survived, ten CH-46 medium helicopters, each with an externally-slung load of 1500kg of supplies, would descend through a smokescreen to release their loads and climb out quickly. In the rear echelon, one helicopter would land in a predetermined zone with replacement men and take out casualties, the position in the echelon and the landing zone being constantly varied. The entire 'Super Gaggle' took less than five minutes.

After dark, when the communists could no longer observe the defenders, supplies would be gathered in from the hillside. Indeed, both to conserve water and avoid casualties, the Marines worked by night; only small observation posts and the supporting arms controllers were about in daylight. Nevertheless, each

positions but, with darkness approaching and Company I's real mission the defence of Hill 881S, the company could only retire to its original positions; it was weaker by 50 Marines than it had been that morning.

Above: Marines rush a casualty to the medics.

Below: A Douglas A-1E Skyraider drops a phosphorus bomb.

Two days later the battle for Khe Sanh began in earnest as the main base was struck by several hundred rounds of large calibre rocket and artillery fire. The barrage created havoc along the base's lifeline – a runway of steel matting without which supplies could not be flown in. The bombardment also exploded 1360 tonnes of munitions in the main ammo dump. While the shelling continued on a daily basis, the NVA attempted to force the Marines off the surrounding hills by cutting off resupply. But for the unique structure of the Marine Air Ground Teams, they might have succeeded. On Hill 881S, for example, two rounds bracketed the landing zone on 22 January just as a helicopter was being loaded with wounded; 22 men were killed or grievously wounded and the helicopter was completely destroyed. The solution to the predicament at Khe Sanh was a carefully rehearsed, perfectly timed and coordinated air/ground resupply operation known as 'Super Gaggle'. First mounted in mid-February, it began with a pre-arranged bombardment by the

morning a muted bugle would sound through the trenches as a torn and bullet-ridden flag was hauled up on an improvised flagpole. Dabney and his men would stand to attention then hit the dirt as soon as the last note sounded. Officially, the American flag was not supposed to be raised alone over South Vietnamese territory but the Marines felt strongly that it was a right they had fought hard to get and, as Marine blood had bought the hill, so the flag belonged there.

As the weather improved, so the American rate of fire support accelerated and that of the NVA decreased. Using Combat Skyspot, a computer system that guided incoming B-52 bombers on to their target, close-in attacks were mounted on NVA positions. The new tactic, allowing hundreds of bombs to be dropped simultaneously in designated target boxes, had a devastating effect. In all, 60,498 tonnes of bombs were dropped in support of the Marines within 25km of Khe Sanh – a greater tonnage than that dropped on all of Germany during 1943. To estimate the number of NVA killed by the B-52 strikes is impossible, but the NVA may have lost as many as 15,000 casualties during the siege, to a Marine loss of 199 killed and 830 wounded. Under such a weight of fire, the NVA simply melted away. Khe Sanh was relieved on 8 April 1968, although skirmishing continued until the middle of the month.

Since disengagement from Vietnam, the US Marine Corps has been organised to carry out seaborne assaults at short notice anywhere in the world. It currently has three ground-force combat divisions – the 1st Division, at Camp Pendleton, California, is available for commitment to the Rapid Deployment Joint Task Force; the 2nd, at Camp Lejeune, North Carolina, is responsible for operations in the Atlantic, Caribbean or Mediterranean; and the 3rd, on Okinawa, is responsible for Pacific operations. These are self-contained fighting formations, each of some 17,000 men. They can be deployed in their entirety as Marine Amphibious Forces (MAFs) but, in peacetime, smaller formations are more suited to security needs. Two Marine Amphibious Brigades (MABs) are therefore maintained – one at Pendleton and the other on Hawaii – while both the US Mediterranean and Pacific Fleets have Marine Amphibious Units (MAUs) of about 1900 Marines each. The Marine Amphibious Unit operating from the US Sixth Fleet in the Mediterranean, for example, was committed to the peacekeeping Multi-National Force in Beirut in August 1982: 239 were killed on 23 October 1983 when a suicide driver crashed a truck packed with explosives into their barracks. Some days earlier, the 22nd MAU, en route to relieve those in Beirut, had been turned back to participate in the US intervention in Grenada. On 26 October 1983 the Marines captured Fort Frederick, a dominant feature of the island's capital, St George's, in a skilful and impressive operation.

It was just the kind of operation for which the Marines were ideally suited and a role that the US Marine Corps has fulfilled successfully now for nearly 200 years.

Below: American soldiers relax as the Stars and Stripes flies in triumph over Grenada after the successful conclusion of Operation Urgent Fury.

82nd AIRBORNE
The 82nd Airborne Division

THE central question surrounding the use of paratroopers has always been one of whether they are cost-effective when the aircraft, specialist equipment and training required have all been taken into account. However, despite threats to their existence, both the 82nd and the 101st Airborne Divisions were retained after World War II. Indeed, in Korea, the 187th Regimental Combat Team, made up of men from both divisions, was dropped by parachute in operations in both October 1950 and March 1951. In doing so, it showed a new-found ability to drop heavy equipment such as 105mm howitzers and made the glider – the usual World War II method of landing support equipment – obsolete. Initially, therefore, the Americans intended to use paratroopers in Vietnam in the traditional manner and went so far as to raise South Vietnamese parachute battalions. However, the development of heliborne forces offered superior flexibility over parachute forces, whose fixed-wing transports were far more vulnerable to ground fire than more manoeuvrable helicopters. In 1968, therefore, the 101st was converted into an airmobile formation, leaving the 82nd alone in the parachute role.

Nevertheless, the requirement for quick-reaction forces capable of worldwide deployment guaranteed the future of the 82nd. In fact, just three years before the conversion of the 101st, two battalions of the 82nd were emplaned on 30 April 1965 and ordered to Puerto Rico in order to be ready to intervene in the deteriorating situation in the Dominican Republic, where anti-government rebels threatened to topple a pro-Western civilian junta. While en route to Puerto Rico, the battalions were diverted to San Isidro airbase in the Republic as President Johnson decided to act. Fortunately, a last-minute decision to airland the men rather than have them drop by parachute saved many casualties since the selected dropping zone was subsequently found to be covered in coral patches. Fanning out from the airbase, the paratroopers quickly established a perimeter and began to work their way towards the capital, Santo Domingo. They met little resistance and were able to halt at the Duarte bridge on the

Above: US airborne troops, armed with M16 rifles, capture a hilltop in Vietnam.

Previous page: Men of the 82nd Airborne on Grenada in 1983.

eastern outskirts to await reinforcements. The rapid build-up of US forces included the remainder of the 82nd, which arrived on 4 May 1965. A buffer zone was successfully established between the rebel and junta forces and the last of the paratroopers were withdrawn in July as Latin American peacekeeping contingents replaced them. US intervention on the island had stabilised the situation.

Some thirteen years later, on 16 May 1978, the 82nd was again put on a similar alert when the invasion of Shaba province in Zaïre by Katanganese 'gendarmerie' threatened the stability of President Mobutu's pro-Western government. In the event, French and Belgian paratroopers rather than men of the 82nd were dropped into Shaba but this in itself demonstrated the flexibility and continuing worth of airborne forces. When, therefore, the US Rapid Deployment Joint Task Force (RDJTF) was established by President Carter in October 1979, the 82nd was one of three army divisions allocated to it. Exercises

History of the 82nd Airborne

United States airborne troops came into existence after America's entry into World War II, the 82nd Airborne Divi-sion being formally constituted as an airborne formation on 15 August 1942. After service in the Torch landings in North Africa later that year, the 82nd took part in Operation Husky – the invasion of Sicily in July 1943. After service in Italy, the division was re-called to Britain to join the 101st Air-borne Division in being dropped behind German lines in support of the D-Day landings of June 1944. As part of Operation Market Garden, which cul-minated in the battle for Arnhem, the 82nd proved its own worth by achiev-ing its objectives at Nijmegen bridge.

Despite being fully trained, however, the 82nd was held back as a strategic reserve during the Korean War when, as an emergency measure, an *ad hoc* 187th Airborne Regimental Combat Team was deployed to South Korea. Korea also saw the first significant use of the helicopter and, as helicopter tech-nology advanced, the concept of sol-diers dropped by parachute from fixed-wing aircraft was questioned. Nonetheless, the widespread use of heliborne troops in the Vietnam War did not signal the end of the paratroop-er and, on 22 February 1967, the 173rd Airborne Brigade was dropped by parachute during Operation Junction City. The 82nd itself again remained in strategic reserve but its 3rd Brigade served briefly in Vietnam in a heliborne role when it was rushed out during the Tet offensive of early 1968.

The hostile environment of the mod-ern battlefield makes large-scale para-chute drops exceedingly hazardous but there remains a need for picked troops who can be rapidly transported vast distances to be dropped on a target with a minimum of delay. Similarly, as sol-diers trained in an independent inter-ventionary role, paratroopers are also ideal as quick-reaction troops in either an air-transportable or heliborne role. Thus the 82nd played an important role in US intervention in the Dominican Republic in 1965 and, more recently, in Grenada in October 1983. The 82nd is also an important component of the US Rapid Deployment Joint Task Force.

Below: UH-60A Black Hawk helicopters of the US Command (Rapid Deployment Force) on exercise in 1982. The Black Hawk saw combat in the invasion of Grenada in 1983.

were conducted in Egypt in 1980 and 1982 by the RDJTF, which was redesignated the US Central Command (CENTCOM) in June 1983. Ironically, however, it was not the Persian Gulf but the Caribbean that was to be the scene of the 82nd's next operation, when the murder of Grenada's prime minister, Maurice Bishop, by members of his own People's Revolutionary Government prompted US and Caribbean intervention.

Some 750 paratroopers of the Division Ready Brigade of the 82nd were flown direct from the divisional base at

Right: US airborne troops and civilians clash in the streets of Santo Domingo, Dominican Republic, in 1965; the occupation was not universally welcomed, but resistance was light.

Below: A US 105mm gun crew receives orders before going into action during the invasion of Grenada.

Fort Bragg, North Carolina, as the second wave to land at Point Salines, site of a new airfield construction project on Grenada. Touching down at about 1400 hours on 25 October 1983, the 82nd had arrived within just seventeen hours of being placed on alert. They came under fire from armoured cars of the Grenadan People's Revolutionary Army but, with the assistance of air strikes, were able to secure the airfield. The fighting was heavier than expected due to the presence of Cuban construction workers, who were all trained infantrymen, and eventually some 5000 men of the 82nd were committed to the operation. On 26 October the paratroopers combed the island for pockets of resistance and, on the following day, supported the army's Rangers in an assault on the Cuban barracks at Edgmont. Most were withdrawn as soon as the island was secured but the 508th Airborne Infantry Regiment was one unit retained as a security force. Thus the 82nd had once more proved its value as a quick-reaction force, its young paratroopers adjusting themselves to combat realities. It remains the sole quick-reaction parachute force at the disposal of CENTCOM.

THE RANGERS
The 75th Infantry (Ranger) Regiment

A British colony for 200 years, Grenada had received its independence in 1974. Until 1979 the island had been ruled by Prime Minister Eric Gairy who, though nominally accountable to a British-appointed Governor-General, had created an increasingly authoritarian regime. Gairy was deposed in March 1979 in a coup led by Maurice Bishop's New Jewel Movement (NJM). A charismatic barrister, Bishop became prime minister but with a doctrinaire Marxist-Leninist, Bernard Coard, as his deputy. A deep division opened between Bishop and Coard, who wished to push the island

into closer alignment with the Soviet Union. Although he had developed ties with the Cuban leader, Fidel Castro, Bishop was finally ordered to share the leadership of Grenada with Coard by the NJM in September 1983. On 13 October, however, Bishop was placed under house arrest. Freed by a large crowd six days later, Bishop was carried triumphantly into the island's capital, St George's, but units of the People's Revolutionary Army (PRA) seized him and five supporters and they were summarily shot dead.

Amid the deterioration of public order on Grenada, the Organisation of Eastern Caribbean States (OECS),

History and training of the Rangers

The first Rangers in American history were formed by John Goreham in 1750 to wage an anti-guerrilla war for the British against American Indian and French forces. They predated the more famous Rangers raised by Robert Rogers by six years.

When, in 1942, the United States began to form commando-style units of volunteers for war in Europe, the name was revived. The 1st Battalion was formed in June 1942 from volunteers from the 1st Armored and 34th Infantry Divisions and trained by British instructors in Scotland. Eventually, six Ranger battalions were formed and, since responsibility for selection fell upon Colonel William Darby, many now remember the formations as 'Darby's Rangers'. The 1st Battalion saw action in the Torch landings in North Africa and, subsequently, Rangers took part in the campaigns in Sicily, Italy and Normandy: the 1st and 3rd Battalions suffered particularly heavy casualties in the landings at Anzio in January 1944.

The Rangers were disbanded after the end of World War II although Ranger 'companies' were deployed by some regiments during the Korean War. No Ranger force then existed until the US Army, anxious to start afresh after the disappointment of the Vietnam War, began recruiting two battalions of Rangers in 1974. They became operational in 1975 as the 1st and 2nd Battalions of the 75th Infantry (Ranger) Regiment, being based respectively at Fort Stewart, Georgia, and Fort Lewis, Washington State. With a total strength of 606 men, the two battalions came under the 1st Special Operations Command in October 1982.

The men, who are all volunteers, are equipped as light infantry and each must be airborne-qualified before becoming a Ranger. The usual route is through the Ranger School at Fort Benning, Georgia – an establishment which survived the earlier dismantling of the Rangers by continuing as an officer and NCO training school. All the arts associated with elite, self-dependent units are taught in a 58-day training programme, which continues for 18 hours a day, 7 days a week. Training includes survival in the wild, close-quarters combat and jungle, desert and mountain-warfare skills. Both battalions received their baptism of fire during the US intervention in Grenada in October 1983 and, in 1984, a third battalion was authorised, to be based at Fort Benning.

Previous page: American medical students on Grenada show their gratitude to the Rangers who have just rescued them. The Ranger at the extreme left is armed with a 12-gauge shotgun. Known as a 'trench gun', this weapon is extremely effective in close-quarter combat and is also used to blow doors off their hinges during rescue operations.

together with Jamaica and Barbados, called upon US President Ronald Reagan to intervene. Reagan was not slow to comply for he wished to restore US influence in an area increasingly dominated by Cuba and to demonstrate that he was prepared to use force to restore the status quo in the turbulent region. It was also intended to eliminate what the Reagan administration perceived as the future military threat posed by the Cuban construction of an airstrip at Point Salines on Grenada. On another level, he argued that the operation mounted – Urgent Fury – was also necessary to rescue several hundred American students at the island's St George's Medical School, who might be used as hostages by the new regime. Among the units selected for the operation were the 1st and 2nd Battalions of the 75th Infantry (Ranger) Regiment whose initial task would be to seize the controversial airstrip at Point Salines.

At 0600 hours on 25 October 1983, as US Marines were already landing at Pearls airport to the east, eighteen C-130 transports approached the airstrip at Point Salines in the west. Aboard were 300 men of the 1st Battalion, 75th Regiment, under the command of Lieutenant-Colonel Wes Taylor and 250 men of the 2nd Battalion, commanded by Lieutenant-Colonel Ralph Hagler. The original plan called for one company to parachute onto the airstrip and secure it so that the remaining Rangers could be airlanded. However, during the flight new orders were issued, based on intelligence gained by AC-130E Spectre gunships using their low-light television cameras and infra-red sensors, which indicated that the runways were obstructed. All the Rangers were now to make a combat jump from only 150m as this would enable their aircraft to approach at a level beneath the effective field of fire of the Cuban anti-aircraft guns also detected around the target. Although Rhodesian security forces had carried out combat jumps from even lower altitudes, no US paratrooper had 'shotgunned' since World War II. A second reason for the low jump was that it would cut down time in the air to 19 or 20 seconds, reducing the Rangers' vulnerability to smallarms fire. As it was, many arrived on the ground to find their chutes riddled with holes from the defenders' fire.

Re-rigging in the aircraft for a low jump with the older T10 parachutes – less sensitive to the effects of a heavy ground-wind over the drop zone, which exceeded the normal safety margin by seven knots – and carrying extra ammunition instead of a useless reserve chute, the first 12-man stick from Company A, 1st Battalion jumped out over Point Salines. They came under so much ground fire that the aircraft following veered away to allow Spectre gunships to suppress the fire before the other Rangers were committed. Some fifteen minutes later, at 0615 hours, the jump was resumed with the remaining Rangers dropping to join the first twelve who were all heavily engaged on the ground. Fortunately, only one Ranger was injured, by breaking a leg in the low-level jump, while another, who was gusted into the sea, was able to get ashore safely notwithstanding the weight of his 50kg pack.

Once the Rangers were all on the ground, they moved to secure the airstrip and to clear the runway of the old drums and other debris that had been strewn over it. The first priority was to take a bluff overlooking the airstrip and suppress the considerable fire emanating from it. After clearing the drop zone, the Rangers set up their mortars and began to bombard the bluff. Spectre gunships and carrier-based A-6 Intruder and A-7 Corsair fighters supported the Rangers who, by 0715 hours, had surged forward to knock out the machine-gun and mortar

Grenada
US Airborne Forces, October 1983

On the morning of 25 October 1983 the United States launched Operation Urgent Fury with an airborne assault on the airstrip at Point Salines and a heliborne landing near Pearls airport. As a second Marine task force worked its way down from Grand Mal Bay, the airborne forces at Point Salines overcame Cuban and Grenadan resistance and pushed northwards. St George's fell late on 26 October and mopping up operations began.

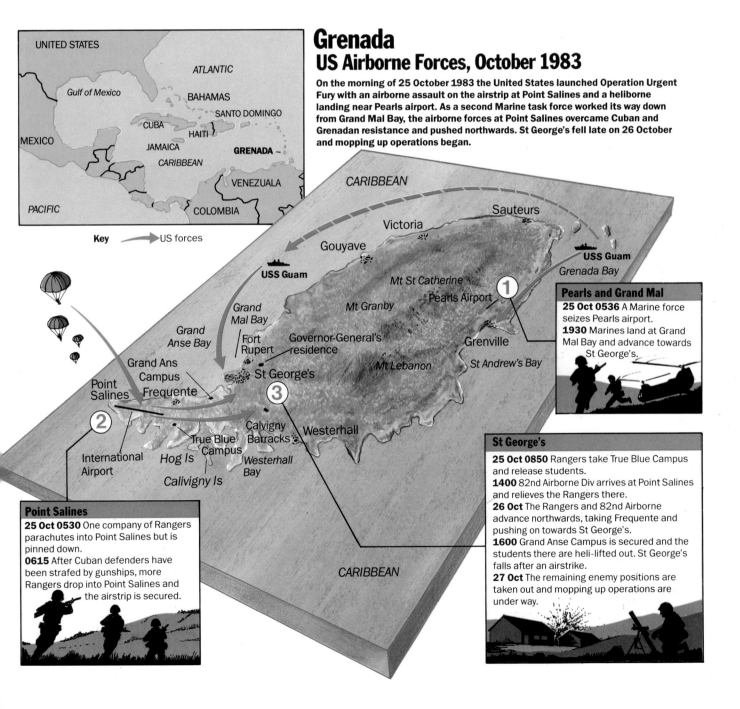

Key → US forces

Pearls and Grand Mal

25 Oct 0536 A Marine force seizes Pearls airport.
1930 Marines land at Grand Mal Bay and advance towards St George's.

Point Salines

25 Oct 0530 One company of Rangers parachutes into Point Salines but is pinned down.
0615 After Cuban defenders have been strafed by gunships, more Rangers drop into Point Salines and the airstrip is secured.

St George's

25 Oct 0850 Rangers take True Blue Campus and release students.
1400 82nd Airborne Div arrives at Point Salines and relieves the Rangers there.
26 Oct The Rangers and 82nd Airborne advance northwards, taking Frequente and pushing on towards St George's.
1600 Grand Anse Campus is secured and the students there are heli-lifted out. St George's falls after an airstrike.
27 Oct The remaining enemy positions are taken out and mopping up operations are under way.

positions on the heights. Two Cuban counter-attacks were beaten back, including one by three BTR-60 APCs (armoured personnel carriers). Using recoilless rifles and LAWs (light anti-tank weapons), the Rangers stopped the APCs, which were then drilled full of holes by 20mm fire from a Spectre overhead.

The Rangers then moved out to rescue 130 American students at the medical school's True Blue campus. Some casualties were incurred but the campus was secured by 0850 hours. By a little after 1400 hours, advance elements of the 82nd Airborne Division had arrived at Point Salines to free the Rangers for further operations inland. On the afternoon of the following day, 26 October, men of the 2nd Battalion were assigned to rescue a further group of American students trapped on the Grand Anse campus some miles to the east of Point Salines. Using Marine helicopters for their lift, the Rangers landed on the northern sector of the campus at 1600 hours. One chopper was shot down but the Rangers in it suffered only minor

Left: This Ranger sergeant on Grenada is armed with the 5.56mm CAR-15. Attached to his LC-2 belt are a fighting/survival knife and two water bottles. The trousers are OD (olive drab) twill jungle fatigues, and the boots are the nylon and black leather jungle type. The three metal chevrons on the collar denote rank, and luminous points at the back of the M1951 patrol cap are for position marking when on patrol.

injuries and continued on foot. A defensive perimeter was established around the campus and the students were airlifted out. As the third day of Urgent Fury dawned, only one large concentration of resistance remained around the Cuban barracks at Edgmont. While airborne forces surrounded the barracks, men of the 2nd Battalion spearheaded the assault in Blackhawk helicopters. Three were killed and fifteen injured, mostly after one chopper pilot was killed and his machine crashed into another on the ground. As it turned out, the barracks were virtually deserted as the defenders had fled, and by the evening of 27 October resistance had all but ceased.

Total US casualties were 18 dead and 113 injured, while more than 1100 Cubans and Grenadans had been taken prisoner. When American units searched the positions wrested from the defenders, large caches of light and heavy weapons were found, as well as documents which suggested that Cuba's interest in Grenada lay far beyond the island itself. The documents were regarded in Washington as a final vindication of US intervention, in which the Rangers had fulfilled their role as a spearhead. Indeed, their motto is 'Rangers lead the way' and, in tribute to their success, a third battalion was authorised to be raised in 1984.

THE SEALs
The US Navy Sea/Air/Land Teams

FOR the American soldier, the great delta where the Mekong river flows into the sea in the southernmost corner of South Vietnam was one of the deadliest and most treacherous areas of the whole Vietnam war zone. It was an area of open water, swamp and rice paddies, criss-crossed by some 6500km of waterways and canals, difficult to navigate and harder still to pacify. For the 80,000 Viet Cong operating in the delta by 1966, it was a stronghold from which to launch savage attacks and ambushes before melting back into the swamps as silently as they had come. It was an unconventional war that required unconventional counter-measures. Many of those who served in Vietnam in special operations would concede that the US Navy SEALs (Sea–Air–Land Teams), committed to the delta in 1966, were amongst the most formidable of all the American special forces.

On arrival in South Vietnam, the SEAL Teams operated by setting up observation and listening posts along the countless waterways and trails used by the VC. Once base routes had been located and identified, SEALs would then mount raids or fight fire with fire by laying ambushes and booby traps to cut VC supply routes. So successful were these reconnaissance missions that, within a year, listening posts were inserted for anything up to a week, during which SEALs would continuously observe and monitor VC movements in their sector. It was not an easy task since it required immense stealth and self-discipline – absolute silence was required and all orders had to be given by hand signal. Moreover, any form of resupply was completely out of the question. But the SEALs mastered these requirements and became experts in their prime aim of searching out and destroying the VC.

SEALs are fundamentally a highly mobile force and, although they are designed to be self-sufficient and able to fight without support, during the insertion and extraction phases of each mission considerable quantities of equipment were made available for their transportation. In early operations in the delta, the SEALs were dropped from 'Mike' boats – heavily armed riverine patrol craft – but, later, 'Boston Whalers'

were introduced for this purpose. These were 16ft glass-fibre craft with a very shallow draft and powered by 40hp or 85hp outboard engines, capable of high speeds should the SEALs have to make a quick getaway. For insertions from submarines or other clandestine operations, the light and silent-running IBS (inflatable boat, small) would be used, capable of carrying seven men and 500kg of equipment. For operations in dense swampland, where the use of boats was impossible, choppers from naval Light Helicopter Attack Squadrons would be brought in, the SEALs abseiling into the water or onto land, or diving into the water from the chopper.

For the execution of their missions, SEALs were equipped with some highly sophisticated weapons and equipment. Firepower was crucial for close-quarters fighting and a typical three-man SEAL fire element would normally be armed with an Ithaca M37 12-gauge fighting shotgun, a 5.56mm Stoner M63A1 light machine gun, and an M16 assault rifle with an M203 grenade launcher attached. On more clandestine operations, SEALs carried the 9mm Smith and Wesson Mark 22 Model O silenced pistol, known as the 'hush puppy', which proved a very

Above: Dressed in 'tiger-stripe' fatigues, a member of a SEAL team waits in ambush, holding a 5.56mm Stoner light machine gun at the ready. The Stoner system was developed in the early 1960s as a multi-purpose weapon which would be quickly converted for several different roles, including sub-machine gun, assault rifle, light machine gun and medium machine gun. In its LMG configuration it held a 150-round drum magazine and was highly regarded by SEALs operating in the Mekong delta.

Previous page: His face liberally covered with cam (camouflage) cream, a SEAL prepares to go into action in the Mekong delta.

effective silent killer for taking out VC sentries. SEALs were also trained in the art of hand-to-hand combat and made good use of fighting knives such as the Randall, Ka-bar and Gerber. Also of interest were the various versions of the special camouflaged combat coat designed to carry everything the SEAL needed; it even had an in-built flotation bladder.

In 1966 SEALs were involved in the ICEX (Intelligence and Exploitation) Program aimed at identifying and destroying the VC infrastructure throughout South Vietnam, and at the same time they were used for intelligence missions over the border inside North Vietnam. Haiphong harbour, the main port of entry for Soviet and Chinese shipments of arms and equipment to North Vietnam, was visited fairly frequently by SEALs. Later, other North Vietnamese harbours and bridges were sabotaged although these missions were never publicly acknowledged. Indeed, it was said that one SEAL team was captured inside North Vietnam but managed to kill its captors and escape despite having been disarmed. In a few cases, SEALs set up security cordons around South Vietnamese ports although, for the most part, such work was entrusted to attack-trained 'killer' dolphins, who may have accounted for up to 60 enemy frogmen.

By 1967, as area commanders began to hear of their significant achievements, requests for the deployment of SEAL teams began to be forwarded in large numbers and the strength of the SEALs in South Vietnam increased. Operating from a main base at Nha Be, as well as from mobile bases on barges, the SEALs continued to mount hunter-killer and intelligence missions in the delta. They also acted as scouts and spearhead forces for larger riverine operations. In Operation Crimson Tide in September 1967 and Operation Bold Dragon III in March 1968, for example, they scouted and blew up a number of VC installations. In the latter operation, they did considerable damage to the VC on Tanh Dinh island and, acting on intelligence from a VC defector, also succeeded in destroying a VC weapons factory. Beyond the delta they were used on wide-ranging patrols, especially in the mangrove swamps of the Rung Rat special zone south of Saigon.

Late in 1967 the US initiated the Phoenix Program, a combination of in-depth intelligence gathering and counter-terror operations. SEALs worked very closely with South Vietnamese Provincial Reconnaissance Units (PRUs or 'prews') in the Mekong, acting as advisers and

History and training of the SEALs

The US Navy SEALs were commissioned as a unit in January 1962 with the aim of expanding greatly the role and capabilities of the already existing combat swimmer force, the Navy Underwater Demolition Teams (UDTs). Most SEAL personnel are former UDT members but, once assigned to a SEAL Team, their training in unconventional warfare is considerably broadened. SEALs are instructed in the demolition of enemy shipping, harbour facilities, rail links, bridges and other riverine installations, and a wide range of counter-guerrilla and clandestine operational techniques. These include jungle warfare, hand-to-hand and un-armed combat skills, escape and evasion techniques, survival, and extensive weapons training. They are also taught reconnaissance and surveillance, and how to organise and work with friendly military or paramilitary units. Finally, parachute training is provided, including both high- and low-altitude jumping techniques.

The basic SEAL tactical unit is the Team, of which there are two under the command of the Naval Special Warfare Groups based respectively at Corona-do Naval Amphibious Base near San Diego, California, and Little Creek near Norfolk, Virginia. Each Team consists of 27 officers and 156 men divided into five platoons and, like most special operations forces, the structure is streamlined so that each platoon is capable of

mounting self-contained operations. SEALs were deployed extensively in South Vietnam, operating against the Viet Cong in the Mekong delta from 1966 until 1971/2 when the last detachments were officially withdrawn. However, there is reason to believe that a few SEALs remained and carried out special operations almost until the fall of Saigon in April 1975.

Most recently, SEALs took part in the US intervention in Grenada in October 1983. One team reconnoitred selected landing sites some 48 hours before the main force was due to arrive. Another 11-man team moved into the residence of the Governor-General, Sir Paul Scoon, at 0536 hours on 25 October 1983 to secure his safety. They came under heavy fire from three BTR-60 APCs and, without anti-tank weapons, were forced to sustain a 'siege'. By the time they were relieved at 0700 hours on the following day, almost all of them had been wounded but they had held out in the best traditions of their service.

Right: From the safety of a Mike boat, SEALs watch as their charges destroy VC bunkers.

Below: This SEAL operating in Vietnam in the 1960s is kitted out in locally-made 'tiger-stripe' fatigues, and his face and hands are camouflaged in the distinctive style of the unit. Nylon and leather jungle boots and a headscarf made from olive-drab towelling complete his outfit. Armament is the M16A1 rifle (fitted with an M203 grenade launcher) and attached to his belt are a USMC Ka-bar fighting knife and a fragmentation grenade.

trainers for the program. Phoenix was particularly successful in the delta and the VC infrastructure there was cut significantly. SEALs also helped to select and train their South Vietnamese equivalents, the Lin Dei Nugel Nghai (LDNN). On 22 November 1970, for example, 15 SEALs and 19 South Vietnamese smashed into a VC prison camp and fought a running battle with the guards, who were forced to flee.

Despite the impressive operational record, only one SEAL won the Congressional Medal of Honor in

Vietnam – Lieutenant Joseph Kerrey, who led an operation in Nha Trang Bay on 14 March 1969 to capture VC political cadre members on an island. Kerrey and his team scaled a 107m cliff to get above

the enemy but, as they descended, they came under heavy fire. Although badly wounded by a grenade, Kerrey still managed to direct his team's fire effectively. He remained conscious and in command while his men secured an extraction site and laid down covering fire as a chopper came in to pull them out. After Vietnam, Kerrey remained with the SEALs and was in training with the British Special Boat Squadron shortly before the outbreak of the Falklands conflict in 1982.

Due to the highly secret nature of their missions, many of the SEALs' operations and exploits, such as those inside North Vietnam, are still shrouded in secrecy. During the Vietnam War they accounted for some 580 VC killed in action and over 300 'probable kills' but they never rested on their laurels and were foremost proponents of the kind of no-questions-asked belligerence known as 'kicking ass and taking names'. It is a role for which they continue to train.

THE GREEN BERETS

The US Army Special Forces

THE exhausting and thorough training programme at Fort Bragg's Special Warfare Center (now known as the US Army John F Kennedy Center for Military Assistance, or USAJFKCENMA) is where the combat skills of the tough professionals of the Green Berets are honed to perfection. The course is still based on that originated in 1954 by Colonel Aaron Bank, but has been constantly updated to accommodate changes in the type and areas of operation that might be needed.

Always at least high-school graduates, new recruits must be tough and in peak physical condition, with an average of three years' military service behind them. Most, who are usually in their early 20s, are airborne-qualified but few have combat experience. As many as 75 per cent of the candidates fail to make the grade in the stringent three-stage programme which tests mental and physical abilities to the full. The first 31 days are given over to developing stamina and basic combat skills. Each of the 17-hour days may well begin with a 10km route march carrying a 20kg pack. Emphasis is also placed on SERE (Survival, Evasion, Resistance and Escape) and candidates can only pass to the second stage of training if they survive a three-day 'manhunt' in which, armed only with a knife, they live in the wild and attempt to evade their pursuers. In the second stage, recruits take one of five specialist courses of varying length chosen from engineering (which includes construction and destruction), weapons, communications, medical skills, and intelligence-gathering. Following this, trainees learn basic operational procedures and participate in a large-scale exercise in the Uwharrie National Forest where they raise 'native' forces while evading aggressor units. Even after successful completion of the basic training, which allows the recruits to wear the coveted green beret, additional skills such as languages still have to be acquired on attachment to US military commands throughout the world.

Green Berets are also trained in the dangerous arts of insertion into enemy-occupied territory. The most common

Previous page: Two Green Berets learn the technique of house clearance – a skill that was much in demand during the Vietnam War.

History of the Special Forces

The origins of the US Special Forces lie with the 1st Special Service Force formed by Lieutenant-Colonel Robert Frederick in 1942 with the intention of raiding hydroelectric plants in Nazi-occupied Norway. Eventually six battalions were raised and these saw service in the Aleutians, North Africa, Italy and southern France. The concept of a specialised raiding force was revived with the formation of the 10th Special Forces Group (SFG) at Fort Bragg, North Carolina, on 20 June 1952. In September 1953, the 77th (later 7th) SFG was constituted and the 1st SFG followed in June 1957. The green beret had been selected as a suitable distinction in 1954 and was first worn in June 1956. Many in the military establishment, however, opposed small elite units and the beret was banned until reinstated in October 1961 by President John F. Kennedy, whose support proved invaluable.

Between September 1961 and March 1964 four new SFGs – the 3rd, 5th, 6th and 8th – were created. The 3rd was assigned to Africa and the 6th to the Middle East. The 8th operated from Fort Gulick, Panama, training Latin American officers in counter-insurgency and undertaking missions in Guatemala, Colombia and Bolivia against guerrillas. Indeed, two Special Forces members were allegedly present when Bolivian Rangers captured and shot Che Guevara in October 1967.

The 5th SFG was sent to South Vietnam in October 1964 to take control of all Special Forces activity there. In fact, 1st SFG personnel had begun training South Vietnamese forces in 1957, while teams from 7th SFG had been committed on six-month tours in May 1960. In December 1961 Special Forces teams established a pilot programme at Buon Enao in the Darlac province of the Central Highlands to organise Civilian Irregular Defense Groups to defend villages against the communists. By 1964 there were over 11,000 CIDG troops along the Cambodian and Laotian borders alone and, by 1966, when 5th SFG itself had grown from 951 men to 2627 men, there was a huge CIDG force under command. The 'Greek-letter projects' – reconnaissance units used to infiltrate enemy-held areas – were also activated in 1964.

Special Forces operations similarly embraced the Studies and Observation Group (SOG), under whose auspices cross-border raids were mounted, such as the attempt to free American POWs held at Son Tay in North Vietnam in November 1970. The Green Berets lost some military support after their departure from South Vietnam in March 1971 but their value for covert operations and counter-insurgency has been recognised. There are now three regular SFGs – the 5th, 7th and 10th – of battalion size under the control of the 1st Special Operations Command of the Joint Special Operations Agency.

Above: Thorough tuition is given before theory can be put into practice. Here recruits are taught the layout of a para-rig.

Above right: Training includes working with a wide range of foreign weapons, including the AK-47 assault rifle, widely favoured by communist guerrillas.

methods used are HELO (High Extraction, Low Opening) and HEHO (High Extraction, High Opening). In the former, the Green Beret free-falls from 35,000ft to the minimum safety height before opening his chute; the latter is a method of gliding down at a rate of half-a-mile per 1000ft of descent, to travel a considerable distance from the jumping point. Green Berets are similarly expert at underwater insertion using the CCR 1000 scuba system, which allows up to four hours' submersion. The basic operational unit is the A-Detachment or, more popularly, 'A-Team', consisting of two officers and ten men. Four such teams are controlled by a 'B-Team', which itself comprises six officers and eighteen other ranks. Three B-Teams are controlled, in turn, by a Special Forces Company or 'C-Team', consisting of six officers and thirteen NCOs. The C-Team assigns objectives and assesses intelligence gathered. A-Teams train local forces while B-Teams can operate in a more active role. When 5th SFG was assigned to South Vietnam in 1964 it had 36 A-Teams, 9 B-Teams and 3 C-Teams. Subsequently, its skills were augmented by Special Action Forces (SAF), which included civil affairs, psychological operations, medical, field security, and engineer units.

Vietnam

A priority for the Special Forces in Vietnam was the eradication of Viet Cong influence among the Montagnard tribesmen of the Central Highlands through raising indigenous troops in Civilian Irregular Defense Groups (CIDGs, or 'cidgees'). Indeed, a single A-Team was theoretically capable of raising 1500 men within a single month. Once a pioneering group had set civic action programmes in motion, teams from the Green Berets and the equivalent South Vietnamese Luc Luong Dac Biet (LLDB) would begin military training. Defensive positions would be built around villages, and tribesmen would receive between two (for militia) and six (for strike-force units) weeks' instruction in the use of the M1 carbine and M3 sub-machine gun. By the end of 1963 there were 18,000 members in strike forces and over 43,000 hamlet milita within the CIDG programme. Moreover, cidgees were no longer passively waiting for attack but were patrolling aggressively in search of VC, especially in the Border Surveillance Program launched along key VC infiltration routes in October 1963. There were problems assimilating some

M14 Rifle

Calibre 7.62mm
Length 111.7cm
Weight 3.88kg
Feed 20-round box magazine
System of operation Gas
Rate of fire (cyclic) 750rpm
Muzzle velocity 853mps

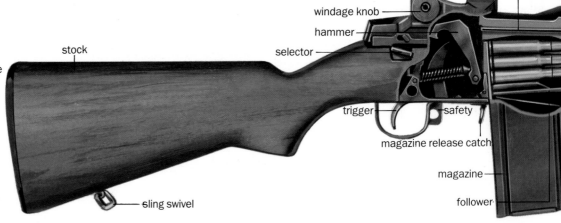

stock

rear sight assembly
windage knob
hammer
selector
firing pin
trigger
safety
magazine release catch
magazine
follower
sling swivel

Top: The M14 rifle was used extensively in Vietnam prior to the introduction of the M16 assault rifle.

Above: Captain Roger Donlon, commanding officer of Special Forces A-Team 726 at Nam Dong.

Far Right: This 5th Special Forces Group captain wears green jungle fatigues with black leather and nylon boots. Armament is an M2 carbine and a .45 calibre Colt M1911A1 pistol.

minority tribal groups and hostility often surfaced between the Montagnards and the LLDB. Nevertheless, the success of CIDG groups in negating communist influence was illustrated by the increasingly concentrated attacks on CIDG camps. On 6 July 1964, for example, the remote Nam Dong camp, just 24km from the Laotian frontier, was attacked by over 900 VC. The garrison of CIDG and A-Team 726, commanded by Captain Roger Donlon, suffered 120 casualties and the camp was set ablaze. But they held out for over two hours until assistance arrived, Donlon winning the Medal of Honor for his inspired leadership: despite a stomach wound he had personally eliminated a three-man VC demolition squad at the camp's main gate.

As a result of such attacks, the Mobile Strike Force ('Mike' Force) was authorised in October 1964. Originally comprising 600 men, it was trained for airborne or airmobile warfare as an elite quick-reaction element of the CIDG Program. Eventually, five Strike Force Commands were established with 11,000 men in 34 companies. The Mike Forces were widely used in 'Blackjack' operations, in which they would reinforce highly mobile teams inserted into enemy-occupied territory ('Indian Country') and exploit the latter's reconnaissance findings by striking with maximum effectiveness. Another specialist CIDG group was the 'Apache' Force who, with Special Forces advisers, would assist in orientating newly arrived American

troops. Later the Apache Force evolved into the combat reconnaissance teams used to prepare the way for Mike Force operations.

By 1967, although many US commanders still failed to employ CIDG troops correctly, their effectiveness was steadily increasing. Border surveillance and fighting camps were being constructed and units were operating from such camps in hard-contested areas such as the notorious War Zone C. When the Tet (Lunar New Year) offensive opened in January 1968, cidgees gained a great deal of respect as urban fighters and inflicted severe blows on VC who attacked centres such as Ban Me Thuot and Nha Trang. After Tet, the cidgees enjoyed greater respect and received M16 and M60 GPMGs (general-purpose machine guns) for the first time in April 1968. By 1970, at which time the Special Forces CIDG Program was closed down and the CIDG units passed to South Vietnamese command, units had even participated in operations in Cambodia and had made a real contribution to curbing insurgency inside South Vietnam.

Project Delta

CIDG Mike Forces had also been closely involved with the Green Berets' 'Greek-letter projects' – Delta, Sigma, Omega and Gamma. Delta, the best known, was activated in 1964 as a self-contained

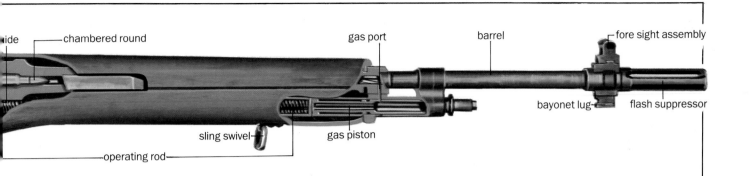

ide ─ chambered round   gas port   barrel   fore sight assembly

bayonet lug   flash suppressor

sling swivel   gas piston

operating rod

Special Forces Vietnam

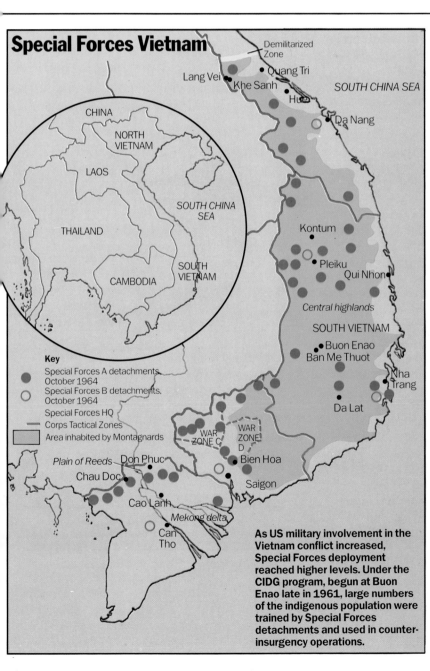

Demilitarized Zone

Lang Vei
Khe Sanh
Quang Tri
Hue
Da Nang

SOUTH CHINA SEA

CHINA

NORTH VIETNAM

LAOS

SOUTH CHINA SEA

THAILAND

CAMBODIA

SOUTH VIETNAM

Kontum

Pleiku

Qui Nhon

Central highlands

SOUTH VIETNAM

Buon Enao
Ban Me Thuot

Nha Trang

Da Lat

Key
● Special Forces A detachments October 1964
○ Special Forces B detachments. October 1964
● Special Forces HQ
── Corps Tactical Zones
▨ Area inhabited by Montagnards

WAR ZONE C
WAR ZONE D

Plain of Reeds   Don Phuc
Chau Doc
Bien Hoa
Saigon
Cao Lanh
Mekong delta
Can Tho

As US military involvement in the Vietnam conflict increased, Special Forces deployment reached higher levels. Under the CIDG program, begun at Buon Enao late in 1961, large numbers of the indigenous population were trained by Special Forces detachments and used in counter-insurgency operations.

Above: Brigadier-General Donald Blackburn headed the study team that developed the operational plan for the raid on Son Tay.

group to carry out hazardous intelligence-gathering and hunter-killer missions along South Vietnam's frontiers. Not to be confused with the later post-Vietnam Delta Force, it was organised into 12 (later 16) tight-knit, highly skilled reconnaissance teams, each made up of two Green Berets and four locals or 'indigs'. Delta also had six (later 12) 'Roadrunner' teams, each consisting of four indigs, whose role was to move along enemy infiltration routes disguised as guerrillas, report back, and call up the 'killer' element in the form of the South Vietnamese 91st Ranger Battalion (Airborne). The 281st Assault Helicopter Company was also assigned to provide Delta with its own organic lift capability. It was time-consuming, strength-sapping and unglamorous work but absolutely necessary for the gathering of intelligence. Its success led to the activation of Projects Sigma, Gamma and Omega in 1966 and 1967.

While Delta was run jointly by US and South Vietnamese Special Forces, the other Greek-letter projects were the responsibility of Green Berets alone, although each involved indigenous personnel working alongside Americans. Indigs were also included in the Green Berets' own reconnaissance teams, which were equally capable of carrying out wider roles such as assassinations, sabotage, psychological warfare, snatches and rescue missions. These teams came under the control of the Studies and Observations Group (SOG) which, at its peak, controlled 2000 US personnel and 8000 indigs. By 1967, co-ordination within SOG had devolved upon three Command and Control (CC) units, the primary operational unit of the CC being a 'Spike Recon Team' of three Green Berets and nine indigs. Recon teams (RTs) were, in turn, backed by 'Hatchet Forces' of five Special Forces personnel and up to 309 indigs and SLAM (Search–Locate–Annihilate Mission) companies who provided the cutting edge in acting upon RT intelligence.

As their function was primarily one of intelligence-gathering, RTs often avoided 'live' contact but they were still walking arsenals. The most common sidearm was a handy Browning 9mm pistol or .22in Ruger automatic with silencer but larger weapons included the

Right: The 7.62mm miniguns of one HH-53 Super Jolly Green Giant were used to demolish the guard towers around the Son Tay compound.

CAR-15 version of the M16, the Swedish K 9mm sub-machine gun and even sawn-off M79 grenade launchers. Armed with this deadly array of ordnance, the RTs would invariably be inserted by helicopter at dusk. On the ground, stealth would be vital and orders would be given by hand or arm signals. Each member would be trained in interpreting and reading any signs left by the enemy and, if it became clear that a trail was in constant use, they might lay an ambush or carry out a snatch to capture a guerrilla. However, to avoid getting involved in a firefight, teams would often leave a calling card: this might take the form of a Claymore mine with a delay fuze, M14 mines planted in a triangular pattern, or trip wires attached to fragmentation grenades.

After completing a mission, the team would rendezvous at an agreed landing site. Helicopters dropping in low and fast at a steep angle was a favoured method of rapid extraction. If under fire or being pursued, teams could also be extracted by a nylon webbing rig. Like a simplified parachute harness, the wearer could attach the rig to a rope hanging from the chopper and be drawn up aloft quickly. Initially, a McGuire rig was used but, later, the 5th SFG Recondo School devised an improved rig known as STABO.

Son Tay

SOG attracted some of the most redoubtable Special Forces officers such as Colonel John Singlaub, Colonel 'Bull' Simons and Brigadier-General Donald Blackburn, a veteran of World War II. Both Blackburn and Simons were involved in one of the most daring of all Green Beret operations during the Vietnam War – the attempt to free American POWs held at Son Tay prison in North Vietnam, some 37km west of Hanoi. Once intelligence had been received in May 1970 that Americans were held at Son Tay, Blackburn as SACSA (Special Assistant for Counter-insurgency and Special Activities) was tasked with a rescue mission. He wanted to lead the mission personally but, because of his knowledge of sensitive

intelligence, the assignment went to Simons.

A special Joint Contingency Task Group (JCTG) of 97 Green Berets was selected at Fort Bragg for Operation Ivory Coast. Training was undertaken on a special mock-up of the Son Tay compound at night – each day it was dismantled to prevent Soviet spy satellites discovering American intentions. During training, Simons solved the crucial problem of eliminating camp guards by equipping his snipers with 'Singlepoint Nite Sites', acquired (like much of the equipment for the raid) from outside normal army supply channels, and introducing an HH-53 Super Jolly Green Giant chopper to bring down the guard towers with its 7.62mm miniguns. From the 97 men originally selected, 14 would actually be deposited inside the prison compound by crash-landing an HH-3 Jolly Green Giant. Another 20 would form a command and security group and Simons would lead a 22-strong support group. Originally envisaged for October, the raid was not authorised by President Nixon until 18 November 1970, conditions for the operation being deemed acceptable on the night of 20/21 November.

On the evening of 20 November, therefore, the raiders who had arrived in Thailand two days earlier were shuttled to Udorn airbase from which the raid was launched at 2318 hours. Carrier aircraft created a diversion over Hanoi as a C-130 flare ship illuminated the area around the compound at Son Tay. The raid began at about 0218 hours in the morning of 21 November. The HH-53 opened up and soon brought the guard towers tumbling to the ground. Shortly afterwards, Major 'Dick' Meadows' assault team crash-landed in the compound, each man pressed against mattresses to cushion the impact. Minutes later the command and security group landed just outside and, even though Simons' group landed 400m off course at what was thought to be a school but proved to be a barracks for Soviet and Chinese advisers, opposition was suppressed within ten minutes. Unfortunately, there were no prisoners in the compound – they had been moved some weeks before the raid. Less than 30 minutes after the raid had begun all were safely back on board with only one man

wounded. It was not a complete failure since Simons' men had killed dozens of the enemy and the raid had proved in a striking fashion that North Vietnamese installations were vulnerable to the kind of attacks Blackburn had been advocating for some time. Indirectly the raid led to some improvements in the treatment of American POWs and the North

Son Tay
US Special Forces, 21 November 1970

In the early morning of 21 November 1970 a crack assault group of US Special Forces staged a daring raid on a North Vietnamese POW camp only 23 miles from Hanoi. The American POWs they hoped to free had been moved out – but the raid was executed with verve and the force pulled out without suffering a single serious casualty.

Song Con

Assault on the compound

21 Nov 0218 Son Tay camp is illuminated by a C-130 flare-ship and strafed. Meadows' assault force lands inside the compound and goes into action, firing and rushing forward to cell blocks 'Opium Den', 'Cat House' and 'Beer House'. The command group under Sydnor lands outside and blasts its way through the compound's south wall.
0226 Having cleared the enemy at the 'secondary school' site, Simons' group is heli-lifted to the Son Tay compound to assist with mopping up enemy forces.
0236 The first helicopter returns from the holding area and withdrawal of the raiding force begins.

Vietnamese, who had lost face with their Chinese and Soviet advisers, were forced to divert additional troops to guard sensitive areas.

Despite the frequent success of the Green Berets, they could not offset the inability of the US forces as a whole to come to grips with waging a war against an unconventional enemy. Thus, as the American commitment in South Vietnam wound down, many of the Special Forces teams were deactivated. On 31 December 1970 the participation of the 5th SFG in the CIDG Program officially ended and the 5th as a whole departed for Fort Bragg on 3 March 1971, although some members remained in advisory or operational roles much longer.

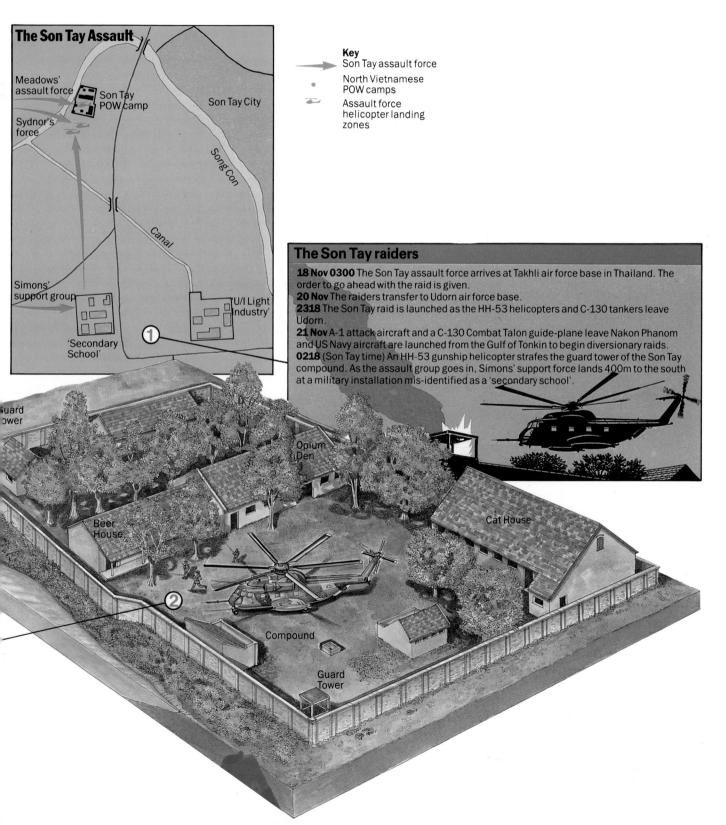

The Son Tay Assault

Meadows' assault force

Son Tay POW camp

Son Tay City

Sydnor's force

Song Con

Canal

Simons' support group

'U/I Light Industry'

'Secondary School'

Key
Son Tay assault force
North Vietnamese POW camps
Assault force helicopter landing zones

The Son Tay raiders

18 Nov 0300 The Son Tay assault force arrives at Takhli air force base in Thailand. The order to go ahead with the raid is given.
20 Nov The raiders transfer to Udorn air force base.
2318 The Son Tay raid is launched as the HH-53 helicopters and C-130 tankers leave Udorn.
21 Nov A-1 attack aircraft and a C-130 Combat Talon guide-plane leave Nakon Phanom and US Navy aircraft are launched from the Gulf of Tonkin to begin diversionary raids.
0218 (Son Tay time) An HH-53 gunship helicopter strafes the guard tower of the Son Tay compound. As the assault group goes in, Simons' support force lands 400m to the south at a military installation mis-identified as a 'secondary school'.

Guard Tower

Opium Den

Beer House

Cat House

Compound

Guard Tower

1st AIR CAVALRY

The 1st Cavalry Division (Airmobile)

WHEN it arrived in South Vietnam in 1965, the 1st Air Cavalry had no 'book' to go by and tactics, which varied from unit to unit, had to be evolved to meet local conditions. In general, however, the basic combat formation was the troop of four platoons, divided up into teams, colour-coded for a particular task. The 'pink' hunter-killer team comprised 'white' aero scouts flying OH-6 Loaches, and the 'red' section of AH-1 Huey Cobra gunships. The 'blue' team consisted of the troop's lift element – eight UH-1D Hueys – and the Aero Rifle Platoon

(ARP). Success depended upon a high degree of co-ordination between the various elements. Pink teams would identify enemy positions, mark suitable landing zones (LZs) and call up the reds to deal with the enemy on the ground. As the ARPs dismounted to form a defensive perimeter, the pink team Cobras remained on station to provide aerial artillery support.

The tactical lynchpin was the helicopters themselves. Known to the troops as the Huey, the UH-1 was the most successful chopper to see service in Vietnam, the UH-1D being the most

History of the 1st Air Cavalry

The early history of the 1st Cavalry Division (Airmobile) is a story of a dedicated few overcoming the prejudices of many. Although helicopters had been used for casualty evacuation in the Korean War and the Marine Corps had carried out some pioneering airborne assault tests, the Pentagon remained lukewarm to the idea. The report of the Howse Board in August 1962 changed all that in stating that the airmobile concept was 'necessary and desirable'. The 11th Air Assault Division (Test) was ordered to put theory into practice and trials in early 1965 proved so successful that it was given the go-ahead to prepare for active service. Men from the 2nd Infantry Division joined the unit and, on 1 July 1965, the 1st Air Cavalry came into being.

A month later the formation – 16,000 strong with 400 fixed-wing aircraft and helicopters and over 1600 vehicles – was en route for South Vietnam. It was a formation under close scrutiny and both sides of the 'airmobility debate' awaited with interest the results of the division's baptism of fire. After establishing a base at An Khe and conducting a few small-scale actions against local Viet Cong, the division got the chance to show its worth in the Ia Drang valley in the autumn of 1965. Its performance heralded a new era in military thinking. The two cornerstones of its success were, first, the quality of its men – the flying skills of the pilots, the inventiveness of the engineers, the determination of the ground troops, and the tactical flair of the commanders – and, second, the new weapons and equipment that were made available to them. The latter transformed the relationship between firepower and mobility. Previously, any increase in firepower could only be made at the expense of mobility (or vice versa), but the airmobility concept added a new dimension to the equation: firepower could now be allied to mobility and an increase in one could enhance the effectiveness of the other.

Through a whole series of engagements over the next five years – Hue, Khe Sanh, A Shau valley and Liberty Canyon, right up to the invasion of Cambodia in 1970 – the 1st Air Cavalry gained for itself the reputation of premier combat division in the US Army. Together with the 101st Airborne Division, which was converted from its parachute role, the 1st Air Cavalry continues to represent the airmobile concept within the American military establishment.

Left: While ground patrols of the 1st Air Cavalry move out of the landing zone, door gunners aboard Bell UH-1H helicopters take up firecover positions to protect both their aircraft and the patrols from possible enemy attack.

numerous of the Huey series. As the divisional assault-troop transport, it was armed with two door-mounted 7.62mm M60 machine guns and could carry 11 or 12 fully-equipped men besides two gunners and two pilots. Fully loaded, it was capable of a maximum speed of little more than 160kph. While Hueys performed the assault role, equally important work was carried out by the division's CH-47 Chinooks, which could transport up to 44 men but were mainly used to transport artillery and heavy supplies. Whole batteries of 105mm howitzers could be flown in to the steepest and most inaccessible positions and, thanks to the Chinook, the 1st Air Cavalry could position a fire-support base virtually at will. Ever resourceful, the 1st Air Cavalry even developed several Chinooks as bombers during Operation Pershing in 1967, dropping from the rear doors tear gas and napalm attached to a static line, which armed the projectiles once they had fallen clear of the chopper.

Another special adaptation of the Chinook was its conversion into a gunship or 'Go-Go Bird' with twin 20mm multi-barrelled cannon, 40mm grenade launchers and 0.5in heavy machine guns. Originally, the UH-1C was used in the gunship role but it was too large and too slow and, in 1967, the Bell Helicopter Company's AH-1 Huey Cobra arrived in Vietnam. The machine's survivability was enhanced by a top speed of over 309kph and a superbly designed forward profile to give all-round visibility, while armoured seats and personal body armour protected the crew. Most impressive of all was its armament. At first, a single 7.62mm minigun was carried but, later, the XM-28 weapons' sub-system allowed other options such as two miniguns, two 40mm grenade launchers, or one minigun and one grenade launcher. The Cobra's stub wings also allowed further armament such as 2.75in rocket packs or, eventually, guided missiles.

While the helicopters were the most visible element of the 1st Air Cavalry, and the one that most readily distinguished itself from other formations, eight infantry battalions and the divisional artillery formed the core. The divisional aviation group was capable of airlifting three battalions – around 2000 men – at any given time while the remaining infantry acted either in an ordinary infantry role or were held

M60 GPMG

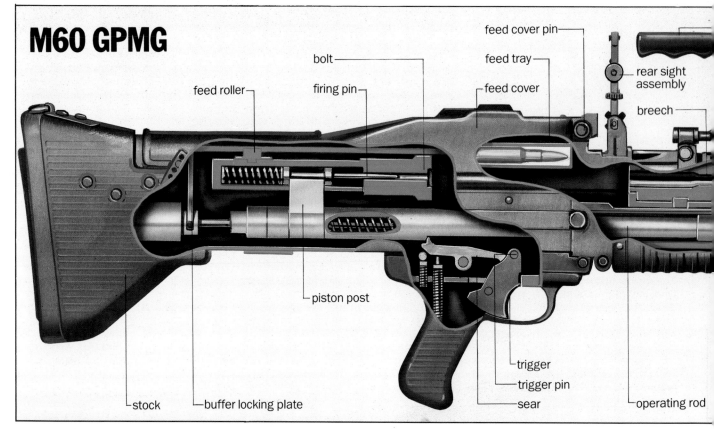

feed cover pin

bolt

feed tray

rear sight assembly

feed roller

firing pin

feed cover

breech

piston post

trigger

trigger pin

sear

operating rod

stock

buffer locking plate

Above: The M60 general-purpose machine gun provided the infantry section of the 1st Air Cavalry with its own firepower. Belt-fed and gas-operated, the M60 was generally popular with the troops, and even if its rate of fire was somewhat low for sustained long-range shooting, it was more than adequate as armament for jungle patrols.

in reserve for later aerial deployment. The weight of artillery support seemed, at first sight, to undermine the 'lean and mean' concept of airmobility but the Chinooks could easily transport three battalions of 105mm howitzers. Later, when a need for heavier firepower was perceived, CH-54 Tarhe Sky Cranes proved equal to the task of carrying a battalion of 155mm howitzers which were attached to the division. In addition, there was the aerial artillery battalion of three batteries, each with 12 choppers armed with packs of 2.75in aerial rockets.

This formidable combination of firepower and mobility was first tested in the Ia Drang valley in the Central Highlands of South Vietnam, some 40km southwest of Pleiku. Initially, on 21 October 1965, only a battalion task force was warned to move to assist South Vietnamese troops under pressure from North Vietnamese Army (NVA) regulars at Plei Me Camp. However, it became apparent that the NVA assault was meant to be the beginning of a full-scale offensive aiming to cut South Vietnam in half, and the presence of at least two NVA regiments provided an opportunity to deploy the 1st Air Cavalry as a whole. As the NVA pulled back from Plei Me on

25 October, the divisional commander, Major-General Harry Kinnard, was given a free hand to pursue the enemy.

It was no easy task to engage in hard-hitting search-and-destroy operations in the dense vegetation of the Central Highlands where rocks, hidden in man-tall elephant grass, could flip a helicopter on its side. Most clearings were too small for even a single Huey and pilots could hack their way to the ground only by the risky process – strictly against regulations – of using the tail rotor as a chain saw. In the first skirmishes, too, many cavalry troopers were disconcerted by the suicidally close range at which they came to grips with the enemy. Several units were almost dropped into the laps of the NVA and firefights took place at ranges less than 20m. It was often difficult to organise artillery support and medevac was delayed because of the lack of equipment to clear the LZ.

For the first 12 days, much of the 1st Brigade was deployed west of Pleiku and involved in fierce fighting. Many operations, however, were successful. On 1 November, for example, a routine reconnaissance patrol spotted unusual activity 12km west of Plei Me. Units

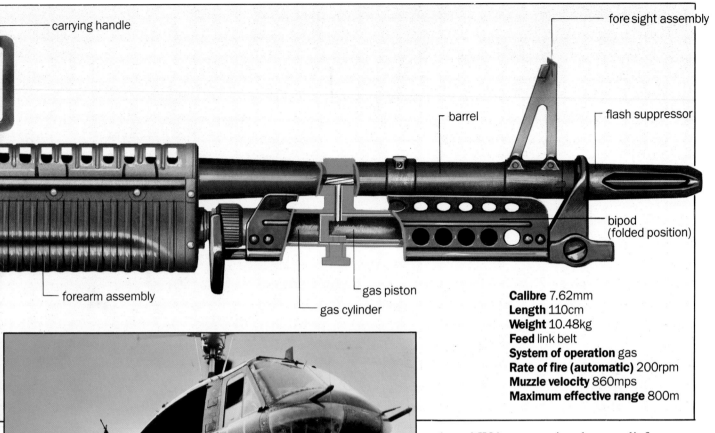

carrying handle

fore sight assembly

barrel

flash suppressor

bipod (folded position)

forearm assembly

gas piston

gas cylinder

Calibre 7.62mm
Length 110cm
Weight 10.48kg
Feed link belt
System of operation gas
Rate of fire (automatic) 200rpm
Muzzle velocity 860mps
Maximum effective range 800m

Above: A quick response to a threat by VC as men jump down from a Bell Huey. A radio operator stays in position, ready to give covering fire.

three NVA companies that a relief operation had to be mounted by Company A, 1st Battalion, 8th Cavalry.

The first combats were often small-scale but, for Kinnard, they were ample justification for the airmobile concept. Scouts were regularly finding the enemy, mobile rifle units were successively fixing the NVA, and massive firepower was inflicting maximum damage. Even night deployments had been successfully attempted and, by the time the 1st Brigade was withdrawn on 9 November, some 200 NVA had been killed and an estimated 180 wounded. More importantly, over 100,000 rounds of 7.62mm ammunition, two mortars and three recoilless rifles had been destroyed.

The 1st Brigade was replaced by the 3rd Brigade, consisting of the 1st and 2nd Battalions, 7th Cavalry, and the 2nd Battalion, 5th Cavalry. By this stage, Kinnard's main concern was to prevent the NVA slipping away and 3rd Brigade's commander, Colonel Thomas W. Brown, was tasked with a vigorous hunt south and southeast of Plei Me. Accordingly, on 14 November, Lieutenant-Colonel Harold G. Moore's 1st Battalion, 7th Cavalry, began a sweep along the base of the Chu Pong range. LZ X-Ray, 10km

were ordered in and not only killed 78 NVA and captured another 57 but also secured a complete NVA field hospital. The 1st Squadron of the 9th Cavalry drew blood two days later in a perfectly executed ambush on an NVA unit of company strength just north of the Chu Pong mountains. But the 9th Cavalry did not have things entirely their own way and their base came under such sustained, almost fanatical, attacks from

west of Plei Me, was chosen as the best place for an opening air assault in the vicinity of NVA positions. At 1017 hours, a preliminary bombardment by 105mm howitzers commenced, followed by the aerial gunships. Company B of the 1st Battalion then landed, and was followed by Companies A and C.

By 1330 hours, however, the NVA had made further reinforcement at X-Ray extremely harzardous, since the LZ was sparse brush ringed with elephant grass and anthills that provided ideal cover for the communists. Several Hueys were hit and, although none was shot down,

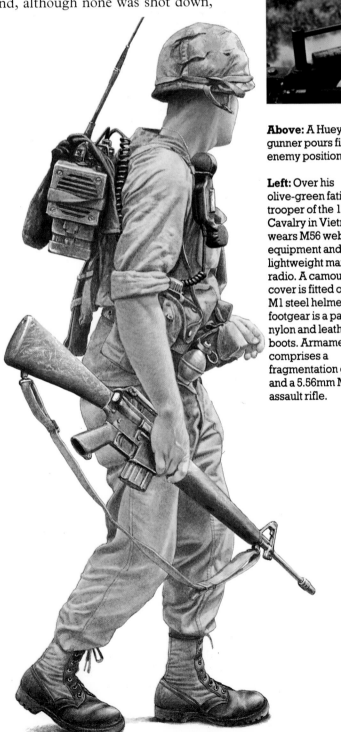

Above: A Huey door gunner pours fire onto enemy positions.

Left: Over his olive-green fatigues this trooper of the 1st Air Cavalry in Vietnam wears M56 web equipment and a lightweight man-pack radio. A camouflage cover is fitted over his M1 steel helmet, while footgear is a pair of US nylon and leather jungle boots. Armament comprises a fragmentation grenade and a 5.56mm M16A1 assault rifle.

Moore forbade further attempts. The LZ was decidedly 'hot' and, by mid-afternoon on 14 November, Moore knew he had a major battle on his hands. Company B of 2nd Battalion, 7th Cavalry, was landed at 1800 hours but it was not until after air strikes and aerial rocket artillery had blasted the NVA out of their positions that 2nd Battalion, 5th Cavalry, could be sent in by noon on the following day. Even then, Moore's men had to hold on until they were airlifted out as leading elements of the 2nd Battalion, 7th Cavalry, arrived on 16 November.

The two-day battle around LZ X-Ray was the high point of the 1st Air Cavalry's campaign in the Ia Drang valley. Moore's men had suffered nearly 200 casualties but the NVA had undoubtedly suffered far more – 634 known dead and 581 supposed dead. One of Company B's platoons had been isolated since the first evening of the operation and had been forced to beat off repeated attacks. Savage close fighting had gone on throughout the LZ. But it was clear that there would now be no full-scale offensive by the NVA in the Central Highlands.

The 3rd Brigade was withdrawn from Ia Drang on 20 November 1965 and the 2nd Brigade by 26 November. In the 35 days it had spent in the valley, the 1st Air Cavalry Division had changed the very nature of the war in Vietnam.

THE TUNNEL RATS

The Tunnel Rat Team, 1st Engineer Battalion, 1st Infantry Division

SERGEANT Robert Batten – 'Batman' as he was universally known – was the most fearsome of the elite, but little-known, Tunnel Rats. The name was unglamorous and brutal but so was the nature of the war they fought underground. Batten was more famous among the VC than his own side and was the only NCO on the VC's '10 most-wanted list'. Four times wounded, he volunteered to stay in Vietnam for two extra tours of duty. It was Batten, too, who coined the Tunnel Rats' motto. He would explain, 'I love getting those gooks out of there. They

think they have it made down in them holes. Well, they have it made like a rat's ass when old Batman comes after them.' So it was that 'Not worth a rat's ass', improbably put into Latin, became the motto.

Between February and July 1969 the team's 'Rat Six' was Lieutenant Jack Flowers. A college drop-out from Indiana, Flowers had been anti-war when conscripted and sought out the safest jobs when assigned to Lai Khe. Then, one day, a helicopter pilot sneeringly insulted him in a particular wounding way. The vicious abuse stung and, surprisingly,

The role of the Tunnel Rats at Cu Chi

Mining and counter-mining operations have characterised countless sieges throughout history. During World War I, tunnelling was an integral part of trench warfare, Britain's Royal Engineers forming special Tunnelling Companies in January 1915. However, although tunnels had been used by the Viet Minh in battles against French forces in Indo-China and by Chinese and North Korean troops in the Korean War, the vast tunnel complex first encountered by American troops during Operation Crimp in South Vietnam in January 1966 was entirely new to their experience.

In all, the Viet Cong had dug a 320km labyrinth of underground tunnels around Saigon, which provided them with barracks, arms factories and hospitals under the very noses of the Americans. Crimp had been designed to establish the 1st Infantry Division ('The Big Red One') and the 25th Infantry ('Tropic Lightning') Division as well as other units in camps around Saigon. Ironically, the 25th's new base at Cu Chi, astride the strategic Route 1 northwest of Saigon, was built right over one of the most important VC tunnel systems and, as late as 1969, the VC were still able to penetrate defences of which they had gained an intimate knowledge.

Attempts to destroy the Cu Chi tunnels proved difficult and, in any case, important intelligence could be obtained in them. As a result, *ad hoc* investigations began. Both the 25th Division and, later, the 65th Engineer Battalion worked at Cu Chi but it was the 1st Engineer Battalion of 1st Division that became the acknowledged tunnel experts or 'Tunnel Rats'. In June 1967 the Tunnel Rat Team was formally constituted within the battalion, consisting of seven or eight men under the command of a lieutenant, known as 'Rat Six', supported by one or two NCOs. Based at Lai Khe, the team members, whose average length of service was four months, served widely in South Vietnam. It was grim, silent work as, armed only with knives and pistols, the Tunnel Rats fought hand-to-hand against an ingenious enemy inside the cramped booby-trapped blackness of the tunnels.

By 1970 the Tunnel Rats had been withdrawn but a decisive blow was struck at the tunnels by American airpower after President Johnson's bombing pause in October 1968 freed B-52s from airstrikes over North Vietnam. The B-52s unleashed a swathe of destruction which finally denied the use of the tunnels to the VC but it did not detract from the supreme courage of the Tunnel Rats.

Flowers accepted the job of commanding the Tunnel Rats. There he met Batten, who expected Flowers to stay out of the way. But Flowers was determined to command, trained hard and, as mission succeeded mission, Batten grudgingly accepted his authority.

In May 1969 Batten was finally sent home after three years with the Tunnel Rats, leaving the army when his final request to return to Vietnam was refused. Flowers drank with him on his last night, when Batten delivered his verdict on his officer: 'You're not a killer, Six, and that's your problem. You're pretty good, the best Six I ever had, but you'll screw up somewhere. Charlie [the VC] hasn't killed a Rat for some time. You'll either let him get you or, what's worse, you'll get yourself.'

Batten's replacement was Sergeant Peter Schultz, a good soldier but too tall and well-built to be an effective Rat. Without Batten, Flowers was exposed and the increasing work and responsibility began to drain him. In one tunnel, an enemy mine completely buried him and it was five minutes before he was dug out, unconscious. The end came in late July 1969 when Flowers' team was on a mission in the 'Iron Triangle', northwest of Saigon, where a VC base-camp complex had been discovered. A succession of holes proved 'cold' and, at length, only one remained. Flowers knew he must tackle this since all his men had been down a tunnel already that day.

After a grenade had been dropped down the shaft – little more than a noisy warning gesture – Flowers was lowered some 5m in a 'Swiss seat' cradle for what he anticipated to be a one-to-one

Previous page: Clearing a tunnel in 1967.

Below: Lieutenant Jack 'Rat Six' Flowers receives the Bronze Star.

To Cu Chi

Above: A VC tunnel is dimly lit by a Rat's flashlight as he fires a special tracer round from his handgun.

Above right: Actors were able to perform in specially built subterranean theatres.

confrontation underground. With Batten's prediction ever-present in his mind, Flowers pictured an enemy leaning against the side of the tunnel with an AK-47 assault rifle set on full automatic fire. His one chance would be to kill with the first shot from his pistol. One metre from the tunnel floor, Flowers signalled to Schultz to release the rope. Hitting the

floor with his pistol firing, Flowers' first shot went through the VC's forehead, the second through his cheek, the third his throat and the fourth, fifth and sixth into his body. Flowers kept pulling the trigger, clicking on empty chambers. He stared dumbly in front of him, disbelieving what his mind had created, for there had been no enemy soldier there after all. Somewhere inside Flowers' head, Batman laughed.

Two days later, Flowers was relieved of command of the Tunnel Rats and shipped quickly out of Lai Khe; there were no farewells and no handovers. Fifteen years later, in the restaurant of a Philadelphia skyscraper, Flowers ruminated on the end of his war: 'Rat Six was dead. He died in some tunnel in the Iron Triangle. Batman was right. Charlie didn't get me. I got myself.'

Below: The tunnels of Cu Chi had all the facilities to feed, shelter and provide storage for the VC.

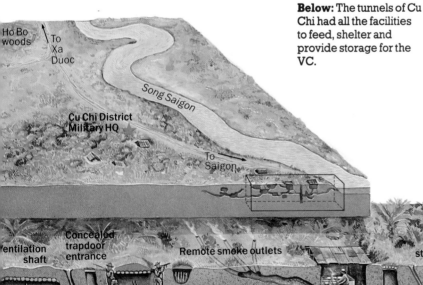

Hồ Bo woods
To Xa Duoc
Song Saigon
Cu Chi District Military HQ
To Saigon

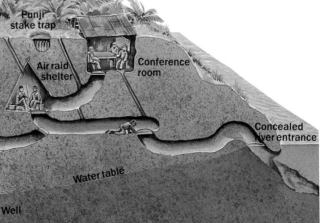

Ventilation shaft

Concealed trapdoor entrance

Remote smoke outlets

Punji stake trap

Firing post

Kitchen

Air raid shelter

Conference room

Dormitory door

Water, gas and blast-proof trapdoor

Tunnel drop (absorbs blast)

Connecting tunnel

First aid station

Well

Water table

Concealed river entrance

3·FORCES IN EUROPE

THANKS to the nuclear 'balance of terror', Europe has been at peace for over forty years. This does not mean that European armed forces have been inactive. On the contrary, the struggle against terrorism and in 'out of area' campaigns in the Third World has seen widespread deployment of troops in a combat role. The challenging nature of these operations has usually led to the use of elite forces, for bitter experience has shown that men of an exacting standard of training and discipline can succeed where inferior troops fail – as at Kolwezi, Zaïre, in 1978.

The response of Western nations to terrorism has involved the creation of small, but highly professional anti-terrorist forces. Some countries – such as West Germany and France – have raised completely new bodies, who have

quickly created a tradition of ruthless efficiency in dealing with terrorist hijacks and sieges. Others, like the Netherlands, have used existing military formations as the basis of their anti-terrorist forces. The response of the liberal democracies to the threat of terrorism was at first slow, but by the mid-1980s Western Europe as a whole had shown itself willing to fight fire with fire, confident of the fighting ability of its superbly trained elite forces.

The Soviet Union has not been faced with the same problems as the West. However, the Russian campaign in Afghanistan shows no sign of ending. Elite Soviet airborne troops, although trained for the very different circumstances of conventional war in Europe, have adapted well to fighting a war of repression in inhospitable terrain. Similarly, Spetsnaz, the Soviet Special Purpose Forces, have fought in Afghanistan although they are intended for covert operations against NATO in a European war.

European special forces will remain an important instrument of policy for the foreseeable future. Overseas commitments, like the French ties to Africa, will not simply go away; French air and ground forces were in action in Chad as recently as February 1986. The terrorist threat too can only be contained, and not completely eradicated. As long as the fear of a hijacking or a seizure of hostages remains, elite forces such as GSG9, GIGN and the Dutch Marines will continue to train, awaiting the call to defend innocent civilians against political fanatics.

FRENCH FOREIGN LEGION

La Légion Etrangère

ELIAHU Itskovitz was barely 20 years old, yet there was murder in his heart. It was the early 1950s, and the young Romanian Jew was serving in the 3ᵉ Régiment Etranger d'Infanterie (3 REI – 3rd Foreign Legion Infantry Regiment) in Indo-China. Eliahu's fixation was not with killing the communist Viet Minh, however – he had a more personal enemy.

Seven years previously, Eliahu had seen a giant Romanian Fascist lead his parents to the gas chamber at Chisinau concentration camp and strangle two of his brothers bare-handed. Much later, after his liberation by the Russians, Eliahu had discovered that his tormentor, named Stanescu, had enlisted in the Legion under a false name and had been sent to Indo-China. There, in the scrub jungle near Bac Ninh, Eliahu finally found Stanescu, which had been his purpose in joining the Legion. 'Stanescu!' shouted the young Jew. Startled, the big man spun round. 'I' said Eliahu with relish, 'am one of the Jews of Chisinau.' And with that he emptied a full magazine from his Sten gun into Stanescu's body.

The French Foreign Legion has been surrounded by more bizarre tales than any other unit that the world has ever known; Eliahu's story is just one.

Left: A legionnaire on lookout duty in the mountains of Algeria.

Far left: Well protected against wind and sand, legionnaires carry out a mission in the Chad desert.

Hollywood epics, books and even comic strips have fostered the idea of a 'Legion of the Damned' – a refuge for the world's criminals, fugitives and men who joined simply 'to forget'. Almost everyone's reaction on hearing the name 'Foreign Legion' is to think of Beau Geste, white képis and stone forts in the desert – but what is the truth about the Legion of today?

The Legion has retained its multi-national character, but is no longer, in the words of philosopher and former legionnaire Arthur Koestler, composed of the 'scum of the earth'. With the onset of mass unemployment, the Legion can afford to hand-pick its men from the

History of the French Foreign Legion

From its inception in 1831 until 1962, the Legion's fortunes were inextricably bound up with North Africa. Its main base from 1845 was Sidi-bel-Abbès, south of Oran in Algeria. From this headquarters the Legion took part in campaigns all over Algeria, Morocco and Tunisia.

The Legion has fought heroically all over the world. In 1863 at Camerone in Mexico, a Legion company was attacked by 2000 Mexicans; the legionnaires held out for 11 hours, killing and wounding 600, but were eventually wiped out. In Dahomey (now Benin) in 1892, 1050 legionnaires took part in a campaign against a fierce native force which included 'Amazon' female soldiers. Only 450 legionnaires survived, most dying of fever.

A total of 43,000 legionnaires fought on the Western Front during World War I, and suffered 5250 fatalities. In World War II, the 13th Demi-Brigade of the Legion served with the British in the Western Desert, covering themselves with glory at Bir Hacheim in May 1942. They later fought in both Italy and Ger-

many. Since 1945 the Legion has campaigned in virtually all of France's colonial wars, most notably in Indo-China, where they fought virtually to the last man at the disastrous siege of Dien Bien Phu, and in the bitter Algerian campaign (1954–62). In more recent times the Legion has been prominent in the interventions in Chad, Djibouti (see pp. 113–116) and Zaïre. Between 1982 and 1984 several Legion units formed part of the Multi-National Force (MNF) which attempted to keep the peace in Beirut.

More than 100 different nationalities are represented in the nine regiments of today's Legion, most being French-speaking. Ironically, it is the diversity of backgrounds that has provided the Legion with its rock-like unity. On one occasion in Morocco, Marshal Lyautey was reviewing a unit when he singled out one individual. 'And what is your nationality?' asked the Marshal. Replied the soldier: 'Légionnaire, mon Général!'

hundreds who flock to the 16 recruiting offices scattered around France. Those selected will be given a fairly cursory medical examination – senses, lungs, heart and blood – and personal details will be taken. It is a time-honoured custom that a man may enlist under an assumed name, but today Interpol is contacted for them to verify that the man is at least not a wanted murderer or international terrorist. However, many petty villains and even deserters from other armies enlist. If he is good enough for the Legion, a man's past is considered to be his own business.

Surprisingly few men are considered to be up to scratch: out of a potential weekly intake of 30 men, often only two or three are taken on for further training. For the 'lucky' ones there follows a year of near brutal training, designed to get bodies and minds into fighting trim. One young British volunteer in the 1980s summed up the process as follows: 'You're given a hard time and you can't relax. If you can't take it, you shouldn't have joined the Legion'. Today's punishment for falling short of the Legion's high standards consists mainly of loss of privileges or spells in the 'glasshouse' (prison), but in the fairly recent past punishments bordered on the savage. In Algeria earlier this century, flogging was not uncommon, and offenders were sometimes spreadeagled on a gun-carriage wheel or buried up to

their necks in sand, which was no joke beneath the searing African sun. Despite being in the desert, if a grain of sand was found adhering to a carefully oiled rifle bolt, the unfortunate owner was liable to have the butt of the weapon smashed over his head or against his jaw by the inspecting NCO.

Every moment of the legionnaire's day was full. First parade was at 0700 – and heaven help any man whose kit was not spotless, teeth not properly cleaned, or ears dirty. This was followed by an 8km run before breakfast. The rest of the day was filled with drill, weapons training, map reading and field craft. In the late afternoon, the young legionnaire would undergo a punishing series of

Above: Putting advanced field skills to the test, these legionnaires try to find evidence of guerrilla movement in Chad.

Below: The French Foreign Legion responded to the Chad government's requests for assistance in 1969, 1978 and 1983.

endurance tests: running with a pack filled with sand, doing press-ups and crawling under barbed wire, each individual performance being recorded in a book.

Physical prowess is, of course, demanded by all armies, but several factors were unique to the Legion. Firstly, there was the fanatical insistence that every man must be able to march great distances, in all weathers and over any kind of terrain, and burdened down with heavy kit. Until 1962, this was a practical necessity for survival, as the average legionnaire would have spent most of his service campaigning in the mountains and deserts of North Africa. The old legionnaire's motto neatly sums it up: *Marche ou crève* (march or bust). The consequences of falling out on a route march in the arduous Rif country did not bear thinking about. Today, as the new recruit at Aubagne – near Marseilles – discovers, there are a few pleasures to offset the pain. The food, for example, is top-rate French cuisine, and wine and beer are plentiful. But perhaps the keenest pleasure a recruit can experience is the thrill of being issued with his white *képi*. This cap is almost as sacred to the legionnaire as the Legion's flaming grenade badge; both symbolise the proud 150-year-old tradition of service. The full kit costs about £500 and contains all the various pieces of uniform that the legionnaire will need during his five-year stint: khaki dress uniform, 'ranger' boots, dress shoes, combat outfit, green ties, shirts, overcoat, green beret, badges, red dress epaulettes tasselled with gold braid, and a blue waist sash.

After his induction at the Quartier Viénot barracks in Aubagne, the new legionnaire moves on to a basic training period of 15 weeks at the Quartier Lapasset at Castelnaudary near Toulouse. Here, batches of 350 recruits at a time are thrashed into shape – each week a fresh group of about 30 *engagés volontaires* (volunteer recruits) arrives, while a similar number passes out.

The basics have changed little since Sidi-bel-Abbès days, although there has been a marked change in details to keep pace with the rapid developments in the science of war, and with the technical knowledge that even the humblest 'squaddie' must nowadays possess. Much

emphasis continues to be placed on physical fitness, but the *Marche ou crève* regime has been somewhat modified, for the Legion's campaigns are now usually of the 'rapid intervention' variety. Recruits may then go on to specialised training with units such as the 2 REP (2e Régiment Etranger de Parachutistes – 2nd Foreign Legion Parachutists) or 1 REC (1er Régiment Etranger de Cavalerie – 1st Foreign Legion Cavalry Regiment). Initially, Legion cavalry units were made up of Cossacks and White Russians who fled Russia after the Bolshevik Revolution of 1917, but today their 'steeds' are AMX10 light tanks.

Since 1960, the fortunes of the Legion have been mixed. From 1954 to 1962 it was involved in the bitter Algerian War of Independence against ALN (Armée de Libération Nationale) nationalist guerrillas. Since 1940 the French Army had suffered a series of humiliating reverses, culminating in the disaster of Dien Bien Phu in 1954. The French were determined to win in Algeria by fair means or foul, and the Legion played a full part in the campaign to keep *Algérie française*. The Legion's two para units, 1 REP and 2 REP, became the linchpin of French counter-insurgency (COIN). They were used as a mobile reserve, generally truck or heliborne rather than airdropped, to hunt

Above: Celebrating Camerone Day (30 April) around a camp-fire. The most important day in the Legion year, it is the anniversary of the battle of Camerone when a company of legionnaires was attacked by a force of 2000 Mexicans. The epitome of courage and discipline, the legionnaires fought to the last man.

and pursue ALN units. The French successfully isolated the ALN by erecting fortified barriers (*barrages*) along the Tunisian and Moroccan borders, thus ensuring that the rebels could obtain no outside assistance. Large numbers of civilians were forcibly relocated – 300,000 being moved from around Constantine alone – cutting off the ALN from internal support and allowing the creation of 'free fire' zones, where French troops were able to shoot to kill.

Parallel to this process of isolation, attempts were made to defeat the insurgent forces in the field. By 1959 300,000 troops were deployed in *quadrillage*, a chequerboard of small garrisons across the face of Algeria. Big pushes were carried out by the Réserve Générale, which was formed from 30,000 elite troops from the paras, Marines and, of course, the Legion. The *quadrillage* units held down the countryside, while the legionnaires and the other crack units sought out the ALN to destroy them – a task in which the French largely succeeded. Politically, however, it became clear to the French by 1960 that they could not maintain indefinite control of

Algeria. Outraged at what they considered to be the treason of newly-appointed President de Gaulle, 1 REP's anger boiled over into mutiny. As a punishment, the unit was disbanded in April 1961.

The Legion's story since 1962 has been much happier. It has adapted to a role protecting French interests all over the globe. A typical operation was the Chad campaign in 1978. A Legion force (2 REP, 1 REC, 2 REI) plus a Marine company were dispatched to prop up the government against dissident attacks. In April 1978 a small force including a para company marched to relieve the town of Ati. After a stiff firefight the government troops cleared the town of rebels, who had been armed with ultra-modern Soviet heavy weapons, including a 106mm recoilless gun and a 120mm mortar. The retreating rebels left behind 80 dead; government losses amounted to only three dead and nine wounded. The legionnaires of the modern era have proved themselves to be as worthy of the honour of wearing the white *képi* as were their predecessors at Dien Bien Phu, Camerone and Algeria.

Below: Legionnaires make their way through the hills of Djibouti. Physical fitness is of prime importance and every legionnaire must be able to move rapidly across difficult terrain carrying a heavy pack on his back.

FRENCH PARAS

2e Régiment Etranger de Parachutistes

AT around 1000 hours on Wednesday 17 May 1978, the telephone rang in the office of the commander of the 2nd Foreign Legion Parachute Regiment (2 REP). As Colonel Philippe Erulin picked up the receiver, he heared a brief but electrifying message: 'General Liron of 2 Para Brigade here; your regiment will be on stand-by at six o'clock'. Two days later, 2 REP's parachutes mushroomed in the sky as they began an extremely hazardous mission: an operational drop in the very heart of Africa.

2 REP is an elite among elites, because it combines the qualities of two different crack corps – the Foreign Legion and the paras. 2 REP take the very best volunteers for the Legion, who, coming from all nations and walks of life,

are united in their strength, courage, taste for danger, and, of course, their desire to fight. Small wonder that 2 REP is the most prestigious unit in the French Army.

Colonel Erulin was a veteran of the savage Algerian war, but this latest mission was his riskiest adventure yet. He was ordered to jump into the hottest spot in Africa: Shaba province in south Zaïre. Formerly known as Katanga, this province had been a source of trouble ever since the Belgian Congo had obtained independence as Zaïre in 1960. Now the news came that Katangan rebels, backed by the Marxist government of Angola, had seized the town of Kolwezi, Shaba's most important centre for diamonds and copper, a rich prize for the malcontents. Some 3000 European residents, mainly French and Belgian mining engineers, barricaded themselves into their homes, fearing the worst. When some of their number were arrested and accused of being 'mercenaries', it seemed clear that Major Mufu, the rebel leader, and his 4000 'Tigers' (some only 15 years old) regarded the white population as potential hostages in the case of a counter-attack.

President Mobutu's appeal to French President Giscard d'Estaing for help took

Left: A sniper of the French paras, armed with an FR-F1 sniper rifle, takes a break during the Kolwezi operation.

place against a background of rising tension. At 1000 hours on 16 May a company of Zaïrean paratroopers were massacred in a disastrous attack on Kolwezi. The survivors ran off into the bush. Inside the town, disorder and indiscipline mounted as drunken and drugged soldiers roamed the streets, murdering anyone whom they considered 'suspect', regardless of race. French intervention was now inevitable.

Previous page: A Legion sergeant in Kolwezi receives orders during a lull in the fighting. The red shoulder scarf was worn so that French troops could easily be identified.

History of the French paras

The French Foreign Legion's 2nd Parachute Battalion (2e Bataillon Etranger Parachutiste, or 2 BEP) was formed in October 1948 at Sidi-bel-Abbès, Algeria. In 1949, 2 BEP moved to Indo-China where it played a prominent part in the savage campaign against the Viet Minh. In 1955, the unit returned to North Africa where it was upgraded to regimental status, absorbing 3 BEP. Under the new title of 2 REP, it was heavily involved in the bitter counter-insurgency operations against nationalist rebels in Algeria from 1956 to 1962, killing 4000 enemy for the loss of 598 Legionnaires. After the punitive disbandment of 1 REP in the aftermath of the abortive 'Generals' coup' of 1961, 2 REP survived as the Legion's only parachute unit.

Since Algeria, 2 REP has transformed itself from a crack but fundamentally conventional force into a rapid reaction unit, capable of deep penetration raids and rescue missions. As such, the Legion paras have been intensively trained in skills that are not usually associated with an airborne unit, such as arctic and mountain warfare, and amphibious operations. The weaponry of the 1300 officers and men of 2 REP is formidable. The Scouting and Support Company, for instance, has 16 Milan ATGW (anti-tank guided weapons) launchers, a platoon of 20mm anti-aircraft guns, and 12 81mm and 120mm mortars. Smallarms include the MAT-49

sub-machine gun or, for the specialist marksman, the FR-F1 sniper's rifle.

From 1962 onwards, 2 REP has largely been committed to the defence of Chad, a former French colony. In 1970, the regiment regrouped at Camp Raffalli, Corsica. One company was permanently stationed in the Horn of Africa at Djibouti, where in 1976 it supported GIGN's rescue of French schoolchildren from Somali-backed rebels.

Since the Kolwezi drop in 1978, 2 REP has seen further action in Chad, and in 1983–84 formed part of France's contribution to the peacekeeping Multi-National Force in Beirut. 2 REP forms part of the 2nd Parachute Division which is a principal component of the Force d'Intervention Rapide, the French equivalent of the American Rapid Deployment Force. 2 REP thus continues in a role designed to protect the interests of France by the use of arms, and, perhaps more importantly, to uphold the honour of the French Foreign Legion.

Right: As a member of 2 REP at Kolwezi, this corporal wears the 'Satin 300' combat uniform, especially tailored for the Legion with short jacket and narrow trousers. Hanging from the webbing belt are a bayonet, a multi-pocketed bag for holding grenades and a leather pouch containing weapon-cleaning equipment. French ranger boots – based on the World War II model – are worn, and headgear is the green Legion beret with the regimental version of the French parachute badge. Rank is indicated by green chevrons fixed to the jacket by a Velcro patch. The black scarf worn over the left shoulder is a field recognition sign used in the Kolwezi operation.

Erulin decided that 2 REP had to jump right into the trouble-spot, close to the outskirts of the town. If the paras dropped into the bush and fought their way in, it was feared that the whites would be massacred. Erulin trusted to surprise and the sheer professionalism of 2 REP to succeed where the native paras had failed.

On the night of 17/18 May, most of 2 REP flew in civilian DC-8s to Kinshasa, the capital of Zaïre. Because of the lack of transport, 4 Company were forced to follow on later. At Kinshasa there were further problems. The Zaïrean Air Force was able to supply only five out of a promised seven airworthy transport planes. The gravity of the situation precluded any thought of delaying the drop, so on 19 May 500 men were crammed aboard the four C-130s and one C-160 available for a terrifying five-hour flight to Kolwezi. At 1540 hours the order was given to jump.

The first assault was onto DZ (dropping zone) Vieille Ville, or Old Town, just beyond the first buildings but close to their objective. The legionnaires floated down in broad daylight, their parachutes bright against the clear blue sky. Fortunately, the rebels were caught off guard, and before they could organise a response, the paras were already regrouping in the tall elephant grass and preparing to move on their objectives. Speed was now of the essence. 1 Company headed for Lycée Jean XXIII. 2 Company, trained as 2 REP's mountain warfare specialists, moved towards the hospital and the mining company buildings, where there was a vehicle park. 3 Company was to seize the Impala Hotel and the Post Office before taking up positions around the bridge connecting the old and new towns. At first the legionnaires met with only desultory fire. The Katangans were numerous, but their morale was far inferior to that of the paras, who, in the words of their war diary, were spurred on to 'superhuman efforts' by the knowledge that they were engaged in a race against time to save the hostages' lives, and by the grisly sights that greeted 2 REP as they moved through the streets of Kolwezi: corpses in the boulevards and pools of blood in the gutters. However, resistance stiffened as they moved forward. Their first fatality, an Englishman named Corporal Arnold, was hit by sniper fire but nothing could stop the ruthless momentum of the paras' attack. As each area of the town was cleared, white residents emerged from cover, shaken and trembling. Tragically, those held in the Impala Hotel were

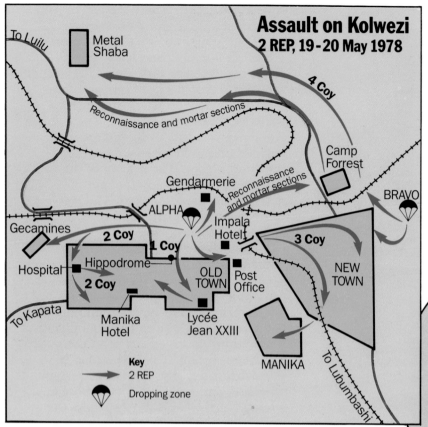

Assault on Kolwezi
2 REP, 19-20 May 1978

Key
2 REP
Dropping zone

positions to the east of New Town, to ensure that no rebels escaped. Once again, there was little initial resistance, but around 1500 hours, 4 Company ran into heavy fighting at Metal Shaba. Support Company had to rush to the aid of 4 Company whose leading platoon was pinned down, its NCO dead. Moving forward in commandeered vehicles, Support Company set up an 81mm mortar barrage which forced the rebels into retreat, but not for long. Suddenly a column of lorry-borne Katangan infantry supported by two light tanks mounted a

killed before the legionnaires could reach them.

Within two hours of the initial jump, 2 REP controlled nearly all the town. They had killed over 100 rebels, but only sustained light casualties themselves. Then the second wave arrived from Corsica in C-130s but Erulin, fearing the dangers of a drop in the gathering gloom, sent them on to Lubumbashi to spend the night there.

A grim ordeal awaited those paras who remained in Kolwezi. Despite the waves of tiredness that assailed them – most had not slept for 70 hours – relentless patrols and constant vigilance had to be maintained to prevent isolated rebels trapped inside the town from escaping into the bush, and to prevent infiltration into Kolwezi from outside. Six legionnaires were wounded during this skirmishing, but the losses of the Katangans were much heavier.

At dawn on 20 May, the second wave of legionnaires dropped on the designated DZs. After regrouping, the now reinforced battalion mounted another sweep through Kolwezi with 4 Company (normally the unit's snipers and sabotage experts) taking up blocking

powerful counter-thrust. At this moment of crisis the legionnaires proved equal to the task. Deploying swiftly to meet this new threat, a hail of fire from the mortars and 89mm anti-tank rocket launchers smashed the Katangan column mercilessly. The rebels fled, leaving behind 80 dead, their lorries ablaze and their tanks crippled.

Although the immediate battle was over, the process of clearing the town went on until 25 May, when a rebel force was wiped out while retreating towards Angola. By 5 June the paras had begun to return to their base in Corsica, having written another glorious page in the annals of the Legion. As many as 90 per cent of 2 REP had had no previous combat experience, yet, in the words of Colonel Erulin, 'as soon as the first shot was fired, they all acted like veterans.' For the modest total of five killed and 20 wounded, these 'veterans' had totally smashed the Katangan threat to Kolwezi.

FRENCH GIGN

Groupement d'Intervention de la Gendarmerie Nationale

History of the GIGN

In the early 1970s, the French para-military Gendarmerie Nationale decided to create a specialist anti-terrorist unit. The murder of Israeli athletes by Palestinian terrorists at the Munich Olympics in 1972 and the siege of the Saudi Arabian embassy in Paris in 1973 added impetus to their activities, and the GIGN was formed on 3 November 1973. GIGN was originally divided into two commands: GIGN 1, based near Paris at Maisons-Alfort, was responsible for northern France; GIGN 2, based at Mont-de-Marsan, was assigned to watch over the south of the country.

Initially, the force consisted of a mere 15 men, working in three five-man teams under the command of Lieutenant Prouteau. In 1976 the two commands were merged and the establishment was increased to two officers and 40 NCOs organised into three strike teams, each comprising two five-man intervention forces, a team commander and a dog handler. Normally each of the strike teams is on full alert, ready for deployment at a moment's notice, for one week in three.

In addition to their role as a counter-terrorist unit, GIGN has also been used to curb prison unrest, notably in the case of the attempted escape from Clairvaux prison in January 1978. At Clairvaux, as at Djibouti in 1976, GIGN marksmen saved several hostages through precision shooting. The force has also been widely deployed to foster French diplomatic interests by training and assisting foreign anti-terrorist units and VIP protection groups. In 1979, for instance, GIGN men helped to train the Saudi Arabian National Guard squad that stormed the Great Mosque that had been occupied by fanatics. GIGN has also trained many other units, especially those of France's former colonies.

Much of GIGN's day-to-day work consists of fairly routine activities such as VIP protection. However, 'Gigène's' vigilance is never relaxed; at this very moment their rapid deployment force is ready to fly to wherever French interests are threatened.

AS the heavy barge approached, the diver lying on the bed of the River Seine experienced mounting panic. Surely the vessel's bottom would crush him as it passed overhead? Fighting down his initial reaction to swim for his life, the diver hugged the river-bed closer as the huge barge passed directly over him with only a few metres' clearance. As the barge slipped away, his claustrophobia subsided and was replaced by feelings of relief and pride at his achievement, for he had cleared another hurdle in the training of the crack French GIGN (Groupement d'Intervention de la Gendarmerie Nationale).

All elite forces have arduous training programmes, but that of the GIGN is one of the toughest of all. Much emphasis is laid on marksmanship; exact shot placement is considered to be of vital importance, since one day a GIGN man may be called upon to eliminate a terrorist before the latter can harm a hostage. GIGN members are expected to be able to engage six targets at 25m within five seconds with a handgun (formerly a 9mm automatic, now a 0.357in Magnum). With his 7.62mm calibre FR-F1 sniper's rifle, fitted with a flash suppressor and other advanced features, he must achieve a minimum of 93 hits out of 100 shots at a target 200m away. Many GIGN men can regularly obtain a higher score than this. Such a standard of accuracy can only be achieved by constant practice: each man will fire more than 12,000 rounds in training each year. The men also practise scoring hits in a variety of adverse circumstances.

All GIGN members are expert skiers and mountaineers and train at the French parachute school at Pau in the foothills of the Pyrenees, making a minimum of five jumps per year. Their skills at swimming are legendary. In addition to the barge exercise described above (which develops confidence and prepares the diver for underwater infiltration), GIGN men are expected to be able to swim for long distances, sometimes towing a 75kg dummy to represent someone being rescued. Another exercise involves diving to the bottom of a deep ditch, answering a question by writing on a waterproof tablet and returning to the surface – all without breathing apparatus. This gruelling exercise develops both endurance and the ability to think rapidly under pressure. Also taught are rappelling techniques (descending by means of harness and rope) – especially from helicopters – and martial arts. The latter are important because the GIGN philosophy is based on the avoidance of lethal force if at all possible. To this end many GIGN men have achieved black-belt status, including Lieutenant Prouteau who commanded GIGN in their first major operation – against the terrorists of the FLCS (Somali Coast Liberation Front).

Previous page: A commando diver of GIGN.

Above: Lieutenant Prouteau, overall commander of GIGN and leader of the team to free the schoolchildren held hostage in Djibouti.

Shortly before 0800 hours on 3 February 1976, a group of four FLCS men hijacked a school bus in Djibouti, the capital of the then French Territory of the Afars and the Issas. They then drove to a point some 180m from a Somali border post, where their demands were made known. Their threat was simple: if immediate independence was not granted to the territory, the 30 hostages (all children aged between 6 and 12 years) would be butchered.

Beneath the pitiless glare of the desert sun, conditions on the coach swiftly deteriorated. The French authorities quickly decided that a military option should be available should negotiations fail, so, in the greatest secrecy, a nine-man GIGN team under Prouteau was dispatched to Djibouti in a specially converted DC-8. Prouteau's problems were not confined to countering the hijackers. An added complication was the presence of Somali troops manning a frontier post a mere 180m away. They had made clear where their sympathies lay by making no effort to prevent a fifth terrorist from boarding the bus in what was an obviously prearranged move. A unit of the French Foreign Legion was drafted in to provide support for the GIGN against any action taken by the Somalis.

GIGN have an extensive range of sophisticated equipment at their disposal, ranging from 'high tech' electronic surveillance aids to various explosives, including stun grenades and 'door opening' charges. On this occasion, however, Prouteau relied purely on old-fashioned skills: patience and deadly accurate marksmanship. Having thoroughly reconnoitred the ground, Prouteau deployed his nine snipers around the hijacked bus.

GIGN tactical doctrine in such a situation called for Prouteau to maintain continual radio contact with the

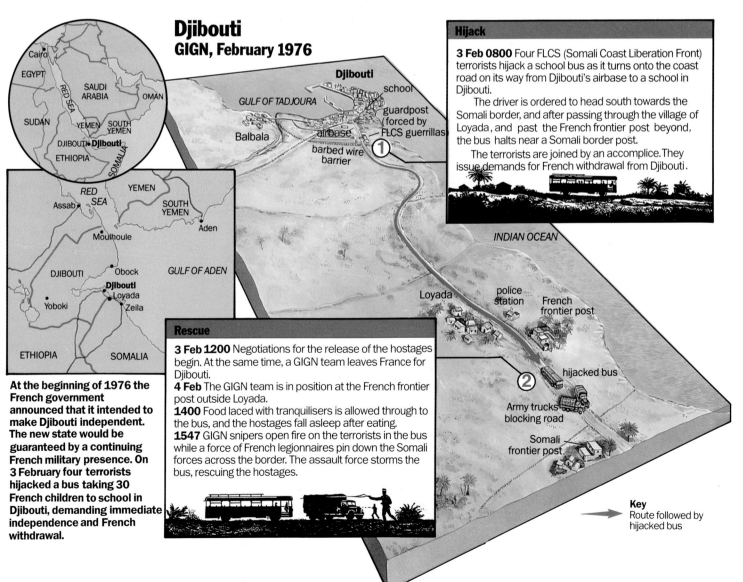

Djibouti
GIGN, February 1976

Hijack

3 Feb 0800 Four FLCS (Somali Coast Liberation Front) terrorists hijack a school bus as it turns onto the coast road on its way from Djibouti's airbase to a school in Djibouti.

The driver is ordered to head south towards the Somali border, and after passing through the village of Loyada, and past the French frontier post beyond, the bus halts near a Somali border post.

The terrorists are joined by an accomplice. They issue demands for French withdrawal from Djibouti.

At the beginning of 1976 the French government announced that it intended to make Djibouti independent. The new state would be guaranteed by a continuing French military presence. On 3 February four terrorists hijacked a bus taking 30 French children to school in Djibouti, demanding immediate independence and French withdrawal.

Rescue

3 Feb 1200 Negotiations for the release of the hostages begin. At the same time, a GIGN team leaves France for Djibouti.
4 Feb The GIGN team is in position at the French frontier post outside Loyada.
1400 Food laced with tranquilisers is allowed through to the bus, and the hostages fall asleep after eating.
1547 GIGN snipers open fire on the terrorists in the bus while a force of French legionnaires pin down the Somali forces across the border. The assault force storms the bus, rescuing the hostages.

Key
Route followed by hijacked bus

Above: A group of GIGN men pose for the camera before a scuba-diving lesson.

marksmen, each of whom was equipped with a throat microphone. Each sniper was assigned to watch over a portion of the bus. Prouteau decided to play a waiting game; only when all of his men had informed him that they had a terrorist lined up in their sights would he give the order to open fire. That was the only way to avoid a massacre of the children. The vital question was – would the terrorists' nerve snap before GIGN had a clear target?

Prouteau was concerned that the hostages were masking the marksmen's line of sight. He therefore decided on a risky subterfuge which, if discovered, could have had calamitous repercussions. At 1400 hours on 4 February, a meal containing tranquillisers was allowed through to the children, who fell asleep and sank away from the bus windows. Finally, after 10 hours' wait, GIGN's long vigil was rewarded. Each terrorist had been given a number; when Prouteau heard all the numbers in his earphones, he knew that all the hijackers aboard the bus were simultaneously visible in the snipers' sights. Scarcely daring to breathe, at 1547 hours Prouteau gave the order to open fire.

Instantaneously, four terrorists were killed and a fifth was hit outside the bus; then all hell broke loose. The Somali border guards opened up on the GIGN men, pinning them down, but help was at hand. As the Foreign Legion men gave covering fire, Prouteau in person led a small party to free the children. They arrived at the bus just too late to prevent a sixth terrorist from boarding the bus, supported by Somali fire, and murdering a little girl. Prouteau's men took swift and bloody revenge, not only on the terrorist but also on the Somalis as the GIGN covering party and the legionnaires poured a withering hail of fire into the border post, killing the leader of the terrorist outrage.

The Djibouti operation was a classic hostage rescue mission. It was carried out at a great distance from the homeland at short notice; the attackers had to gather intelligence rapidly, plan an attack, wait patiently for the right moment and then put in a devastating blow with no margin for error; out of 30 children taken hostage, 29 were saved. Since its formation, GIGN have rescued over 250 hostages: a fine record, befitting one of the world's toughest elite forces.

DUTCH MARINES
Korps Mariniers

CROUCHING beside the hijacked train, the Marines knew that this time it was for real. The two earlier sieges of December 1975 had ended without a storming. This time, however, there were no easy answers; the Dutch Marines had to resolve the siege in their own fashion – at the point of a gun. As the seconds ticked remorselessly away to zero hour, keen ears could just pick up the distant rumble of aero engines. The Starfighters were commencing the run-in to their supporting attack.

The BBE (Bizondere Bystand

Previous page: A member of the Royal Netherlands Marine Corps on a training exercise in Scandinavia.

Eenheid – literally, the Different Circumstances Unit), the crack anti-terrorist squad of the Dutch Marine Corps had been rushed to De Punt in northern Holland in response to an act of terrorism committed by South Moluccan extremists. At 0830 hours on 23 May 1977 a commuter train had been seized by members of the VZJ (Vrije Zuidmolukse Jongeren – Free South Moluccan Youth Organisation). Next, they issued their demands for the safe release of the hostages: that the Dutch government exert pressure on Indonesia (formerly the Dutch East Indies) to grant independence to their homeland; that other Moluccans be released from Dutch prisons; and that a Boeing 747 be provided at Schipol, Amsterdam's international airport. To prove that they were not bluffing, the hijackers killed the train driver in cold blood, and threw his body onto the tracks. Within hours the BBE had arrived on the scene.

Based at Van Braam Houckyeest barracks, the BBE – like the Marine Corps as a whole – is comprised largely of regular troops, with a leavening of conscripts; at the end of their national service, the latter can join the reserves or sign on as regulars. Officers and NCOs serve for seven and four years respectively. The BBE, in the course of their rigorous training, learn to use many weapons including the GPMG (general-purpose machine gun) and the FN FAL rifle. For close work – of the type that is inevitable when storming a train, aircraft or building – Heckler and Koch automatics and Smith and Wesson police special pistols are favoured.

The degree of success of counter-terrorist work almost invariably depends on the quality of the intelligence available. It is essential to know as much as possible about an enemy before an assault is launched. For that reason the Dutch government spun out the

History of the Dutch Marines

Founded on 10 December 1665, the Dutch Marine Corps is one of the world's oldest military formations. They have served, in the words of their motto, *Qua Patet Orbis* – 'Wherever the World Extends'. In the course of their distinguished history the Corps has fought campaigns in the East Indies, in Spain during the War of the Spanish Succession, and in China during the Boxer Rebellion, to name but a few.

During World War II they fought hero-ically in the defence of Rotterdam in 1940, and later in the famous 'Princess Irene' Dutch Brigade in northwest Europe in 1944–45.

The present-day Royal Netherlands Marine Corps numbers some 2800 men, including the world-renowned Marine Band of the Royal Netherlands Navy. The Corps' strength is divided between two regional commands – the Dutch Antilles, based in the Caribbean, and the Netherlands, which is assigned a NATO role. The latter consists of 1st Amphibious Combat Group (1 ACG), a commando unit of 700 men based at Doorn, who regularly exercise with helicopters as part of their training. Also stationed at Doorn are two 'quick reaction' forces, drawn from 1 ACG, which are ready to be dispatched to any quarter of the globe at 24 hours' notice. The other Marine units based in the homeland are worthy of mention. These are the crack anti-terrorist unit, the BBE, and the 7th Netherlands Special Boat Section, which is based at Den Oever and trained specifically for long-range reconnaissance and anti-terrorist oper-ations on oil rigs.

One the Corps' earliest battle honours, 'Chatham', recalls the first time that British and Dutch Marines met in action, in the Anglo-Dutch War of 1665–67. Later, in 1704, Dutch and British Marines fought side by side at Gibraltar, thus providing an historical

precedent for today's close co-oper-ation between the two corps. In time of war Royal Marines and Dutch Marines would be deployed to NATO's northern flank together as the UK/NL amphibious force.

In 1951, following the failure of a rebellion against Indonesia, some 15,000 Moluccans were exiled to the Netherlands. The anger and frustration of second-generation Moluccan immi-grants boiled over in the 1970s when they began to carry out acts of terrorism to draw attention to their struggle for independence from Indonesia. On 2 December 1975 seven armed men hi-jacked a train, and two days later six others occupied the Indonesian consul-ate in Amsterdam. Despite the murder of two hostages, both sieges were ended by negotiation.

The sieges of a train and primary school in May–June 1977 were followed by another act of terrorism, when on 13 March 1978, 71 hostages were seized in government offices at Drenthe. Five passers-by were wounded and one hostage shot dead. On the following day Dutch Marines successfully stormed the building.

Since 1978 the Dutch policy of com-bining the 'carrot' of improved social conditions with the 'stick' of heavy jail sentences appears to have been effec-tive in eliminating Moluccan terrorism; their nationalist aspirations, however, remain.

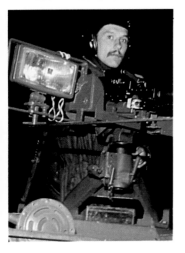

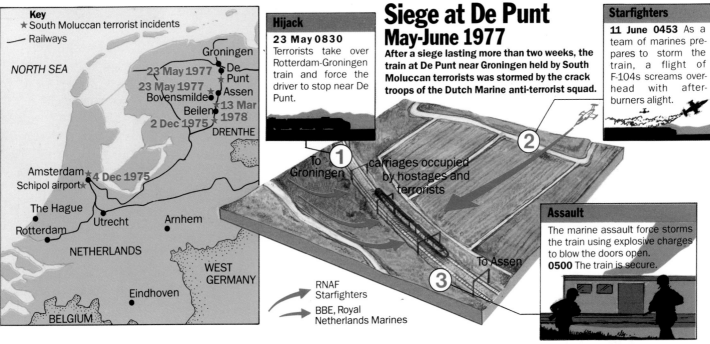

Siege at De Punt
May-June 1977

After a siege lasting more than two weeks, the train at De Punt near Groningen held by South Moluccan terrorists was stormed by the crack troops of the Dutch Marine anti-terrorist squad.

Hijack
23 May 0830 Terrorists take over Rotterdam-Groningen train and force the driver to stop near De Punt.

Starfighters
11 June 0453 As a team of marines prepares to storm the train, a flight of F-104s screams overhead with afterburners alight.

Assault
The marine assault force storms the train using explosive charges to blow the doors open.
0500 The train is secure.

Key
★ South Moluccan terrorist incidents
— Railways

NORTH SEA

Groningen
23 May 1977 — De Punt
23 May 1977 — ★ Assen
Bovensmilde ★ 13 Mar
Beilen ★ 1978
2 Dec 1975 ★
DRENTHE

Amsterdam ★ 4 Dec 1975
Schipol airport ★
The Hague
Rotterdam ● Utrecht
Arnhem ●
NETHERLANDS
WEST GERMANY
Eindhoven ●
BELGIUM

To Groningen ①
carriages occupied by hostages and terrorists
②
To Assen ③

→ RNAF Starfighters
→ BBE, Royal Netherlands Marines

Top: Dutch Marines manned a tight cordon to seal off the area immediately surrounding the hijacked train at De Punt

negotiations for nearly three weeks until 11 June. During this time, invaluable snippets of information were gathered about the hijackers' positions, numbers and weapons, from many sources, including 'Red Cross' personnel (in reality, disguised military policemen) who took food up to the train, and the Dutch SBS (Special Boat Section). The SBS, under the cloak of night, planted sophisticated listening devices underneath the carriages, as well as explosives on the tracks in front of the train. On the fourth day the authorities achieved a major coup. They managed to negotiate the release of a pregnant woman who provided information of excellent quality about the situation inside the train. By the time that the Marines were ready to go in, on 11 June, the Dutch knew that

there were 13 hijackers and that they were armed with automatics and grenades. They had also discovered that several hostages had fallen prey to the 'Stockholm Syndrome' – a curious psychological process by which hostages begin to identify and even sympathise with their kidnappers. Most important of all, the Dutch learned that the hijackers spent much time in one particular carriage.

In the early hours of 11 June, a platoon of Marines inched their way to the pre-set fire positions around the carriages. They were to provide covering fire for the assaulting platoon, as were a squad of crack snipers from the Dutch Rijks Politie, armed with Heckler and Koch 7.92mm rifles. Extremely accurate, these rifles incorporate a psychological weapon: a sight that focuses a red dot on the target. Any terrorist finding such a dot on his body would immediately freeze or take cover – leaving him little time to murder a hostage. Also on hand were three British SAS men to offer advice.

In the minutes before the 'go' order, each man of the assault platoon carefully checked his equipment. A loose buckle or open pocket might snag on something in the train and cost vital seconds – and in an action of this type seconds can literally mean the difference between life and death. Meticulous checking of equipment also served to distract the men from the ordeal by fire that lay ahead. Finally, faces and hands smeared with camouflage cream, the storming party stealthily approached their starting positions. The time was zero hour minus 30 minutes.

Three Marines placed small explosive charges against the door of the train; others put scaling ladders into position. At zero minus five, all the troops donned earphones and nervously awaited the commencement of the diversions. And then it happened. Bang on time, at 453 hours, six F-104 Starfighters of the Royal Dutch Air Force screamed in at rooftop level, sweeping low over the train. As they did so, the pilots turned on their afterburners. The effect was instantaneous and, for the people in the train, terrifying. The whole train shuddered with the vibration produced by the jets, and the hostages hurled themselves to the floor in fear. Seconds later, the train was again rocked by the explosive charges placed on the tracks by the SBS. Simultaneously, the covering platoon opened a blistering fusillade into the carriages containing the terrorists.

Then, with a tremendous explosion, the carriage doors were blown off their hinges and the Marines poured in. Straightaway a firefight developed, as the rescuers raced through the train shouting to the hostages to take cover. The assault party ensured that as they entered a carriage they were all facing in the same direction; thus anyone who was both armed and facing them was a terrorist, to be cut down mercilessly. Using these simple but brutally effective tactics, the BBE accounted for six hijackers and captured seven others in little more than

a minute. At zero hour plus five minutes the train had been captured and the hostages freed at the cost of one slightly injured Marine.

Tragically two hostages died in the firefight, so the Marines saw the mission as only a partial success, despite the liberation of 80 or so hostages in almost impossible circumstances. The Royal Netherlands Marine Corps has never gone in for the 'gung-ho' self-promotion of certain other elite units. It believes, rightly, that actions speak louder than words.

Left: Armed with a 9mm Uzi sub-machine gun, this member of the Dutch Marines anti-terrorist section is wearing an armoured flak jacket over a woollen pullover, combat trousers and a US M1 helmet. On his belt he carries a haversack for grenades, a pouch for medical equipment, a water bottle in a US-type cover, a revolver and a fighting knife.

WEST GERMAN GSG9

Grenzschutzgruppe 9

EDGING warily towards the rear of the hijacked Lufthansa Boeing 737, the crack West Germany commandos of Grenzschutzgruppe 9 (GSG9) were painfully aware that more than the fate of 79 hostages rested on their shoulders. As they prepared to assault the airliner, they knew that at one blow they could wipe out the memory of the national humiliation suffered five years before at the Munich Olympics. On that dreadful occasion, Palestinian terrorists had massacred Israeli athletes almost before the eyes of a horrified world. The consequences of another

failure were not something the GSG9 cared to contemplate.

GSG9's commander at Mogadishu was Colonel Ulrich Wegener. In the wake of Munich he had been given virtually a free hand to create an elite anti-terrorist formation. Wegener's experience had shown him that a successful unit of this type needed to be composed of small, close-knit groups of men capable of both subtlety and extreme ruthlessness. Only the very best material is considered; recruits must have two years' service in the border police, and then pass a gruelling three-day selection

course that tests their endurance and skills to the limit. Nearly 70 per cent are rejected at this stage. The survivors proceed to five months' basic training, and later still to another three-month stint. During this time the vital skills of teamwork and small-unit assault tactics are taught, including the art of stopping a speeding car by pouring sub-machine gun fire into the engine compartment from a helicopter.

GSG9's equipment is as sophisticated as its tactics. The 9mm Heckler and Koch and .38in revolvers which proved unsatisfactory at Mogadishu have since been replaced by handguns such as Heckler and Koch P9S or P7 revolvers. GSG9 also deploy the MP5A2 sub-machine gun, fitted with the advanced ZPP 'low light' sight for night operations. Nothing is left to chance: at their base in St. Augustin is a $9 million underground range, which includes mock-ups of likely terrorist targets. Thus GSG9 had gone through the motions of assaulting a dummy airliner many times before they were called upon to attack the real thing.

The dramatic events which led to GSG9's debut in the international arena began at 1300 hours on 13 October 1977, when Lufthansa Flight LH181 lifted smoothly off the runway of Palma airport, Majorca. The 737's pilot, Captain Jürgen Schumann, routinely set course for the southern coast of France, but his aircraft (call sign: 'Charlie Echo') was fated never to reach its destination. An hour after take-off, air traffic controllers were stunned to hear Schumann nervously report that his aircraft had been hijacked and that he had been ordered, at gunpoint, to fly to Rome. Shortly afterwards the near-hysterical voice of Mahmoud, the

terrorist leader, was heard. Speaking in broken English, he demanded not only the release of the leaders of the notorious Red Army Faction (Baader–Meinhof gang), who were imprisoned in West Germany, but also an enormous ransom of £9 million. If these demands were not met, threatened Mahmoud, the 79 passengers and crew would die.

While refuelling at Rome, Captain Schumann managed to signal to the authorities by dropping four cigars out of a flight-deck window. This information was correctly interpreted as meaning that there were four terrorists aboard. In sending this coded message, which proved to be of vital importance to the success of the operation, Schumann had

Above left: Learning to shoot left-handed increases GSG9's effectiveness as a security force.

Above: Mercedes Benz saloons are used in high-speed chases.

Previous page: The ability to rappell from a border police helicopter enables GSG9 to deploy men on the tops of buildings or trains. These men are armed with Heckler and Koch MP5A2 and MP5A3 sub-machine guns.

acted with considerable personal courage.

The 737 headed for Cyprus after Rome, and then set out on a flight around the Middle East that took in Bahrain, Dubai and the People's Democratic Republic of Yemen (South Yemen), eventually ending in Mogadishu, the Somali capital. It was pursued, unbeknown to the hijackers, by Wegener at the head of a GSG9 commando group. The stakes had been raised dramatically when Mahmoud killed Schumann for allegedly communicating with the Yemeni authorities. As the refuelled 737 (flown now by the co-pilot, Jürgen Vietor) headed towards Somalia on 17 October, it was clear to the West Germans that time was running out for the hostages. Once the plane was on the tarmac at Mogadishu, Mahmoud set a deadline for his demands to be met, after which he threatened to blow up the aircraft. The terrorist leader brutally underlined the reality of the threat by having Schumann's body thrown onto the runway.

To gain a few precious hours, the West Germans employed a successful, though risky, ruse. The negotiators succeeded in convincing Mahmoud that

11 Baader–Meinhof terrorists were about to be freed from German prisons, and the terrorists extended their deadline to 0230 hours on 18 October. This buying of time was of vital importance; now Wegener, acting on orders from his government, could set into motion Operation Magic Fire – the plan to storm the aircraft.

GSG9 had prepared for the assault with meticulous thoroughness. Towards midnight, a small group of GSG9 scouts

Right: Defiant to the end, the seriously wounded Palestinian woman terrorist is taken away to hospital at Mogadishu.

Below: The body of Jürgen Schumann, the captain of the hijacked Lufthansa aircraft, is carried to an ambulance on the tarmac at Mogadishu.

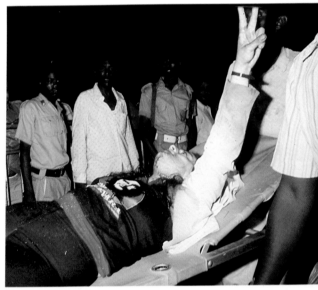

approached unseen to within 30m of the 737. Through infra-red night glasses they confirmed that two hijackers (including Mahmoud) were in the cockpit, but the group could not pinpoint the precise location of the other two terrorists. Armed with this crucial, if incomplete, intelligence, Wegener issued the storming party with their final orders. Once inside the aircraft, he would give the command 'Heads down', and anyone left standing was to be shot. Wegener believed that the hostages would duck behind their seats – an assumption that ultimately proved to be correct. At 0100 hours on 18 October 1977, GSG9 moved out into the desert. Their numbers included specialist marksmen, troopers armed with grenade launchers, and two British SAS men, Major Morrison and Sergeant Davies.

At 0150 hours precisely, Operation Magic Fire began. While the terrorists were kept talking by the control tower, GSG9 moved into position. One group crouched beneath the tail; another sheltered beneath the wings and nose of the airliner. Metal scaling ladders were positioned against the fuselage, and magnetic charges were placed on the front and rear doors on the right-hand side of the aircraft. Then, at 0207 hours, a mere 23 minutes before the terrorists' final deadline was due to expire, the assault went in. A sudden bright light – a flaming oil drum – lit up the night sky directly in front of the 737's nose. Startled, the hijackers were unable to

react before the aircraft was rocked by a massive explosion as the doors were blown in. This was followed immediately by stun grenades hurled by Morrison and Davies.

Under the cover of the blinding flash and deafening roar of the stun grenades, the GSG9 men smashed their way into the airliner. Wegener in person led the group that raced through the front door; two other groups clambered over the wings while a fourth entered from the rear of the 737. All four groups walked into a firefight. One terrorist was killed instantly, but Mahmoud proved as tough in combat as he was ruthless in terrorism. Showing himself in the doorway of the flight deck, he was immediately riddled with .38 bullets fired by a GSG9 trooper. They did not stop him; he was able to hurl two grenades before he was cut down by a burst of fire from a Heckler and Koch MP5. Fortunately, the grenades exploded harmlessly. A woman terrorist was shot in the head; the fourth hijacker was badly wounded.

Five minutes after the GSG9 commandos had begun their assault, three terrorists were dead or dying and the other was a wounded prisoner. All the hostages were freed; only four were slightly injured. Distracted by the flaming oil drum, disorientated by the stun grenades, attacked from four sides simultaneously, the hijackers were overwhelmed by the sheer professionalism of GSG9.

History of the GSG9

GSG9 is not a military unit, but constitutes part of West Germany's paramilitary border police. It was formed after the murder of Israeli athletes at the 1972 Munich Olympic Games had revealed the inadequacy of West German preparedness for dealing with the terrorist threat. Previously, for historical reasons, the government had been wary of forming a specialist unit with a national role because, until 1972, all

the states of the Federal Republic controlled their own police forces. In that year, however, Hans-Dietrich Genscher, the Federal Minister of the Interior, ordered Colonel Ulrich Wegener to raise and train a crack anti-terrorist unit.

Wegener was a recognised expert on terrorism. He had joined the border police in 1958 and trained with the FBI in the United States and also with the Israeli secret service. Indeed it is rumoured that Wegener took part in the Israeli rescue of hostages at Entebbe airport in 1976. By early 1973 Wegener's new force was ready for action, and in that year it adopted the now coveted green beret with its gold eagle badge. While raised initially as an anti-terrorist unit, GSG9 has also evolved techniques to protect VIPs,

guard sensitive government installations and carry out other covert operations. The original strength of GSG9 was set at 188, but the unit's size was raised to 219 men after 1977. Three or four strike units of between 30 and 42 men form the core of GSG9, and these are supported by not only an HQ, communications and intelligence sections but also engineer, technical and training units.

Wegener became a national hero following the Mogadishu rescue in 1977, and is now in overall command of West Germany's border police, although he remains responsible for decisions on deployment of GSG9. Since 1977 the unit has maintained a low profile, which is in itself testimony to its success in curbing terrorism in West Germany.

SOVIET AIRBORNE
The 105th Guards Airborne Division

AKM

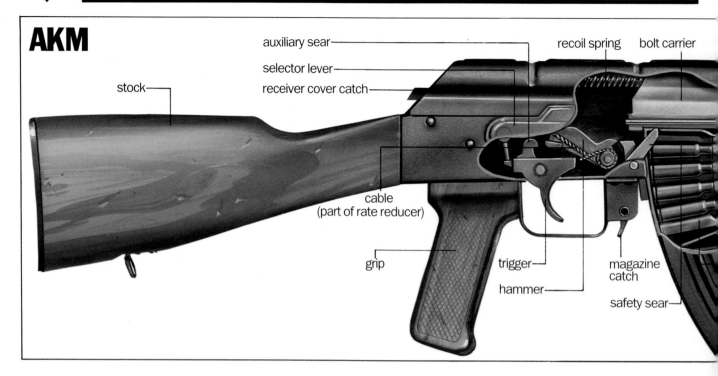

auxiliary sear

selector lever

receiver cover catch

stock

recoil spring   bolt carrier

cable
(part of rate reducer)

grip

trigger

hammer

magazine
catch

safety sear

Above: First produced in 1959, the AKM assault rifle is a modernized version of the highly popular AK-47. The use of stamped steel, rather than machined steel, for the receiver and riveting for the asembly make the rifle more economic to manufacture than its predecessor.

Right: Soviet airborne troops confer while on service in Afghanistan.

Previous page: Members of a Soviet airborne division proudly parade their colours. The blue berets and striped shirts are the hard-earned symbols of their status as an elite force.

AFGHAN service personnel paid little attention to the giant Soviet transport planes landing at Bagram airbase, north of Kabul, towards the end of December 1979. After all, large numbers of Russian advisers were already assisting the Afghan Army in its operations against the tribesmen in rebellion against the Moscow-orientated government in Kabul. In recent weeks these instructors had persuaded one Afghan unit after another to hand in its weapons which, it was claimed, were to be replaced by modern equipment from the USSR. These latest arrivals, however, were different. They wore the light-blue berets and striped vests of crack airborne troops. They were in fact the 105th Guards Airborne Division, normally stationed in the Turkestan Military District of the USSR, and they had arrived to give orders rather than advice – at gunpoint if necessary. By that evening, Christmas Eve, the 105th's advance party was in complete control of the airbase. The Soviet invasion of Afghanistan had begun.

The paras of the 105th are an elite indeed. All members undergo pre-service training, which in itself makes them the pick of the twice-yearly conscript crop. Not only are they all jump-qualified, but they must make a minimum of ten jumps every year in order to retain their coveted status as parachutists. However, the

reason why the 105th can claim to be the Soviet Union's finest conventional troops lies not in their physical prowess, important though that is, but in their ability to break away from official tactical doctrine and adapt to circumstances. Soviet troops are not renowned for showing initiative, but the 105th has carefully studied the lessons of the American experience in Vietnam and applied them to their own counter-insurgency (COIN) operations against the Mujahidin, the rebel tribesmen.

In the early days the Soviets began escorting their convoys with tanks, for it soon became clear that the Russian writ extended only as far as the areas controlled by their garrisons. In the mountainous terrain of central Afghanistan, tanks proved to be worse than useless, as their main armament could not be elevated beyond +15 degrees. The guerrillas soon learned to site their own positions beyond the range of the tanks. Typically, an early convoy escorted by motor rifle troops (trained, of course, for a very different style of warfare on the flat plains of northern Germany) would have been halted by the explosion of a mine or by the rocks of a man-made avalanche. The rebels would then knock out a vehicle near the convoy's tail, trapping everything in between. A blistering fusillade would erupt from the hillsides, the slow tac-tac-

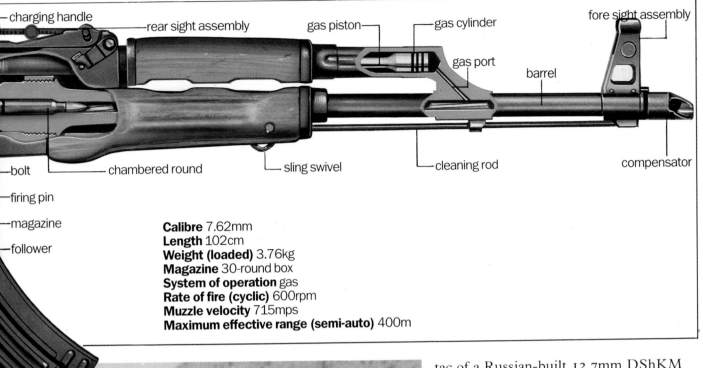

charging handle
rear sight assembly
gas piston
gas cylinder
fore sight assembly
gas port
barrel
bolt
chambered round
sling swivel
cleaning rod
compensator
firing pin
magazine
follower

Calibre 7.62mm
Length 102cm
Weight (loaded) 3.76kg
Magazine 30-round box
System of operation gas
Rate of fire (cyclic) 600rpm
Muzzle velocity 715mps
Maximum effective range (semi-auto) 400m

tac of a Russian-built 12.7mm DShKM heavy machine gun competing with the crump of mortars and smallarms fire from AK-47s and AKMs, and even from venerable British SMLEs (Short Magazine Lee-Enfields) that had last seen service on the Northwest Frontier. Often the tanks were the only survivors of an ambush, having fought their way out covered with wounded, but sometimes they too fell victim to RPG-7 rocket launchers.

The 105th's approach to COIN was somewhat different. As an airborne formation it did not employ tanks, and its comparatively few (18) ASU-85 airborne assault guns possessed even less elevation and were clearly unsuited to mountain warfare. On the other hand they did operate 128 BMDs (Airborne Infantry Combat Vehicles). BMDs had a 73mm smooth-bore gun, which could elevate to +33 degrees, enabling it to search out rebel positions with high-explosive (HE) shells. The success of the BMD forced the Soviet Fortieth Army to withdraw the motor rifle division's tanks from convoy escort duties and replace them with their BMPs – a heavier infantry version of the BMD, but similarly armed. Some sources claim that a proportion of the 105th's BMDs have been re-equipped with the 30mm AGS-17 automatic grenade launcher, a ferocious weapon in a close-quarter ambush.

It soon became apparent that the 105th were a worthy opponent, even for an enemy as tough as the Mujahidin. On convoy escort, the paras usually carried within the BMD were deployed to form a dismounted reaction to ambushes. At the beginning of the war, the response of some Soviet infantry to being attacked was ambiguous. This was a reflection of the fact that a large proportion were Moslems recruited in Uzbekistan and Turkestan who were sympathetic to the religious aims of the Mujahidin, who are also Moslems. No such conflict of loyalties affected the 105th, who swiftly became a byword for aggression and fitness, time after time beating off rebel attacks.

The 105th's activities were not, however, confined to ground action. As Soviet communications systems improved, ambushed columns could call in rapid-reaction heliborne relief forces, and conventional airstrikes directed onto rebel positions. Flying jet aircraft in mountains requires a high degree of skill, and the time available for target

Left: Since the Soviets have made use of the BMP, an armoured personnel carrier fitted with a 73mm gun, the Mujahidin have had to exercise greater caution when setting up ambushes.

identification is severely limited. Much of the HE payload was thus being wasted, so the Soviets turned to the use of napalm and, reputedly, chemical weaponry which affected whole areas and needed less accuracy in its delivery. Even so, inexperienced MiG and Sukhoi pilots still had an alarming tendency to fly straight into the ground, to the natural and ill-concealed delight of the Afghan rebels.

Right: A Mil Mi-24 Hind gunship flies in low over a Soviet base near Kabul. Protected by titanium armour and heavily armed, the Hind has proved to be a formidable opponent to the Mujahidin.

History of the Soviet airborne forces

The genesis of the USSR's airborne forces occurred in the late 1920s. Ex- periments with parachute troops began in 1928, and in 1936 a force of 1500 men was dropped from aircraft before an audience of military experts, an event which made a distinct, if short-lived, impact on Western military observers. An unusual variation on the usual mode of parachuting used in the late 1930s/ early 1940s was the dropping of men without parachutes, who landed safely in deep snow-drifts. From the early 1940s onwards, Soviet airborne troops were regarded as a crack force, and consequently received the designation of 'Guards' units in recognition of their elite status.

In 1941 the Red Army possessed about 50,000 airborne troops, roughly the same number as today. They fought valiantly in the 'Great Patriotic War' (the Soviet name for World War II) against Nazi Germany, the title of 'Hero of the Soviet Union' being awarded to 126 men, but made little impact in an air- borne role. At Vyazma in 1942, for instance, roughly 10,000 paras were dropped in three stages from 27 Janu- ary to 24 February. Lacking artillery and air support, and committed piece- meal to battle, they fought well but failed to take their objectives.

After the war, the Soviets did not begin to rebuild their airborne forces until 1956. Since then they have not been used in a parachute role, although troops were airlanded during the inva- sions of Czechoslovakia in 1968 and Afghanistan in 1979.

The Soviet airborne division normal- ly includes three airborne regiments, each of three battalions, an artillery regiment, signals, transport, air- defence and engineer battalions, plus reconnaissance, NBC (Nuclear, Biologi- cal, Chemical) and parachute-rigging companies. Each airborne regiment has attached anti-tank and mortar bat- teries plus ancillary units. Only one airborne regiment is fully equipped with BMDs; the other two regiments have one BMD-equipped battalion apiece.

The divisional artillery consists of 18 122mm howitzers, 18 multi-barrel rock- et launchers, 18 ASU-85 assault guns and a battalion equipped with anti-tank guided weapons. The total strength of a division is approximately 8800, but for its intervention in Afghanistan the 105th was considerably reinforced by drafts of riflemen from the 103rd and 104th Guards Airborne Divisions together with the appropriate number of BMDs, thus giving the division a much higher proportion of infantry to supporting arms than normal.

It is not surprising that a crack formation like the 105th Guards Airborne should not be content to remain on the defensive for long. Naturally, an airborne division was used to thinking in three rather than two dimensions and it soon developed tactics that utilised helicopters as gunships and transports to allow them to get to grips with the elusive Mujahidin. Primarily, the Soviets needed to protect the road-bound convoys from marauding Afghan rebels. The Russians developed techniques reminiscent of the tactics employed by British columns on the Northwest Frontier. When a convoy was ready to move along a valley, the heights on either side were occupied in advance by troops helilifted onto the summits. Once the column had passed safely by, the advance party was lifted out and moved to hills further along the valley. Fire support to the brave men carrying out this dangerous task was provided by helicopter gunships armed with machine guns and rockets.

To deal with a guerrilla band hidden in the hills, helicopter gunships would attempt to pin them down and soften them up. Paras would simultaneously be lifted into blocking positions to cut off the rebels' retreat while other parties would be airlanded onto dropping zones from where they could converge on the Mujahidin, to winkle them out and destroy them. The 105th have also made

intelligent use of the helicopter as a flying command post. In their large-scale search-and-destroy missions in the wild interior of Afghanistan, Soviet senior officers have been given a bird's-eye view of the operations unfolding beneath them, and are better able to co-ordinate the movements of their troops.

The Mujahidin have not been defeated, and they probably never will be defeated. However, as long as the Soviet Union seeks to impose its will on Afghanistan by force, the 105th Guards Airborne Division will remain the finely-honed razor edge of the Russian military effort.

SOVIET SPETSNAZ
Special Purpose Forces

CREEPING stealthily along the rooftops of Downing Street, the Spetsnaz operatives had little difficulty in reaching their target unobserved. Simultaneously, their comrades eliminated the policeman guarding No. 10, the Prime Minister's residence. Minutes later, it was all over. The British Prime Minister lay slumped over her desk in a pool of blood, a single neat bullet hole in her forehead fired from a silenced PRI automatic pistol. A horrified public awoke the following morning to find the nation leaderless, and

Structure and history of Spetsnaz

The spearhead of the Soviet Armed Forces – the Special Purpose Forces, or Spetsnaz – were virtually unknown in the West until recently. However, as the result of counter-insurgency campaigning in Afghanistan, and the statements of defectors such as 'Viktor Suvorov' (the pseudonym of a former Intelligence Officer), Spetsnaz has assumed a higher profile since the late 1970s. Any writing about Spetsnaz must, however, remain speculative.

It would seem that one Spetsnaz company of 115 men is attached to each Soviet army (41 in all) and one Spetsnaz 'brigade' is deployed at each of the army fronts (a total of 16 brigades). A further four naval 'brigades' are attached to the four Soviet fleets. These brigades consist of between 1000 and 1300 men organised into an HQ, an anti-VIP company, three or four battalions and supporting units. Naval brigades include midget submarines and combat frogmen. The structure of a Spetsnaz company ensures great flexibility in the field. Comprising nine officers, 11 warrant officers and 95 soldiers, the company can deploy as a single unit or break up into as many as 15 independent groups.

The previous history of Spetsnaz is obscure, although Soviet Special Forces' 'battle honours' would certainly include the invasion of Czechoslovakia in 1968. On that occasion Prague Airport was seized before the arrival of the main Warsaw Pact invasion forces. Similarly, a joint KGB–Spetsnaz force was infiltrated into Kabul in December 1979 to pave the way for the Soviet invasion of Afghanistan. Spetsnaz troops have played a leading role in the bloody war of hit and run that has continued in the mountains ever since.

It is widely believed that naval Spetsnaz troops have made at least 150 clandestine landings along the coast of Norway – part of NATO's northern flank – and neutral Sweden to spy out the route for a future invasion of Scandinavia and to reconnoitre naval bases and other coastal installations. In 1984 frogmen were observed several times in the vicinity of Karlskrona, a major Swedish naval base, but none was caught.

Spetsnaz, for all their training, have never faced well-equipped modern troops and have only limited experience of COIN. For this reason, Spetsnaz must be regarded as a shadowy threat – but a threat nonetheless.

Left: During training, Spetsnaz teams wear the uniforms of conventional forces; these men on infantry exercises are dressed as if they were members of the Red Banner Black Sea Fleet.

that Soviet armoured formations were pouring into West Germany.

Fiction? Of course, but not wildly implausible fiction. Western defence experts believe that 'anti-VIP' units of Spetsnaz, the crack Soviet Special Purpose Forces, would be deployed to assassinate NATO leaders at the beginning of a war. Soviet strategists hold that the shock to national morale of such attacks in London, Washington and Bonn would be devastating. To conceal their existence, these highly secret units are detached from their parent brigades to become 'athletics teams', and, as sportsmen, they are welcomed into Western countries. One such Spetsnaz man was Valentin Yerikalin, a silver-medal winner for rowing at the 1968 Olympic Games. Some time later he was arrested by Turkish police after attempting to recruit Turks into an undercover network run by the Spetsnaz brigade attached to the Black Sea Fleet.

Anti-VIP companies are just one element among the Soviet Special Forces which, with a peacetime complement of 30,000 men, greatly outnumber similar forces of other nations. Most Spetsnaz personnel are conscripts, which is unusual for an elite formation, and they serve for two years. Training is rigorous, intense and unremitting throughout their period of service. Officers tour recruiting depots looking for tough, intelligent youngsters, preferably with linguistic and sporting abilities. Out of the 100 or so selected, only about 20 will pass the induction course. One gruelling test is to send recruits on a 30km cross-country run – in gas masks. If one unfortunate wrenches his mask off to gulp down fresh air, the entire squad are made to start again. Once they reach their training units, recruits are taught free-fall parachuting, use of explosives and silent killing techniques.

Training does not end on joining a unit. In order to maintain combat-readiness, Spetsnaz units are frequently mobilised without warning and airdropped into a desolate region such as Siberia, usually at night. They then have to cover vast distances – sometimes as much as thousands of kilometres – to reach their objective, which are often real Soviet installations, guarded by crack KGB troops. The Spetsnaz men then have to 'overcome' the guards: it is alleged that these exercises are so realistic that many young soldiers have died as a result.

The role of the more 'conventional' Spetsnaz unit in time of war would be that of 'desant', that is, dropping as much as 500km behind enemy lines and wreaking havoc by carrying out acts of sabotage and long-range reconnaissance. To make training as realistic as possible, Spetsnaz train in areas that closely resemble their intended theatre of operations; the Baltic coast, for instance, has terrain that is similar to northern Germany. Spetsnaz also carry out practice attacks on purpose-built mock-ups of NATO bases, complete with guards wearing Western uniforms and with inflatable models of Cruise and Pershing II missiles and fighter aircraft such as the Mirage and F-16. Saboteurs are as harshly trained as other Spetsnaz troops. Frequently they are ordered to parachute into blazing forests, or in adverse weather conditions that would certainly prompt an 'abort jump' order in the British or US armies.

Above: Officer cadets train to achieve peak physical fitness.

Right: This Spetsnaz soldier wears full camouflage overalls complete with hood, in a pattern designed for warfare in temperate climates. Armament comprises a 5.45mm AKS-74 with a plastic 30-round magazine, and a 5.45mm PRI automatic pistol carried in a black leather holster.

In time of war, Spetsnaz operatives would try to create havoc behind NATO lines by wearing NATO uniforms and issuing false orders, by spreading rumours and other nefarious acts. This threat is not underestimated in the West; Admiral Lord Hill-Norton, a former British Chief of Defence Staff, has estimated that a mere 1000 English-speaking Spetsnaz men, infiltrated into Britain 'could make it very difficult for us to operate effectively' in wartime.

Because of the nature of their task, Spetsnaz soldiers do not use heavy weapons or equipment. However, their armoury is still formidable. Each man is issued with a 5.45mm Kalashnikov assault rifle, 300 rounds and a silenced P6 pistol. Every team carries one RPG-7D rocket-launcher, and on some missions SA-7 SAM (surface-to-air) missiles as well. Naturally enough, 'diversionary' troops wearing NATO uniforms would carry NATO-issue weapons.

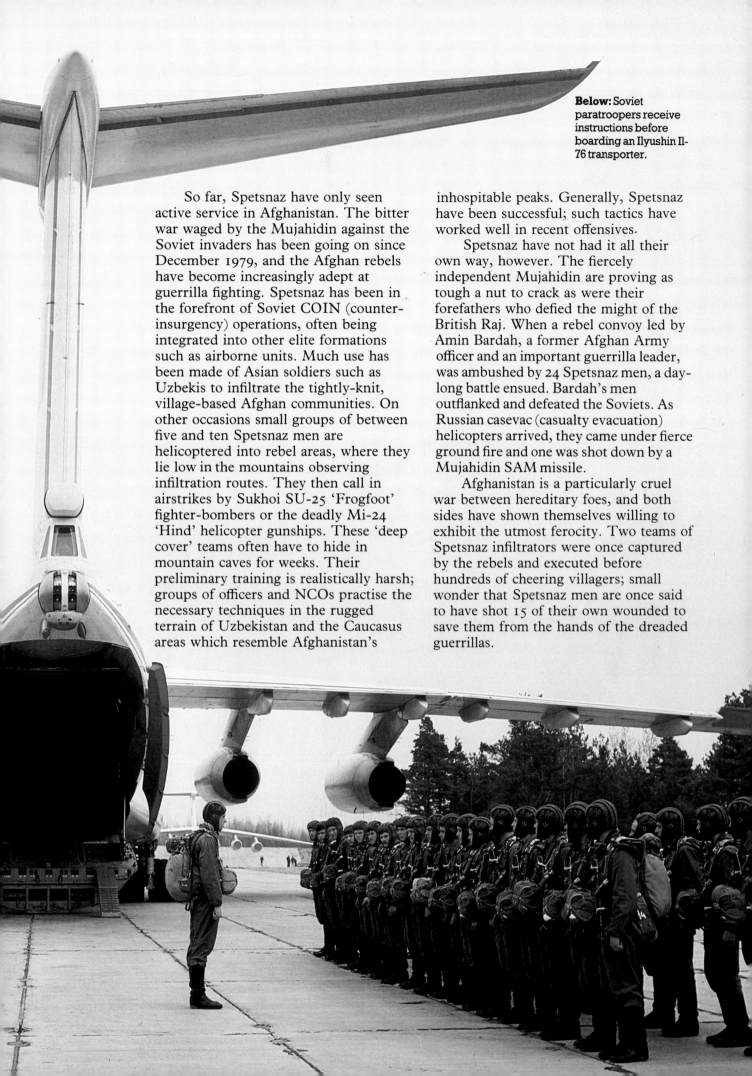

Below: Soviet paratroopers receive instructions before boarding an Ilyushin Il-76 transporter.

So far, Spetsnaz have only seen active service in Afghanistan. The bitter war waged by the Mujahidin against the Soviet invaders has been going on since December 1979, and the Afghan rebels have become increasingly adept at guerrilla fighting. Spetsnaz has been in the forefront of Soviet COIN (counter-insurgency) operations, often being integrated into other elite formations such as airborne units. Much use has been made of Asian soldiers such as Uzbekis to infiltrate the tightly-knit, village-based Afghan communities. On other occasions small groups of between five and ten Spetsnaz men are helicoptered into rebel areas, where they lie low in the mountains observing infiltration routes. They then call in airstrikes by Sukhoi SU-25 'Frogfoot' fighter-bombers or the deadly Mi-24 'Hind' helicopter gunships. These 'deep cover' teams often have to hide in mountain caves for weeks. Their preliminary training is realistically harsh; groups of officers and NCOs practise the necessary techniques in the rugged terrain of Uzbekistan and the Caucasus areas which resemble Afghanistan's

inhospitable peaks. Generally, Spetsnaz have been successful; such tactics have worked well in recent offensives.

Spetsnaz have not had it all their own way, however. The fiercely independent Mujahidin are proving as tough a nut to crack as were their forefathers who defied the might of the British Raj. When a rebel convoy led by Amin Bardah, a former Afghan Army officer and an important guerrilla leader, was ambushed by 24 Spetsnaz men, a day-long battle ensued. Bardah's men outflanked and defeated the Soviets. As Russian casevac (casualty evacuation) helicopters arrived, they came under fierce ground fire and one was shot down by a Mujahidin SAM missile.

Afghanistan is a particularly cruel war between hereditary foes, and both sides have shown themselves willing to exhibit the utmost ferocity. Two teams of Spetsnaz infiltrators were once captured by the rebels and executed before hundreds of cheering villagers; small wonder that Spetsnaz men are once said to have shot 15 of their own wounded to save them from the hands of the dreaded guerrillas.

4·FORCES IN THE MIDDLE EAST

ON 14 May 1948 the last British troops left Palestine. Under UN auspices the country had been divided into two between the Jews and Palestinians. That very night, however, armies of five Arab states (Egypt, Syria, Jordan, Iraq and Lebanon) crossed into former Palestinian territory in an attempt to destroy Israel at birth. In this, the first of six wars so far between the Arab states and Israel, the young state showed its fighting spirit. Outnumbered and outgunned, fighting on three fronts, it defeated all five Arab armies to secure its existence. It was a baptism of fire.

More wars inevitably followed as the Arabs attempted first to re-establish Palestine, and then to recover the territory occupied since 1967, while Israel tried desperately to improve its position of strategic vulnerability.

In 1956 the Israelis attacked south to remove the Palestinian menace on the Gaza Strip, and to inflict a crushing military defeat on Egypt. Again, 11 years later, after a hugely successful pre-emptive airstrike, Israel defeated the Egyptians to gain control of the Sinai, secured the West Bank of the River Jordan, and acquired a foothold in the Syrian-controlled Golan Heights. In just six days the Israelis won what was a mammoth victory. In reply, President Nasser of Egypt began a 'War of Attrition', in which the Arabs attempted to use their greater resources to inflict defeat over a longer time-span. Lasting from 1968 to 1970, the war quickly developed into a stalemate, and was in serious danger of escalating to a direct conflict between the two superpowers.

Three years later, in 1973, the Egyptians counter-attacked during the holiday of Yom Kippur (6th October). Caught by surprise, the Israelis suffered a series of setbacks in the Sinai, before an armoured counter-attack of their own once again pushed the Egyptians back over the Suez Canal.

After five wars in 25 years, a non-military solution was now sought, culminating in the Camp David accords of 1978. Sponsored by President Carter, the Israeli and Egyptian leaders agreed to a 'framework for peace' for the Gaza Strip and West Bank. An uneasy truce therefore settled on Israel's southern and eastern fronts.

In the north, however, raids from Palestinian terrorists based in Lebanon intensified, provoking an Israeli invasion in 1982. The invasion, Operation Peace for Galilee, was another stunning military success for Israel. Pulling out of Lebanon proved much more difficult, though, and the northern border with Syria and Lebanon remains a source of concern.

Throughout these wars Israeli strategy has been to seek a quick resolution. Outnumbered and surrounded, Israel has neither the men nor machines to fight a long war on a number of fronts. Instead, relying on sophisticated technology, high-quality troops and blitzkrieg

tactics, it has succeeded in inflicting a series of devastating military defeats in very short campaigns (the attacks in 1967 and 1982 both lasted a mere six days).

An important component of this strategy is the use of elite forces, performing specialist roles and willing to accept high casualty rates to ensure a speedy advance. Enemy strongpoints (such as Beaufort Castle in 1982) have to be eliminated quickly, lest they threaten the advance's lines of communication. To do this, elite units such as the paras and the Golani Brigade are heavily relied upon. In addition there are units such as the 7th Armoured Brigade which have attained elite status through merit.

Finally, Israel is not alone in its possession of elite forces in the Middle East. The Jordanian Arab Legion, particularly under its British leader Glubb Pasha, was one of the most formidable units in the region, while Egypt, following the pattern of many other states, has created a commando force capable of performing a variety of demanding missions. Both are elite units in their own right and, along with the Israeli units, have been involved in decisive military actions.

ISRAELI PARAS
The Paratroopers

SHORTLY before 0800 hours on 5 June 1967, Colonel Rafael Eitan saw Israeli jets streak across the Sinai. The commander of the crack 202nd Parachute Brigade now knew the war had begun. Moments later the order to advance was broadcast. As part of Major-General Israel Tal's armoured division, the 202nd was charged with clearing the Gaza Strip. Against them were ranged the 7th and 20th (Palestinian) Infantry Divisions, with 150 extra tanks to stiffen the defences. Eitan's

plan was to sweep around the southern edge of the Egyptian defences at Rafah, and then head north to take their positions from the rear in an outflanking movement, as the 7th Armoured Brigade attacked from the northeast.

As the 202nd headed south, one of its more western units was attacked by Egyptian forces. Although one Israeli tank was hit, the unit's young commander quickly spotted and destroyed the Egyptian tanks. Striking the southernmost Egyptian forces side

History and training of the Israeli paras

Following demobilisation in 1949, Israel's armed forces suffered a sharp decline. When General Moshe Dayan was appointed Chief of Staff in December 1953, he realised that an elite combat unit was required to inspire confidence in the regular infantry. Accordingly he merged the small, elite anti-guerrilla force, code-named Unit 101, with the army's best standing formation, the parachute battalion. By combining Unit 101's aggression and the paras' discipline, a fine military machine was created. Under its innovative commander, Ariel Sharon, the growing *esprit de corps* was exploited in bold, high-risk tactics. In 1955 the basic paratroop unit was expanded to a full brigade, while the 1967 War saw at least three full brigades in action, and in the mid-1980s there are no fewer than five elite paratroop brigades.

To be a para, each recruit has to complete an exhaustive training programme. After induction, the volunteers are sent on a basic training course with heavy emphasis on combat skills. Successful candidates are then passed on first to a parachuting course, and then to a course in combined operations. Joint manoeuvres with tank and artillery units are organised, and each recruit is taught how to work with helicopters, assault craft, and APCs. After completing a squad commander's course, in which the roles of a junior NCO are taught, each man is trained in a specialised skill. A percentage of recruits is then selected for Officer School. After serving with a brigade, paras remain on the reserve list for a number of years, during which time they undertake refresher courses at the School of Infantry.

on, the 202nd encountered fierce resistance on its right flank, but on the left flank, the enemy's rear, the Israeli forces were able to scythe through the 'soft' defences and quickly reach the road between Rafah and El Arish.

Meanwhile, Eitan's HQ had been separated from his other units and was fighting for its life against the Egyptian rearguard. Holding a radio set in one hand and a sub-machine gun in the other, Eitan informed Tal of his precarious position. Tal immediately decided to send an armoured unit to Eitan's aid, only to be persuaded by Eitan that the crisis would pass. After two hours of vicious fighting, the 202nd's commander was finally able to re-form his HQ, and with his left flank pushed towards Rafah junction to relieve pressure on his hard-pressed right flank.

Once Rafah junction had been captured, though, it was clear that the right flank was in a desperate situation. With mounting casualties it was separated from Eitan by over 4km of enemy-held territory. Realising that the battle rested on a knife edge, Eitan had to reach his right flank at all costs. Of his five remaining tanks, some had no ammunition left, and few had more than one hour's fuel. Nevertheless, leaping into the lead vehicle, Eitan ordered the tanks forward. The move was decisive. Despite the heavy opposition, Eitan was able to relieve his right flank by sunset. As if by magic, hundreds of Egyptians fled their trenches.

Left: An Israeli paratrooper, armed with an Uzi sub-machine gun, in the Gaza Strip during the Six-Day War, 1967.

Below: Paras in a half-track take cover from Egyptian sniper fire.

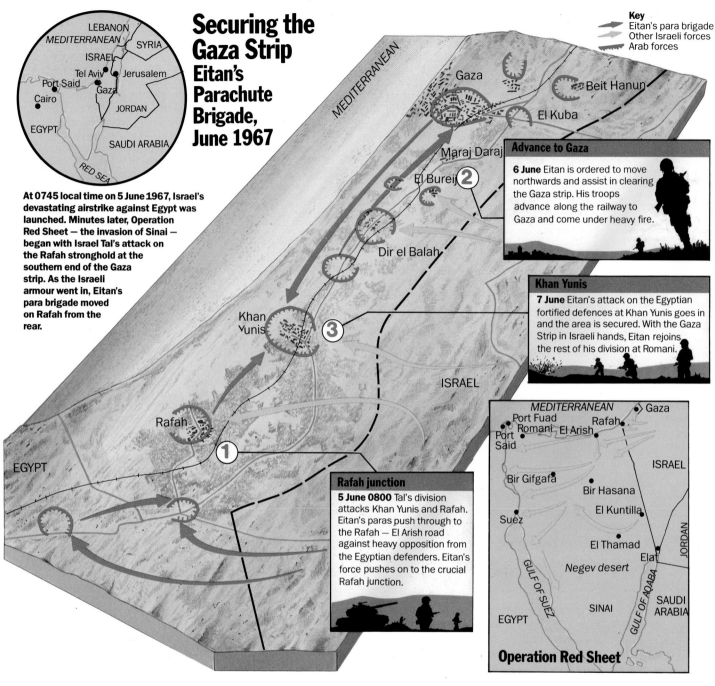

Securing the Gaza Strip
Eitan's Parachute Brigade, June 1967

At 0745 local time on 5 June 1967, Israel's devastating airstrike against Egypt was launched. Minutes later, Operation Red Sheet — the invasion of Sinai — began with Israel Tal's attack on the Rafah stronghold at the southern end of the Gaza strip. As the Israeli armour went in, Eitan's para brigade moved on Rafah from the rear.

Key
Eitan's para brigade
Other Israeli forces
Arab forces

Advance to Gaza
6 June Eitan is ordered to move northwards and assist in clearing the Gaza strip. His troops advance along the railway to Gaza and come under heavy fire.

Khan Yunis
7 June Eitan's attack on the Egyptian fortified defences at Khan Yunis goes in and the area is secured. With the Gaza Strip in Israeli hands, Eitan rejoins the rest of his division at Romani.

Rafah junction
5 June 0800 Tal's division attacks Khan Yunis and Rafah. Eitan's paras push through to the Rafah — El Arish road against heavy opposition from the Egyptian defenders. Eitan's force pushes on to the crucial Rafah junction.

Operation Red Sheet

At nightfall the 202nd regrouped, and the full story of the right flank's bitter struggle was told. At times even the medics had been forced to fight Egyptian tanks at ranges of only a few metres.

They next day the 202nd were ordered north to help clear the Gaza Strip. As they approached the town of Khan Yunis, a mine disabled the lead tank, and a unit straying into the town came under heavy fire. To leave a strong enemy force untouched in the rear would have been a major mistake, and so the 202nd resolved to take out the town. The

attack on 7 June went in as planned, and after only a brief skirmish the Israelis captured the key Egyptian positions and smashed their will to resist. As the fighting died down, Eitan received an urgent message warning him to expect an attack from the north. The 202nd's commander was somewhat surprised at this, since the area to the north had been reported cleared the previous day. Gathering together an impromptu force of jeeps and tanks, Eitan headed north to investigate. Some 2000m from the village of Dir-el-Balah the force stopped and, through their binoculars, searched the

Right: Two AMX13 tanks lead an Israeli column through the Gaza Strip.

Below: Paras bed down in a field beside their transports and try to get some sleep.

streets ahead. Immediately in front of them lay a unit of tanks turning to aim their gun barrels in the 202nd's direction. At the last moment Eitan realised the 'enemy' was a force of Israeli tanks. Ordering his own tanks to lower their gun barrels as a recognition signal, Eitan turned back to Khan Yunis.

Later that morning, the 202nd was ordered south along the coast to pick up an artillery unit at Romani, and then to head for the Suez Canal. With the exception of one attack by Egyptian MiG-21s, the movement south was uneventful. As they approached the Canal, several Israeli Mirage jets screamed overhead and agreed to scout for the 202nd. The jets identified Egyptian forces ahead in the city of El Qantara and, using their cannons, destroyed three tanks. The remainder were left for the 202nd.

With his command unit leading the way along the road, Eitan spread his jeeps on the left, and the tanks and infantry on the right, with the artillery unit providing covering fire. Contact was quickly made with the Egyptians. On the left several tanks massed against the 202nd's jeeps. Warned by Eitan, the jeeps organised a 'reception committee' with their 106mm recoilless rifles. Taken unawares, the tanks were quickly despatched. An anti-tank missile flew past Eitan, smashing into a telephone post less than 5m away, only for his vehicle to be hit moments later by more enemy fire, severely wounding Eitan. Despite the loss of their commander, the 202nd pressed home the attack, smashing Egyptian forces at El Qantara, and on the fourth day of the war reached the banks of the Suez Canal. Exploiting their mobility to the full in a series of daring actions, the 202nd had played a significant role in Israel's victory in the Sinai, pushing the Egyptian forces back to the very banks of the Suez Canal.

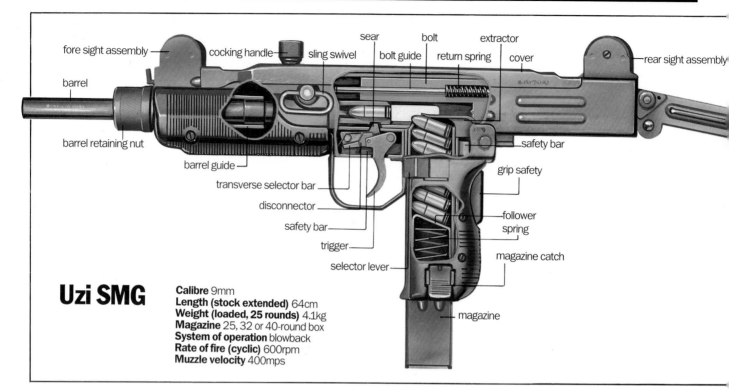

fore sight assembly — cocking handle — sling swivel — sear — bolt — extractor — rear sight assembly

bolt guide — return spring — cover

barrel

barrel retaining nut

barrel guide

transverse selector bar

disconnector

safety bar

trigger

selector lever

safety bar

grip safety

follower

spring

magazine catch

magazine

Uzi SMG

Calibre 9mm
Length (stock extended) 64cm
Weight (loaded, 25 rounds) 4.1kg
Magazine 25, 32 or 40-round box
System of operation blowback
Rate of fire (cyclic) 600rpm
Muzzle velocity 400mps

Above: Designed in the late 1940s by Major Uziel Gal and first manufactured in 1951, the Uzi sub-machine gun was widely used by the Israeli forces in the Battle for Jerusalem in 1967. The gun is easily mass-produced since its components are metal stampings and heat-resistant plastics.

Right: The role of the Israeli 55th Parachute Brigade in the Battle for Jerusalem. At 1100 hours on 5 June Jordanian forces began attacking targets in Israel. In order to defend the corridor to Jerusalem against a Jordanian advance, the Israelis deployed an armoured brigade to secure the high ground lying to the north of the corridor; the paras then began their attack on Jerusalem.

Jerusalem

While the 202nd were racing across the Sinai in a highly mobile campaign, Colonel Mordechai Gur's 55th Parachute Brigade were fighting a very different war. To them was granted the privilege of being the first Israeli unit to enter the Old City of Jerusalem. Containing such holy places as the Temple Mount and the Wailing Wall, its capture was an act of enormous religious and psychological importance to the young state of Israel. To enter it had been the dream of countless generations of Jews, and this privilege had been hard earned by the 55th. In two days of courageous and skilful fighting, they had wrested control of northern Jerusalem from the well dug-in forces of the Jordanian Army and reversed a situation of strategic vulnerability into one where they held the initiative. Against them were ranged the crack Jordanian 27th Infantry Brigade under Brigadier Ata Ali. Commanding a complex series of deep concrete bunkers, trenches, minefields, and barbed wire, they could also call on additional support from other brigades to the north and south, and from a tank battalion kept in reserve. Two elite units were thus fighting for the most cherished

prize in the Middle East, Jerusalem.

As the war began, Mordechai Gur's plan was for the 66th and 71st Battalions to attack in the middle of the night along a front running from the Mandelbaum Gate to a point opposite the Jordanian-held Police School. The 28th Battalion would exploit any breakthrough, pushing southwards towards the walls of the Old City. With minimal support from a few tanks, Gur was only too aware that he was asking his men to fight their way through a formidable set of obstacles.

After some delays while units struggled to find their places, the covering barrage eventually began. With buildings on the Jordanian side bursting into flames and lines of tracer flicking through the darkness, the first Israeli platoons approached the Jordanian positions. Thrusting Bangalore torpedoes (tubes packed with explosive) below the coils of barbed wire, they quickly pulled back and hit the deck. The failure of several Bangalore torpedoes to explode, and the presence of further barbed-wire obstacles, delayed the 71st Battalion. Men moving forward to exploit the expected breach produced overcrowding, presenting a tempting and very vulnerable target to the enemy. Eventually the way through was cleared.

The 66th Battalion was to push northwards through the Police School,

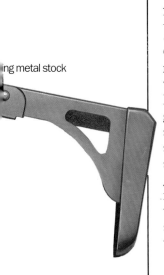

ng metal stock

taking the important position of Ammunition Hill, while the 71st Battalion was to move through the Sheikh Jarrah area and the American Colony towards the Wadi El-Joz. The men of the 66th in particular knew they would face enormous difficulties. Heavily laden with extra ammunition and grenades, they found their mobility severely restricted, while giant searchlights and flares lit up the whole scene, making it impossible to see where Jordanian smallarms fire was coming from. Not bothering to search for enemy trenches, and ignoring constant Jordanian shelling and the heavy loads they carried, the 66th pushed on to its main objective.

First into the Police School was A Company. Four-man groups cleared the rooms, two throwing in grenades and then spraying the room with fire, while the other two moved on to the room next door. In the pitch-black corridors the paras kept tripping and falling, so that the officers were forced into the dangerous option of using torches to light the way. Having cleared the building, A Company moved with D Company towards the Ambassador Hotel, while B and C Companies moved towards Ammunition Hill. As dawn broke, the fighting on the hill had developed into an exhausting battle. Often unable to tell friend from foe, hampered by deadly snipers, and fast running out of ammunition, the paras cleared the hill

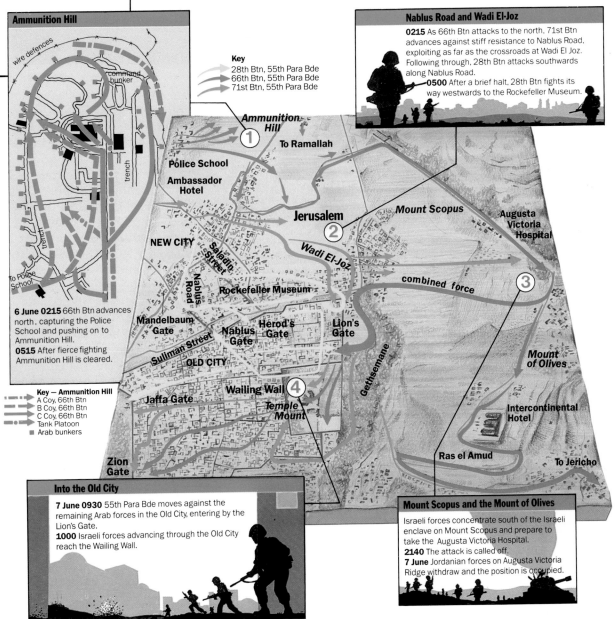

Ammunition Hill

wire defences

command bunker

trench

trench

To Police School

Arab bunkers

6 June 0215 66th Btn advances north, capturing the Police School and pushing on to Ammunition Hill.
0515 After fierce fighting Ammunition Hill is cleared.

Key — Ammunition Hill
A Coy, 66th Btn
B Coy, 66th Btn
C Coy, 66th Btn
Tank Platoon
Arab bunkers

Key
28th Btn, 55th Para Bde
66th Btn, 55th Para Bde
71st Btn, 55th Para Bde

Nablus Road and Wadi El-Joz

0215 As 66th Btn attacks to the north, 71st Btn advances against stiff resistance to Nablus Road, exploiting as far as the crossroads at Wadi El Joz. Following through, 28th Btn attacks southwards along Nablus Road.
0500 After a brief halt, 28th Btn fights its way westwards to the Rockefeller Museum.

Ammunition Hill
①
To Ramallah
Police School
Ambassador Hotel
Jerusalem
②
Mount Scopus
Augusta Victoria Hospital
NEW CITY
Saladin Street
Nablus Road
Wadi El-Joz
combined force
③
Rockefeller Museum
Mandelbaum Gate
Nablus Gate
Herod's Gate
Lion's Gate
Gethsemane
Mount of Olives
Suliman Street
OLD CITY
Jaffa Gate
Wailing Wall
④
Temple Mount
Intercontinental Hotel
Zion Gate
Ras el Amud
To Jericho

Into the Old City

7 June 0930 55th Para Bde moves against the remaining Arab forces in the Old City, entering by the Lion's Gate.
1000 Israeli forces advancing through the Old City reach the Wailing Wall.

Mount Scopus and the Mount of Olives

Israeli forces concentrate south of the Israeli enclave on Mount Scopus and prepare to take the Augusta Victoria Hospital.
2140 The attack is called off.
7 June Jordanian forces on Augusta Victoria Ridge withdraw and the position is occupied.

Right: Israeli paras stand beside the Wailing Wall and await orders for a final advance against Jordanian troops still within the Old City.

and the final 'Great Bunker' by 0515 hours.

Meanwhile the 71st Battalion was also meeting with stiff resistance. With only photographs to guide them, their task was further complicated by the need to clear hidden enemy positions in fierce hand-to-hand combat. Taking the Jordanians in the street leading to Wadi El-Joz by surprise, though, the paras were able to reach their objective. By this time casualties were mounting, with even the brigade's support units coming under heavy fire. The 28th Battalion now moved in, following the 71st through a breach in the wire. Many of their officers had been lost when the battalion HQ was hit by a Jordanian 25-pounder. When the men of the 28th reached the Jordanian side of the wire it was already dawn, but they fought on southwards. Enemy snipers and artillery found the daylight conditions much easier to operate in, however, and frequently infiltrated back into areas previously cleared by the paras.

The 28th Battalion's objective was the imposing new Rockefeller Museum which dominated the northeastern approaches to the Old City. Deafened by the roar of tank guns in the enclosed spaces, the paras moved down Saladin Street and Nablus Road to take not only the Museum but the Rivoli Hotel too, whose kitchens and baths were quickly pressed into service.

The 55th Brigade had performed brilliantly, securing all of its objectives by 0800 hours. After heavy fighting and

Below: Israeli paras take cover from Jordanian sniper fire as they near the Old City. Behind them is the site of the Garden of Gethsemane.

horrific casualties, the paras now saw themselves as blooded veterans, and were desperately keen to push on into the Old City itself. Gur was ordered to take the last Jordanian strongpoint in the region, the Augusta Victoria Hospital on the ridge to the south of Mount Scopus, before entering the Old City. The paras waited until 1930 hours before beginning their assault under cover of darkness. At 2140 hours, with only four Shermans left, Gur was told that 40 enemy tanks had been seen on the reverse slope of where his men were attacking. Gur immediately decided to withdraw until air support could be guaranteed the next morning. At 0804 hours on 7 June, after a fitful night's sleep, the paras were finally cleared to take the Old City. Sweeping up from the Kidron Valley and across from Mount Scopus, with full air cover, they stormed the hospital. Then at 0930 hours Gur was able to give the historic order to his men. With their commander in the lead, the paras entered through the Lion's Gate, and by 1000 hours had reached the Wailing Wall. Resistance was incredibly light: realising that he had been cut off, the Jordanian commander had skilfully pulled his brigade out of the Old City earlier that day. As the 55th's ordnance officer passed round a bottle of whisky, the paras realised they had won a victory few would forget.

Suez

As in 1967, so in the Yom Kippur War of 1973, Israeli paras were involved in decisive actions. On the northern front with the Golani Brigade they captured the strategically important Mount Hermon; a regular brigade was dispatched to the Gulf of Suez to stop Egyptian armour rushing southwards to the Abu Rhodes oilfields; while a reserve brigade under the experienced Brigadier-General Danny Matt prepared to defend the crucial Mitla and Gidi passes in the Sinai. The paras were also involved in the counter-attack across the Suez Canal, with Danny Matt's reservists the first IDF (Israeli Defence Forces) unit to cross the Canal in the early hours of 16 October. The Israelis were unable to secure the lines of communication with this bridgehead, however, due to stubborn Egyptian resistance on the East Bank. As a result Matt's beleaguered forces were left unsupported for several days. Eventually, with the help of the regular para brigade brought up from the Gulf of Suez, the Israelis were able to secure the approach roads to the Canal. In one classic battle, known as Chinese Farm, Israeli paras and tank units fought and overcame two Egyptian divisions in a bloody encounter which raged for hours on end. Finally the way was open for a crossing in strength.

One of the paras' toughest actions came right at the end of the war. On 25 October, an Israeli armoured brigade led by Colonel Arieh Keren rolled into the Egyptian-held town of Suez. It was intended as an easy mopping-up operation. Behind them, under the command of Lieutenant-Colonel Yossi, was a unit of around 100 paras in eight captured half-tracks, a jeep, and a bus. As the tanks entered the town, heavy fire poured down on them from all sides. Standing in their open turrets, 20 of the 24 tank commanders were killed or wounded within minutes.

Leaping from their vehicles, the leading company of paras ran to clear the nearest building. As fire intensified, the unit was split up. While leading two platoons to the safety of a house, the company commander, 'Buki', was killed along with several of his men. The rest of the company followed Yossi's half-track to the shelter of the police station. Before it could reach safety, the half-track was hit by an anti-armour weapon, killing four and wounding four others, including Yossi. The battalion second-in-command, who was bringing up the rear, managed to turn his half-track round and escape from the town after a fierce fight with dozens of Egyptians. In another vehicle at the rear of the column, the HQ platoon commander dropped off his men to evacuate wounded tank crews. When he returned to the town there was no sign of his men – they were all dead.

The situation inside the police

Below: With the lead man carrying a rocket-propelled grenade, a group of Israeli paras move carefully over waste ground on the outskirts of Suez.

station was chaotic, as a number of Egyptian policemen attempted to resist the paras. The intelligence officer, Tzachi, took some men outside to cover stray paras still arriving, and managed to repel the initial Egyptian counter-attack. In the other building, occupied by the remnants of Buki's two platoons, the situation was even worse. A total of 30 men were holed up there in three groups, each group unaware of the other's presence and that the remainder of the battalion was less than 30m away. The Egyptians surrounded the house, laying mines to prevent Israeli reinforcements arriving, and began several unsuccessful assaults.

At the police station, with all other officers dead or severely wounded, First Lieutenant David Amit was promoted from platoon commander to senior officer. By the end of the day ammunition was running out fast, there was only sufficient water for the wounded, and in a nearby five-storey building the Egyptians had found an ideal position to fire down onto the two-storey police station. The paras were cut off, outnumbered, and divided into no less than four separate groups. Artillery or air support was impossible since HQ was unable to locate their exact positions, and though they sent in a relief force that night, the force was unable to find the paras and had to withdraw. Finally establishing brief radio contact, the brigade commander ordered Amit to break out under cover of darkness. Amit flatly refused since it would mean leaving the wounded behind.

At dawn, a desperate raid by the paras recovered some water and ammunition from the half-tracks, and morale was further boosted when a group of four paras was located in the other building. Using radios, Amit and the commander of the four, First Lieutenant Gil, began planning to bring the group into the police station under cover of darkness. Having arranged identification signals and covering fire if necessary, Gil and his men began to move warily out of their apartment. Suddenly they heard the sound of men in an adjoining apartment. Inexplicably, perhaps miraculously, nobody fired. The sounds came from another group of 18 paras. Their mutual surprise and joy was increased when,

attracted by the sound of Hebrew being spoken, the final group of eight came out of hiding. Instead of four, 30 paras now made their way safely across to the police station, to be received in an almost festive atmosphere.

With almost 80 men at his disposal, Amit decided to risk a breakout. Having had no food or sleep for two days, the other paras were unwilling to give up the 'safety' of the police station, and so Amit postponed the attempt until 0200 hours the next day. Now the positions of all the units were known, Israeli artillery was able to give covering fire on all sides, leaving just an 'empty box' for the paras to move through. To avoid slowing the force down, the wounded insisted on walking rather than being carried on stretchers. Keeping as quiet as possible, the paras crept through the Egyptian lines. Passing right under the enemy's nose, the Israelis could hear Egyptian soldiers shouting to each other, but amazingly no shots were fired. The Egyptians were either too concerned with the shelling, mistook the force for one of their own, or simply failed to notice the Israelis. Two hours later they reached the water at the edge of town. Turning west along the channel they headed for a distant bridge which would take them to safety. Almost immediately they came upon an unmarked bridge, clear of mines and booby traps. On the other side an Israeli armoured unit was waiting for the 80 tired and hungry survivors.

Below: Israeli self-propelled artillery is ferried across the Suez Canal to prepare for the final thrust against the Egyptian Army.

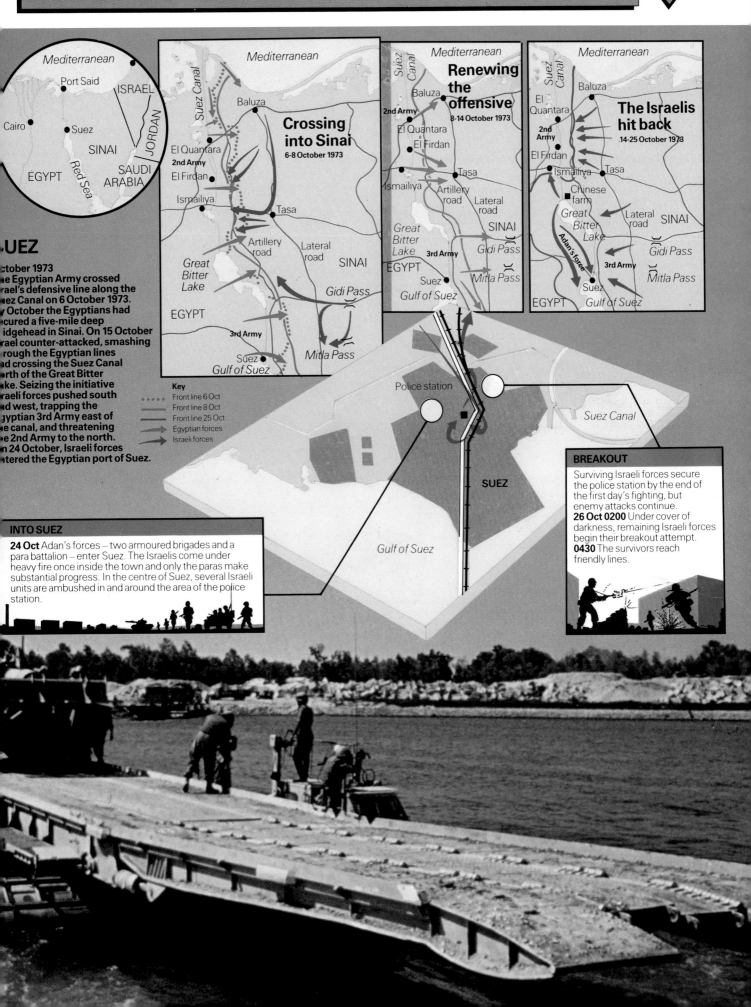

Crossing into Sinai
6-8 October 1973

Key
- Front line 6 Oct
- Front line 8 Oct
- Front line 25 Oct
- Egyptian forces
- Israeli forces

Renewing the offensive
8-14 October 1973

The Israelis hit back
14-25 October 1973

-UEZ

October 1973
the Egyptian Army crossed
rael's defensive line along the
uez Canal on 6 October 1973.
October the Egyptians had
cured a five-mile deep
idgehead in Sinai. On 15 October
rael counter-attacked, smashing
rough the Egyptian lines
d crossing the Suez Canal
rth of the Great Bitter
ke. Seizing the initiative
raeli forces pushed south
d west, trapping the
yptian 3rd Army east of
canal, and threatening
e 2nd Army to the north.
n 24 October, Israeli forces
tered the Egyptian port of Suez.

INTO SUEZ

24 Oct Adan's forces – two armoured brigades and a
para battalion – enter Suez. The Israelis come under
heavy fire once inside the town and only the paras make
substantial progress. In the centre of Suez, several Israeli
units are ambushed in and around the area of the police
station.

BREAKOUT

Surviving Israeli forces secure
the police station by the end of
the first day's fighting, but
enemy attacks continue.
26 Oct 0200 Under cover of
darkness, remaining Israeli forces
begin their breakout attempt.
0430 The survivors reach
friendly lines.

Entebbe

Shortly before dawn on 3 July 1976, specialist units of the Israeli paras loaded their equipment. At a nearby airfield they drove their vehicles into the bellies of four Hercules transports. Elsewhere on the field, final checks were made in a Boeing 707 fitted out as a mobile hospital. By early afternoon the transports were airborne, heading for Ophira at the southern tip of the Sinai; the Boeing headed for Nairobi airport. Operation Thunderball, the plan to rescue 105 Jewish hostages held by terrorists at Entebbe (Uganda's international airport), was under way.

The crisis began at 1230 hours on 27 June, when four terrorists from the Baader–Meinhof gang and PFLP (Popular Front for the Liberation of Palestine) hijacked Air France Flight 139 from Tel Aviv. On board were 12 crew and 246 passengers. Refuelling in Libya, the plane landed at Entebbe early on the 28th, where it was welcomed by the Ugandan dictator Idi Amin. The next day the terrorists issued their demands: the release of 53 known terrorists held in Israel, France, West Germany, Kenya, and Switzerland. With the release of all but the Jewish hostages, senior Israeli political and military leaders decided to risk a daring rescue plan. After a day of intensive preparations, the assault teams left Ophira on 3 July. Behind them flew a second Boeing, with senior officers and a communications team. This would act as a link between the assault force, the medical plane, and the planners in Israel.

Flying low to avoid radar the planes crossed into Ethiopia, only for bad weather to force them north near the Sudanese border. Later, on the approach to Lake Victoria, the aircraft hit storm clouds towering in a solid mass from ground level to 40,000 feet. As they ploughed their way through them, the crews could only console themselves with the fact that such a storm would prevent radar detection.

As the first aircraft approached Entebbe's main runway, the others circled in the storm, keeping to a precise timetable. In the cargo compartment, Lieutenant-Colonel Jonathan 'Yoni'

Right and below: The rescue of 105 Jewish hostages at Entebbe airport by Israeli paras on 3/4 July 1976.

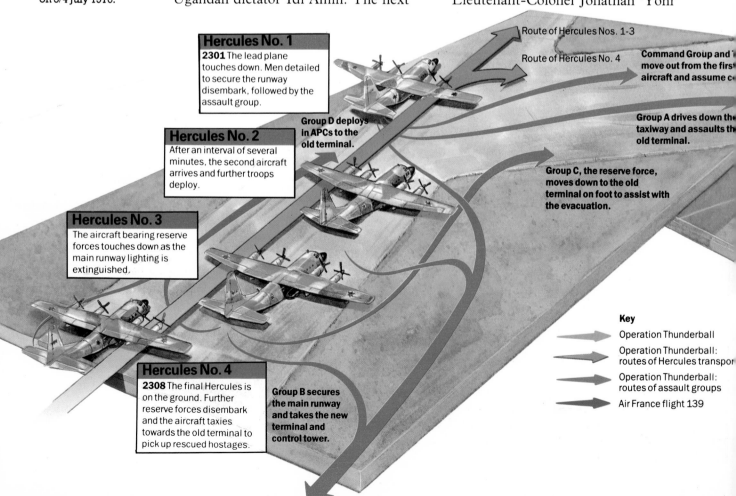

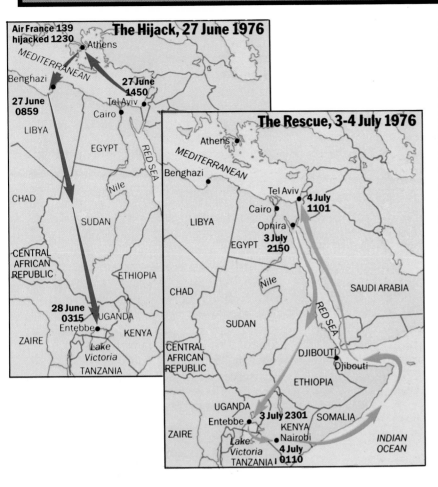

The Hijack, 27 June 1976

Air France 139 hijacked 1230
Athens
MEDITERRANEAN
Benghazi
27 June 0859
27 June 1450
Tel Aviv
Cairo
LIBYA
EGYPT
RED SEA
Nile
CHAD
SUDAN
CENTRAL AFRICAN REPUBLIC
ETHIOPIA
28 June 0315
UGANDA
Entebbe
KENYA
ZAIRE
Lake Victoria
TANZANIA

The Rescue, 3-4 July 1976

Athens
MEDITERRANEAN
Benghazi
Tel Aviv 4 July 1101
Cairo
Ophira
3 July 2150
LIBYA
EGYPT
Nile
CHAD
SAUDI ARABIA
SUDAN
RED SEA
CENTRAL AFRICAN REPUBLIC
DJIBOUTI
Djibouti
ETHIOPIA
UGANDA
3 July 2301
Entebbe
SOMALIA
KENYA
Nairobi
ZAIRE
Lake Victoria
4 July 0110
TANZANIA
INDIAN OCEAN

Netanyahu's men were piling into a black Mercedes disguised to resemble Idi Amin's personal car, and two Land Rovers. With the runway lights on, the aircraft touched down at 2301 hours, just 30 seconds behind schedule. Before the plane stopped, the vehicles were out on the ground, making their way to the old terminal building where the hostages were being held. Two Ugandan sentries ordered the vehicles to stop. There was no choice, and no time to argue. Shooting at the sentries, the paras leapt from their vehicles and raced the 40m to the building. Led by Netanyahu's second-in-command Muki, they found the first entrance blocked off. Tearing to the second door, Muki was fired at by a Ugandan. Muki shot him, only for a terrorist to step outside the main door and retreat rapidly inside. With two others Muki reached the door. The terrorist who had ventured out was now standing to the left of the door. Before he could react, the paras shot him. Across the room another terrorist rose and fired, this time at the sleeping hostages sprawled around him. With just two shots Muki took care of him. Over to the

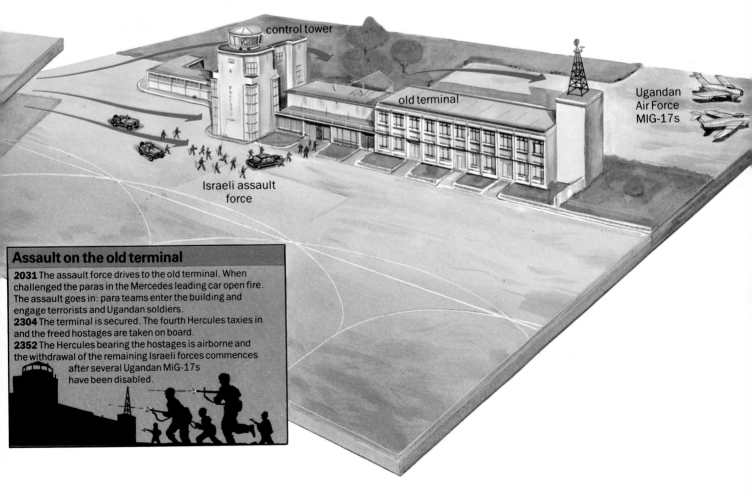

control tower

old terminal

Ugandan Air Force MIG-17s

Israeli assault force

Assault on the old terminal

2031 The assault force drives to the old terminal. When challenged the paras in the Mercedes leading car open fire. The assault goes in: para teams enter the building and engage terrorists and Ugandan soldiers.
2304 The terminal is secured. The fourth Hercules taxies in and the freed hostages are taken on board.
2352 The Hercules bearing the hostages is airborne and the withdrawal of the remaining Israeli forces commences after several Ugandan MiG-17s have been disabled.

right a terrorist let loose a burst, missing the paras and shattering a glass window. The para on Muki's right shot him, while the one on the left shot the fourth terrorist. In the background a loud-hailer was booming: 'This is the IDF. Stay down.' A young man launched himself at the trio in the doorway and was cut down. Later they realised he was just a bewildered hostage.

The second assault team had meanwhile raced through another doorway into a hall where the off-duty terrorists relaxed. Two men in civilian clothes walked calmly towards them. Assuming that they were hostages, the soldiers held their fire. Suddenly one of the men threw a concealed grenade. The paras dropped to the gound. A machine-gun burst eliminated the terrorists and the grenade exploded harmlessly.

Netanyahu's third team moved to silence any opposition from Ugandan soldiers on the floor above. On their way

Above left: Field-Marshal Idi Amin Dada, dictator of Uganda at the time of the rescue.

up the stairs they met two troopers, one of whom opened fire. The paras killed them.

While his men calmed the hostages and tended the wounded, Muki was called out to the tarmac. Netanyahu had remained outside the building, supervising the assault, only to be shot in the back from the top of the control tower. The paras silenced the fire, but for 'Yoni' the wound was to prove fatal.

The old terminal had been taken in under three minutes, and now the three other Hercules could land. With clockwork precision the paras secured all access roads and raced to the new terminal and control tower. A team of air force technicians were already hard at work preparing to transfer Idi Amin's aviation fuel into the Hercules' thirsty tanks – a long process which would take well over an hour.

Although they were ahead of schedule, the situation was still precarious. The Ugandans would soon be bringing up reinforcements, whilst those already there were firing tracer at random – extremely dangerous since, with the engines still running, the Hercules' fuel tanks were very vulnerable. Having secured refuelling rights at Nairobi, there was no point in hanging around. The fourth Hercules was brought up to the old terminal and, guarded by a line of paras on each side, the hostages straggled out. Behind them lay the bodies of thirteen terrorists.

Above: Lieutenant-Colonel Jonathan 'Yoni' Netanyahu, the assault force's commander, was the only member of the raiding party to be killed.

At 2352 hours, the hostages were airborne and on their way to freedom. Inside the Hercules, doctors tended to the seven wounded. Two others had died during the rescue, and a third, moved to a Ugandan hospital before the raid, was later murdered. At the other end of the airfield, an infantry team fired machine-gun bursts into seven Ugandan MiGs; there was no point in inviting pursuit. The paras left at 0012 hours, just over an hour after landing, their job well done.

Refuelling at Nairobi, and then landing at an air force base in central Israel for food and medical treatment, the hostages finally arrived at Tel Aviv mid-morning on the 4th. Watched by a jubilant crowd of thousands, the Hercules released its cargo into the outstretched arms of friends and relatives. The ordeal was over, but more than that, the Israelis had shown their determined response to terrorism in the most effective and dramatic way possible.

Above left: A black Mercedes, disguised as Amin's personal limousine, was used to confuse the Ugandan airport guards.

Above: A jubilant crowd welcomes the freed hostages and their rescuers on their arrival at Lod airport, Tel Aviv, on 4 July.

Below: One of the Israeli Air Force's four C-130 Hercules transports used in the rescue mission taxies to a halt at Lod airport.

Sidon

On 9 June 1982, a force of Israeli paras was faced with the dangerous task of clearing the town of Sidon of 1500 PLO (Palestine Liberation Organisation) guerrillas entrenched there. The guerrillas, from Al Fatah's El Kastel Brigade, had established a closely-knit defence based around a network of high-rise buildings and concealed bunkers. They were further reinforced by Palestinians in the refugee camp of Ein El Hilwe, and by units retreating from the south. Although the paras had support from tanks, artillery and aircraft, much of the fighting had to be hand-to-hand through streets and buildings well known to the enemy, and offering excellent defensive positions.

Operation Peace for Galilee, the Israeli invasion of southern Lebanon, had begun on 6 June 1982 with a combined sea and land assault. Although intended as a swift, deep advance skirting round pockets of resistance (which would be dealt with later), the PLO's secure entrenchment in Sidon, and the town's strategic position on the coast, made it impossible for Sidon to be bypassed. The paras were therefore put ashore on 7 June, some 3km north of Sidon, in the largest amphibious landing ever attempted by the IDF. By the end of the morning the IDF had surrounded the town, and the paras had begun taking the northern suburbs in a smooth, professional operation. At noon, units of the Golani Brigade began advancing on Ein El Hilwe in the southeast, while a combined force of Golani infantry and armour advanced from the east.

The paras were then ordered to open the main road running through Sidon north to Beirut, and having secured that to proceed to link up with the Golanis further south for an attack on Ein El Hilwe the next day. At noon on the 8th the paras therefore began their advance. To save time they ignored any building not known to be a terrorist emplacement. Under the command of Colonel 'Y', they advanced down the main street in two lines, close to the buildings on both sides. Tanks and the more lightly armoured 155mm SP (self-propelled) guns

followed, the latter a necessity due to the limited elevation of the tanks' guns. Resistance was slight at first with just sporadic bursts from snipers, countered by the SP guns. The deeper the paras advanced into Sidon, the heavier the sniper fire became. The tank and artillery commanders were prime targets for the PLO defenders, making the advance achingly slow and dangerous. Two Syrian MiGs made a bomb-run over the column, causing no casualties, but adding to the tension. By evening it was clear that neither the paras nor the force to the south could finish their tasks that day, and so they both withdrew for the night.

On the morning of the 9th it was decided to give maximum support to the paras' operation. Clearing the main road was now a priority in order to maintain the flow of supplies north to the armoured units pushing towards Beirut. The attack on Ein El Hilwe was therefore postponed, and all the artillery transferred to the paras. With this support, they began moving in. Clearing the main street was strange, dangerous, and exhausting work. The paras would climb up 20 flights of stairs in a residential block, expecting to be fired upon at any moment, to find death

Below: Israeli armoured personnel carriers and tanks make an amphibious landing on a Lebanese beach during Operation Peace for Galilee, 1982.

lurking round every corner. Often the sights they saw had an almost unreal quality: they found a 105mm anti-tank gun standing in the middle of one plush living room and it was obvious that it had been frequently fired from that position.

Colonel 'Y' quickly decided that this was not the sort of battle for flashy gestures and vain self-sacrifice. Instead he concentrated upon a slow, methodical advance, keeping casualties to a minimum. Sniper fire would be suppressed by artillery barrage, the paras would enter, mop up, exit, rest and regroup – then do it all over again. In this painstaking way they finally winkled out the defenders and cleared the street.

The job was not yet complete, however. Still remaining were the Ein El Hilwe refugee camp (the centre of PLO activity), and the ancient Casbah, whose narrow, twisting alleyways provided an ideal site for a last stand by the PLO. The IDF had foreseen the problem of the Casbah in their pre-invasion planning, and had been warned of the folly of attempting street fighting there. After calling on the PLO to surrender and firing a series of warning shots, the Israelis launched a devastating artillery barrage on the Casbah, rather than risk

the lives of their own men. The defenders were forced to surrender, picking their way out of the rubble and destruction. The paras then headed off to join up with the Golanis and take the refugee camp.

Once again the paras had shown their mettle, successfully taking a strategically important and heavily defended position with the courage and professionalism that is their hallmark.

Right: A participant in the Israeli invasion of southern Lebanon, this para corporal wears Israeli-produced webbing equipment over an olive-green uniform. Behind the new-pattern nylon helmet are fins of rifle grenades carried on the back; the waist pouches contain spare magazines for the powerful and accurate 5.56mm Galil assault rifle.

ISRAELI 7th BRIGADE

The 7th Armoured Brigade

THE reputation of the 7th Armoured Brigade had been established by its successes in the Sinai in 1956. In 1967 the brigade, still with some of the officers and men from the war of 11 years before, was required to repeat its remarkable feats on the same battlefield. As part of General Tal's division in the northern sector, the 7th Brigade was to be the 'mailed fist' which would break the strong Egyptian defensive line stretching back 12km from Rafah to El Arish. This was to be done as quickly as possible, regardless of cost, and then exploited in a rapid dash to the Suez Canal.

History of the 7th Brigade

With the end of the Palestine Mandate in 1948, the new state of Israel had just nine operational brigades with which to oppose the combined Arab armies. One week before independence, however, Colonel Shlomo Shamir began gathering together another brigade which was to become not only one of Israel's most famous forces, but the beginning of the 'mailed fist' – the heavy emphasis upon armoured units.

This new unit, the 7th Armoured Brigade, was at first ill-equipped and poorly organised. Its core was an armoured battalion consisting of half-tracks and light tanks captured from the enemy. The second infantry battalion consisted almost entirely of men scraped together from other units, whilst the third battalion was led by staff from the training establishment, and manned by immigrants as they arrived. In their first action, they were asked to open the main road to Jerusalem. Not surprisingly, when confronted by troops from the crack Jordanian Arab Legion, the brigade suffered heavy casualties. Later in the war, though, with the raw recruits now blooded veterans, and under the brilliant leadership of the Canadian Ben Dunkelman, the 7th Brigade gave more than a fair account of itself.

From these humble beginnings, the growth of Israeli armoured units has been remarkable. In the early 1950s they purchased AMX13 light tanks from France, and in the 1956 campaign the 7th Brigade began to establish its formidable reputation. On 31 October 1956, in the face of fierce Arab opposition, it took the town of Abu Aweigila, and with the 202nd Parachute Brigade brilliantly exploited this opening to reach the banks of the Suez Canal. Armoured formations had made their mark. As Centurion tanks and then M48s and M60s were introduced, so the devastating power of the 'mailed fist' became one of the most feared tools of the IDF. Finally, in 1982, the Israelis introduced onto the battlefield their own tank – the formidable Merkava – maintaining a tradition of Israeli armoured supremacy.

Above: Major-General Rafael Eitan (left) briefs men of the 7th Armoured Brigade under his command as the fighting continues during the Yom Kippur War, 1973.

Left: A tank commander of the 7th Brigade scans through binoculars for signs of the enemy during the Yom Kippur War.

With the paras outflanking Egyptian positions from the south, the 7th Brigade attacked at 0800 hours on 5 June from the northeast, near the town of Khan Yunis. Against the Israelis were ranged four infantry brigades dug-in beyond heavily fortified anti-tank positions, surrounded by minefields with artillery and over 100 tanks in support. With their turrets open to improve visibility, the Israeli tanks charged through the Palestinian and Egyptian defences. The fighting was tough, with over 35 Israeli tank commanders killed, but the position had to be taken. One battalion destroyed 20 tanks, then the artillery they had been protecting, then another 20 tanks. General Tal could hardly hear his commanders on the radio above the thump of 105mm tank guns and the chatter of machine guns.

As soon as the defences had been breached at Khan Yunis, the 7th Brigade moved on to Sheikh Zuweid, the next Egyptian defensive position. Once again the fighting was tough and unremitting, as the Israelis battled against an infantry brigade and a battalion of ancient T34 tanks emplaced in defensive positions. With one battalion of Centurions using their high accuracy and good protection in a frontal assault to draw enemy fire, the Pattons moved north and south in outflanking movements to take the position. In Rafah the resistance was even tougher, with one Egyptian battalion suffering 1000 casualties before being overrun. The fighting has been so hard that, at one stage, only one company could carry on without rest or reorganisation. At this critical time a further Egyptian brigade revealed itself, attempting to destroy a helicopter which had landed to pick up casualties. Leading his last tank company, the 7th Brigade's commander attacked and destroyed the Egyptians.

Before they reached El Arish, the Israelis had to pierce one final Egyptian strongpoint – the heavily fortified El Jiradi. In the dark the Egyptian tanks gave their positions away with their opening rounds, making themselves vulnerable to the greater firepower and armour of the Centurions. Much more dangerous were the anti-tank guns: firing from well-concealed bunkers, their salvoes were almost impossible to spot. It was only when the tanks were on top of them that they could be taken out – usually by crushing them.

Even when El Jiradi was taken it proved to be a problem. As the 7th Brigade pushed on, so Egyptians infiltrated back, re-taking their positions, and causing the Israeli rearguard severe problems. After a see-saw battle in which control of El Jiradi changed hands on several occasions, the Israelis finally cleared the position of Egyptians.

Now the 7th Brigade could concentrate on the push for El Arish. Although Egyptian artillery caused some casualties, the position was relatively lightly defended and fell quite quickly. The remnants of the brigade then turned south to take the airfield. With air support they achieved this by 0730 hours on the 6th. Tal's division was then ordered south to help relieve Brigadier Yoffe's forces on the central front. Yoffe's advance was being held up by a Soviet-style defensive position at Abu Aweigila. Facing southwards, the position was more vulnerable to attack from Tal's forces in the north. Tal's tactics now changed. Previously his tanks had charged at rigid enemy positions with reckless abandon, punching a hole through the defences at almost any cost. Now the Centurions undertook long-range 'sniping', picking off enemy positions with their highly accurate

105mm guns, while the more mobile Pattons were sent eastwards in an outflanking movement. Under such pressure from several directions, the Egyptians were forced to withdraw.

The 7th Brigade had therefore fought successfully in two very different types of exchange against brave and determined defences. By the third and fourth days of the war, however, signs of collapse were appearing in the Egyptian armed forces. A two-hour tank battle with elements of the Egyptian 4th Armoured Division late on 7 June was indecisive, but the next day Tal's division cleared the Ismailia Pass and, encountering comparatively light opposition, reached the Gulf of Suez at 0030 hours on 9 June. As in 1956, armour had been decisive in a stunning Israeli success, and as in 1956 the 7th Brigade had been at the forefront of the operation.

Above: A column of Israeli M48s and Centurions cross a ridge in the Sinai Desert during the Six-Day War, 1967.

Above: Israeli troops and armour take a break to rest and refuel during their advance into Syria in 1973.

Golan Heights

The 7th Brigade had made its name in the Sinai, with dramatic breakthroughs across the desert. In the 1973 War its role was very different. Suddenly deployed on Israel's northern border in the mountainous Golan, its task was to defend Israeli positions against the massive Syrian attack. This time there was to be no race across the Sinai, but the brigade's role was to be just as crucial.

On 5 October 1973, the eve of the Jewish festival of Yom Kippur, the 7th Brigade was moved from its permanent base in the south to reinforce Major-General Rafael Eitan's forces along the Syrian border in the Golan. Time was so short that only the crews could arrive in time; they had to be equipped with tanks from Eitan's own division to be ready for combat the next day.

Although the Israeli border in the northern Golan had no natural obstacles to hinder a Syrian attack, the Israelis had constructed 17 strongpoints, surrounded by minefields and ditches. The 7th Brigade was deployed on the north of this line and the Golani's Barak Brigade on the south. It was hoped that any Syrian attack would be so blunted by the accurate tank fire from these defensive emplacements that it would be slowed down, allowing Israeli reserves to mobilise. Against them the Syrians deployed five divisions with over 1700 tanks (including the newly acquired T62s) and an abundance of artillery and anti-aircraft batteries. Outnumbered fifteen to one, the Israelis had only their own skill and determination to rely on.

The Syrian plan was to begin with a firestorm from over 1000 guns onto the Israeli positions. Then the 5th, 7th and 9th Infantry Divisions, backed by almost 1000 tanks, were to smash through the Israeli defences, opening the way for the 1st and 3rd Armoured Divisions to drive into the rear of the line.

The offensive began at 1400 hours on the 6th, concentrating on the central and southern sectors of the front rather than the northern sector under Eitan's command. On the night of 6/7 October, a company of eight tanks from the 7th Brigade, under the command of Captain Meir Zamir, was ordered to assist in the defence of the town of Kuneitra further south. In a night battle, at medium and close range, Zamir engaged the Syrian 43rd Armoured Brigade. With his tanks cleverly positioned, the company commander was able to halt and destroy the entire brigade. In a simple, brilliant manoeuvre, the company had prevented the collapse of the central sector.

Right: A participant in the Six-Day War, this Israeli tank officer wears an olive-green uniform and the Israeli version of the US tank crewman's protective helmet. Hanging from his neck is a junction box for the armoured vehicle communication system. Rank – in this case First Lieutenant – is shown by the two green bars on the khaki slide attached to his shoulder strap. As befits his officer status, a revolver is carried on the web belt.

With the Israelis thus holding the Syrians in the southern and central sectors, attention shifted to Eitan's northern sector. On 8 October, with 500 tanks and 700 APCs (armoured personnel carriers), the Syrians attacked between 'Booster' Hill and Tel Hermonit. Against them, in what became known as the 'Valley of Tears', was the 7th Brigade. With no reinforcements available, every officer and man of the unit knew that they were on their own. All that could help them now were their own strength and fighting qualities.

Under heavy artillery cover, the Syrian vehicles approached. Israeli artillery replied at just 4km distance, but were unable to stop the advance. Piercing the minefields, the Syrians converged on the anti-tank ditch with their Soviet-made MTU bridgelayers. The Israelis had turned all crossing points into 'killing grounds', taking a heavy toll of the MTUs and tanks. But still the Syrians came on. Displaying great courage, infantrymen with entrenching tools succeeded where MTUs failed. Ignoring heavy casualties and the obstacles in their path, they pushed on relentlessly until they had got to within a few metres of the Israeli defences.

The Israeli 7th Brigade was now in deep trouble. Fast running out of ammunition, the Syrian shelling had destroyed lines of communication with their supply dumps. Fresh ammunition could not be brought to the front line, so the tanks had to go and get it themselves. This left gaps in the front line which the Syrians could exploit to devastating effect. Often a tank would return to find its position overrun, and the Syrians threatening to break through. In these dire straits, neighbouring Israeli tanks would turn through as much as 180 degrees to fire upon the exposed rear armour of enemy vehicles. At such close range the Israeli Centurions wrought untold damage on the first wave. Turning back again, at only a few metres' distance, they then destroyed the second wave.

The battle continued well into the night, becoming if anything more intense in the dark. With their sophisticated nightsights the Syrians had a major advantage, while Israeli communications had almost totally broken down. Only by

Below: A Centurion of the 7th Brigade dug in facing the Syrian border.

When the massed armour and artillery of the Syrian army crossed the Purple Line on 6 October 1973, the crack 'tankers' of the 7th Armoured Brigade held their ground against overwhelming odds for three days. After regrouping, the 7th Brigade struck back, spearheading a counter-attack that brought the Israelis within 30km of the Syrian capital, Damascus.

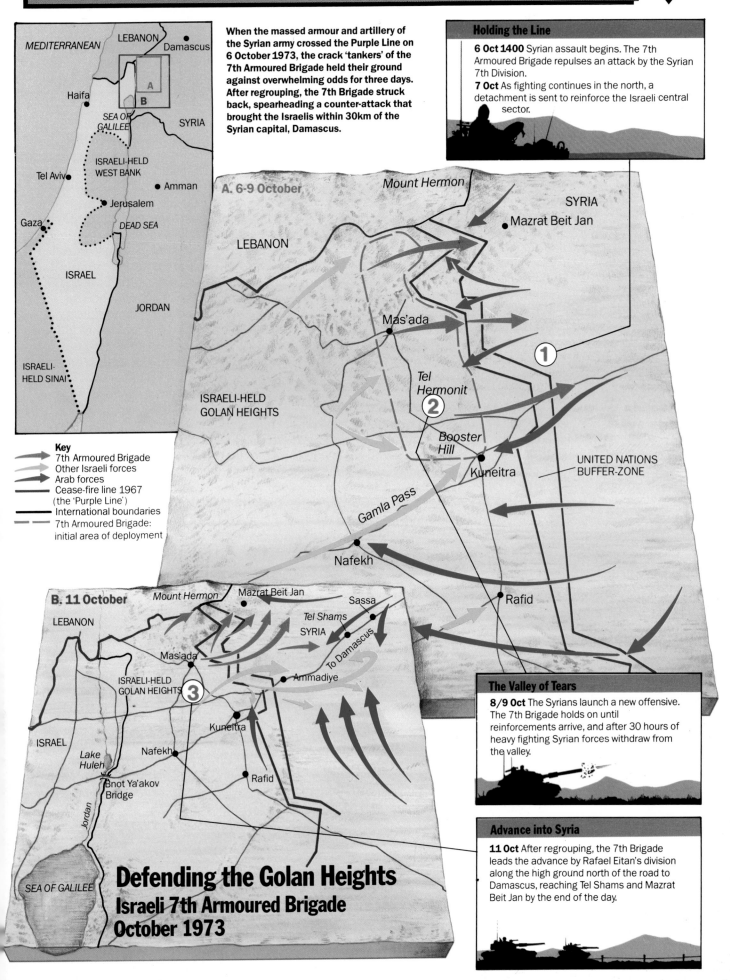

Holding the Line

6 Oct 1400 Syrian assault begins. The 7th Armoured Brigade repulses an attack by the Syrian 7th Division.

7 Oct As fighting continues in the north, a detachment is sent to reinforce the Israeli central sector.

Key
7th Armoured Brigade
Other Israeli forces
Arab forces
Cease-fire line 1967 (the 'Purple Line')
International boundaries
7th Armoured Brigade: initial area of deployment

A. 6–9 October

Mount Hermon
SYRIA
Mazrat Beit Jan
LEBANON
Mas'ada
①
Tel Hermonit
②
ISRAELI-HELD GOLAN HEIGHTS
Booster Hill
Kuneitra
UNITED NATIONS BUFFER-ZONE
Gamla Pass
Nafekh
Rafid

B. 11 October

Mount Hermon
Mazrat Beit Jan
Sassa
LEBANON
Tel Shams
SYRIA
To Damascus
Mas'ada
ISRAELI-HELD GOLAN HEIGHTS
③
Ammadiye
Kuneitra
ISRAEL
Nafekh
Lake Huleh
Rafid
Bnot Ya'akov Bridge
Jordan
SEA OF GALILEE

Defending the Golan Heights
Israeli 7th Armoured Brigade October 1973

The Valley of Tears

8/9 Oct The Syrians launch a new offensive. The 7th Brigade holds on until reinforcements arrive, and after 30 hours of heavy fighting Syrian forces withdraw from the valley.

Advance into Syria

11 Oct After regrouping, the 7th Brigade leads the advance by Rafael Eitan's division along the high ground north of the road to Damascus, reaching Tel Shams and Mazrat Beit Jan by the end of the day.

Inset (overview map)
MEDITERRANEAN
LEBANON
Damascus
Haifa
A
B
SEA OF GALILEE
SYRIA
Tel Aviv
ISRAELI-HELD WEST BANK
Amman
Jerusalem
Gaza
DEAD SEA
ISRAEL
JORDAN
ISRAELI-HELD SINAI

using personal nicknames could the Israelis confuse the Syrians listening in on their radios.

By now it was clear that the Battle of the Valley of Tears was going to be decisive; if the Syrians broke through, there was nothing to stop them reaching the River Jordan. The 7th Brigade responded magnificently. 'We are not moving,' said one officer. 'Not one step, not one centimetre; the fate of the state is in our hands.' With a few reinforcements trickling through, a small force was organised in the Israeli rear early on the 9th. Consisting of repaired tanks, manned mostly by wounded crews, Eitan threw them into the battle at the critical moment. With most of his front-line tanks down to three or four shells each, this new force of 20 tanks attacked suddenly from the Syrian flank. Fighting with great skill and determination, they set about destroying the Syrians. At noon on the 9th, a post of Golani infantry reported seeing Syrian vehicles turning back. It was the beginning of the retreat. With their strength almost exhausted and down to their last few rounds, the men of the 7th Brigade had defeated the last Syrian attack. They had won. As the smoke of battle cleared, they saw the full extent of their victory. Below them, in a mass of twisted, burnt-out wrecks, lay the cream of the enemy's troops. The men of the 7th Armoured Brigade had destroyed over 500 tanks, APCs and other fighting vehicles. Of their own force, only 40 out of 90 tanks remained undamaged. After over 30 hours of combat, the Israelis were too tired even to climb out of their tanks and celebrate.

Just 48 hours later, though, the 7th was back in action, its new task to organise a counter-attack aimed at breaking through to the east of the Golan. The tired, filthy and bearded veterans were now reinforced with fresh crews. With spirits soaring, they easily broke through the Syrian defences, suffering few losses. By the end of the war they had established control of the Golan, and pushed to within 30km of the Syrian capital of Damascus.

For Israel the war had ended as yet another success, but at one stage only the courage and professional excellence of the 7th Armoured Brigade had saved them from catastrophic defeat.

Southern Lebanon

In early 1982, the 7th Armoured Brigade formed part of Brigadier-General Kahalani's much respected 36th Division, but for Operation Peace for Galilee, the Israeli invasion of southern Lebanon, the brigade was transferred to Immanuel Sakel's 252nd Division. This division, along with the 90th Division, made up Task Force East, and was charged with securing the slopes of the Hermon range in the Golan, and the Syrian-controlled Beqaa valley. This task was crucial: if they failed, the flank of the entire IDF would be exposed to Syrian attack. Moreover, it had to be done quickly: any delay would allow the Syrians to move up more units to support their troops already in Lebanon. Yet against them were experienced PLO guerrillas with an intimate knowledge of the mountainous terrain, and regular Syrian units equipped with some of the most sophisticated weaponry available.

The plan for the 252nd Division was to attack out of the Golan along two axes of advance. The first axis led along the foothills of Mount Hermon and through the Wadi Cheba, while the second ran

Right: Part of the 252nd Division's armoured column during the advance into southern Lebanon in 1982.

Below: A low profile and an uncluttered turret are important design features of Israel's Merkava main battle tank, which first saw combat service during the 1982 invasion of southern Lebanon, where it performed well against the tanks of the Syrian Army. Its most important design characteristic, however, is crew protection.

lower down through the valley, striking out for the towns of Hasbaiya and Koukaba, before reaching the main road and sweeping right to Rachaiya. In so doing, the Israelis hoped to outflank the Syrians already in Lebanon, and to be in a position to cut off any retreat.

As the tanks rolled, the difficulty of the task became all too clear. The narrow gorges forced the tanks to move slowly,

making them easy targets for defenders hidden in the heights above. Even when they moved out of the heights, poor roads made the going slow, while enemy artillery had already ranged in on the roads, making them potential death-traps. Under heavy PLO fire, supplemented by Syrian artillery and anti-tank weapons, the Israelis battled on. At one stage their engineers were forced to cut a 20km strip through the Wadi Cheba to allow the advance to continue, while, encouraged by the Israelis' difficulties, small PLO tank-killer teams pressed home attacks with light mortars and grenades.

In these difficult conditions, the skill and courage of the 7th Armoured Brigade shone through. By 7 June they had taken Hasbaiya and Koukaba, and had begun their move towards Rachaiya. With the Israelis stunningly successful across the whole battle front, and now threatening to outflank the Syrians in the east, the Syrian position was disintegrating rapidly. The going was never easy, though, with constant harassment from commando units and helicopter gunships. Despite this, Immanuel Sakel's force battled on and by the cease-fire on 11 June had secured the Israeli right flank, limiting the Syrian threat from the east.

Once again the 7th Armoured Brigade had displayed their skill and determination in moving rapidly and under heavy enemy fire to secure crucial strategic objectives.

ISRAELI GOLANIS
The Golani Brigade

ON Friday 9 June 1967, four days into the Six-Day War, Colonel Yona Efrat finally received his orders to attack. The commander of the elite Golani Brigade had seen his fellow IDF units engaged in the fighting for several days, and had been pleading with the General Staff for his men to be allowed some action. Now was his chance: the brigade was to be put to the test, and to be given the chance to prove it was at least as good as any other elite unit in the IDF. Looking around him, Efrat was only too aware of the determination and enthusiasm of his men.

Above: The distinctive badge of the Golani Brigade.

Formed in February 1948, the Golani Brigade was charged with the defence of Israel's northeast border with Syria. Occupying this crucial position meant retaining a high degree of combat-readiness and professionalism. Selection for the brigade was tough, training even tougher. Only the most motivated recruits, almost all volunteers, survived the six-month basic training course, the last stages of which specialised in work with APCs (armoured personnel carriers), and which finished with a devastating hike to the summit of Mount Hebron. There the successful received the coveted the brown beret of the Golani Brigade.

Efrat's orders on 9 June were simple. His brigade had to destroy the front line of fortified Syrian emplacements on the Golan Heights, overlooking the road from Israel's Hula valley to the Syrian town of Kuneitra. Once the road was secured, armoured units of the IDF could push into Kuneitra and from there into the very heart of the Golan. The mission was crucial to the battle of the Heights, yet the task seemed almost impossible. The only means of attack was a direct assault up the almost sheer face of the Golan. Each Syrian fortress was a mass of well-placed trenches and bunkers, with clear fields of fire, able to give supporting fire to neighbouring forts. They were held by well-trained Syrian troops, supported by heavy artillery and tanks, and surrounded by anti-tank and anti-personnel minefields.

The Golani's primary objectives were to take the two largest forts: Tel Faher and Tel Azzaziat. Tel Faher was to be taken in an outflanking movement from the east by the Barak (Lightning) Battalion, using armoured half-tracks and a company of tanks. They would then move on to the covering fortress of Bourj-a-Bawil where they would give supporting fire for the Bokim HaRishonim Battalion's attack on the second fort, Tel Azzaziat. The Gideon Battalion would be kept in reserve until later, when it would capture the Syrian army camps at Baniyas and then join up with the main force for the attack on Kuneitra.

Of all the Syrian positions on the Golan, Tel Faher appeared virtually impregnable. Built on two knolls protected by three double-apron barbed-

wire concertinas and minefields, it was almost impervious to air attack, and could easily be reinforced by large numbers of tanks and men from the nearby Syrian 11th Brigade. Already in place was a company of the Syrian 187th Infantry Battalion, backed by two 57mm M43 anti-tank guns, two 82mm B10 anti-tank guns, heavy machine guns, and a battery of 82mm mortars. Within 1500m of their advance, the Golani Brigade came under intensive heavy artillery bombardment, and while the Barak Battalion deployed at 1300 hours for its attack on Tel Faher, Syrian tanks and anti-tank weapons opened fire. The brigade soon realised its mistake: instead of outflanking the fort and attacking from the 'soft' rear, the Barak Battalion was attacking from directly in front of the fortress. Syrian fire was intense, accurate and unremitting, destroying several half-tracks. To make matters worse, two of the Golani's precious tanks were stopped by mechanical failure, while the terrain forced the attackers into smaller units, thereby losing much of their cohesion. With the half-tracks of A Company bogged down, and the tanks beginning to be hit, Lieutenant-Colonel 'Moussa' Klein had a difficult decision to make. He ordered the remaining tanks into a frontal assault to relieve the pressure, but disastrous results ensued: all the tanks were hit and put out of commission. With mounting casualties and only part of the battalion still mobile, Klein ordered his remaining half-tracks to re-form and attack at speed – the very thing the Golani Brigade had been trained for.

In the attack casualties were heavy. The command half-track was hit, as were four out of seven half-tracks in A Company. In this perilous situation Major Alex Krinski brought new orders for the company commander, Captain Vardi. The half-tracks were abandoned, and Tel Faher was stormed by a frontal infantry assault. The Syrians reacted with everything they had, so that by the time Vardi and Krinski reached the fort, only 25 out of the 60 men who began the assault were still standing. Against them were at least 50 Syrians in well-placed trenches, protected by two concertinas of barbed wire. Taking 12 men, Krinski attacked from the north, while Vardi took the remaining 13 and attacked from the

Left: Men of the Golani Brigade move down from the Arnoun Heights on 7 June 1982 after successfully storming Beaufort Castle.

Left: Mounted on US-supplied half-tracks, Golani infantry wait for the order to advance into Syria.

south. Vardi's men were unable to cut the barbed wire. A Bangalore torpedo was pushed in, but failed to explode. In desperation Private David Shirazi threw himself on the wire, shouting for the rest of the force to climb over him. When the last man had done this, Shirazi crawled through and joined the fierce hand-to-hand fighting in the trenches. After two hours of bitter struggle, Vardi was left with just two unwounded men. A soldier was sent for reinforcements, only to be shot after just a few steps. Reinforcements eventually arrived, and the mopping-up of the southern sector was completed. Only then could the wounded be seen to.

In the northern sector, fighting was just as tough. As hand-to-hand fighting began, Major Krinski was shot. The battalion commander, Klein, followed up, only to find Krinski dying amongst wounded soldiers. Only one man remained unharmed. A Syrian soldier suddenly appeared before Klein. Klein shot him, only to be killed himself moments later by a sniper's bullet. As more and more paths were discovered off the main trench, so the brigade had to split up into ever smaller units, often led by sergeants and corporals. Finally, at 1800 hours, Tel Faher fell to the determined assault and the Israeli flag was raised over the fortress.

Now the focus shifted to the second objective: the heavily fortified Tel Azzaziat. The leading force of seven half-tracks and three Shermans closed in from the rear – the fort's only weak point. The 70-strong garrison had already survived heavy Israeli shelling, and now its commander ordered the mining of the rear approach road to stop the attack. With one Sherman already destroyed, an Israeli sapper bravely confronted the mines. Under heavy fire he cleared the road for the motorised attack. As the half-tracks approached, the Syrians regrouped, and a second series of mines

Below: Men of the Golani storm the heights.

Tel Azzaziat and Tel Faher
Golani Brigade, June 1967

On the morning of 9 June 1967, the forces of the Israeli Northern Command crossed the Jordan and began their assault against the Syrian strongholds on the Golan Heights. The infantrymen of the crack Golani Brigade were tasked with outflanking the fortress of Tel Azzaziat and securing the strategically important road to Mas'ada and Kuneitra.

Tel Faher

9 June As the Israeli forces in northern Israel launch their offensive against Syrian positions in the Golan Heights, the Golani Brigade advances on Tel Faher.
1800 After fierce hand-to-hand fighting against well-entrenched positions, the Golani Brigade secures Tel Faher.

Tel Azzaziat

Having outflanked the enemy, the Golani Brigade moves on Tel Azzaziat from the rear. By nightfall, the position is in Israeli hands – and the Golani infantry begin their drive towards Baniyas.

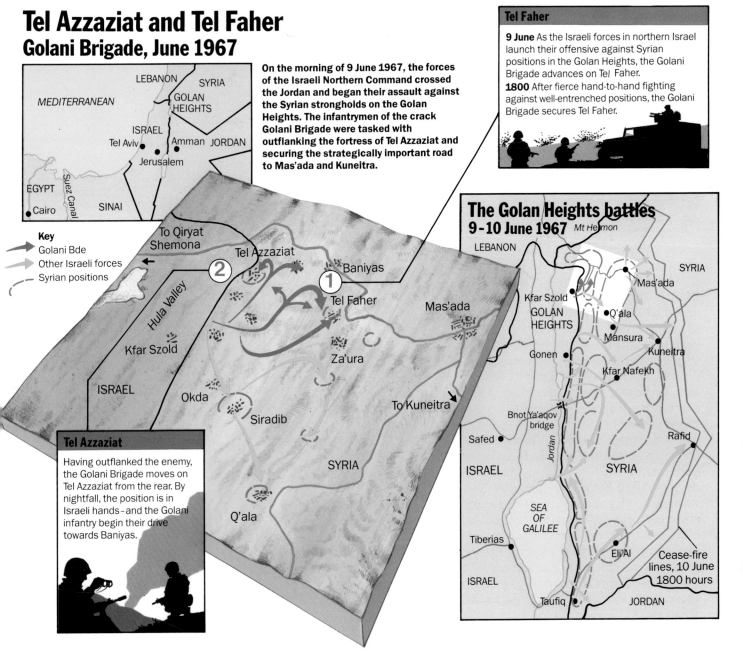

destroyed a half-track, completely blocking the entrance. The attackers dismounted and ran the final few metres to the trenches. In the hand-to-hand fighting that followed, 30 Syrians were killed and 26 captured. For the attackers everything went like clockwork. They had learned the plans of the fort by heart, and knew every trench and firing position. It was a classic battle, showing the Golani Brigade to possess all the fighting qualities of an elite force.

Despite the hard fighting on 9 June, the brigade was ready for action the next day, spearheading the attack on Kuneitra and taking Syrian positions at Baniyas. By mid-morning the Syrians were in full retreat. Taking advantage of the disarray, a detachment of the Golani Brigade was helilifted to Mount Hermon, where they took charge of abandoned Syrian defences. At 1830 hours the UN-arranged cease-fire began, and the victorious Golanis could celebrate. In a short but remarkable campaign they had taken no less than 13 enemy positions on the Golan. Above all, through courage and improvisation, drawing upon their high level of training and morale, and in the face of heavy casualties, they had taken the 'impregnable' fortress of Tel Faher. In the words of the brigade commander, 'Golani has passed through the sound barrier'.

Mount Hermon

Thanks to the Golani Brigade's actions in the Six-Day War, the IDF had managed to establish a small fortress on Mount Hermon some 600m below the Syrian-controlled summit. Although poorly defended, the summit occupied a crucial strategic position. The highest point in the Middle East, Mount Hermon dominates the northern Golan Heights at the junction of the Syrian, Israeli and Lebanese borders. From there, looking across the plain to Damascus, Israeli observers had noted the steady Syrian build-up preceding the 1973 War. Shortly after the beginning of the attack on 6 October 1973, assault teams from the crack Syrian 82nd Parachute Battalion and a specially trained ranger unit launched a helicopter-borne attack on the Israeli position. Despite stubbon IDF resistance, the fortress fell. The next day the Brigade was ordered to recapture the position.

That same morning, the Golanis began their counter-attack. Moving up the winding road to the fort, they were ambushed by Syrian commandos. With 24 men dead, the Golanis were forced to withdraw and postpone the recapture until 21 October. The new plan involved a two-pronged assault. Helicopter-borne paratroops were to land at the top of the mountain, storm the Syrian positions there, and work their way downwards. The Golani Brigade was to work its way upwards to the Israeli fort. Led by five Centurion tanks on the main road, the Golanis approached under cover of darkness to the scene of the Syrian ambush. Once again a battalion of Syrian commandos engaged the Golanis. Using telescopic night sights and shooting from carefully chosen positions scattered amongst the rocks above the road, the Syrians picked off the Golanis. Stopped by a road-block, the tanks and APCs now came under rocket-propelled-grenade fire. An APC was hit, and both the brigade commander and the battalion commander were wounded. The Golanis were now in serious trouble – without commanders, pinned down, and suffering heavy casualties. But the Brigade Operations Officer took charge, and

before reinforcements could arrive, he led a desperate assault.

Under heavy fire the Golanis slowly fought their way up through the boulders, mopping up Syrian commandos as they went. Split into small groups, each drawing upon reserves of courage, fighting bitter exchanges as they went, they edged their way upwards. By dawn, and against strong Syrian opposition, the reconnaissance squadron had captured the crucial upper ski-lift. Once again the Brigade Operations Officer led the Golanis into a final assault. Fighting against exhaustion and determined Syrian opposition, they finally recaptured the fortress, and raised the Israeli flag on one of the antenna masts. The Golanis had suffered 51 killed and over 100 wounded, but by 1000 hours on 22 October Mount Hermon was once more in Israeli hands, thanks to the fighting qualities of the Golani Brigade.

Top: Israeli soldiers express their delight after the retaking of Mount Hermon in 1973.

Above: The scene at Mount Hermon after it had been taken by the Israelis.

Right: Involved in the fighting on the Golan Heights in 1967, this infantryman of the Golani wears distinctive battledress of French origin, and his headgear, covered with sand-coloured sacking and camouflage net, is a US M1 steel helmet. Webbing is of Israeli manufacture. His armament is the 9mm Uzi sub-machine gun.

Beaufort Castle

At 1100 hours on Sunday 6 June, 1982, some nine years after the Yom Kippur War, the Bokim HaRishonim Battalion of the Golani Brigade crossed the border into Lebanon. Spearheading one of the main thrusts of the Israeli invasion, its task was to neutralise the PLO base in the ancient Crusader castle of Beaufort. Standing astride a narrow ridge in the Arnoun Heights which drops 700m in a sheer cliff face, Beaufort could only be approached from the PLO-controlled north. Inside the castle, the PLO commanded a complex series of tunnels, trenches, sandbag defences, and gun positions, making Beaufort seemingly impregnable. From here the PLO had an ideal forward observation post and artillery position covering Galilee and southern Lebanon. For the Israelis, Beaufort and the Arnoun Heights were key targets, without control of which it would be impossible to bring up their main forces for the twin-axis thrust into the heart of the PLO-controlled areas of Lebanon.

As the tanks and APCs ground

Right: Sheltered by a tank, a man of the Golani Brigade takes a break from the action to capture Beaufort Castle.

forward up the mountain road to Arnoun, a heavy artillery barrage rained tons of explosives onto the PLO emplacements. In the sky over the Heights, aircraft of the Israeli Air Force flew sortie after sortie in an attempt to dislodge the determined defenders. The Golani's advance was too slow, though, and as the day wore on it was clear that the main assault could not begin as

Galil

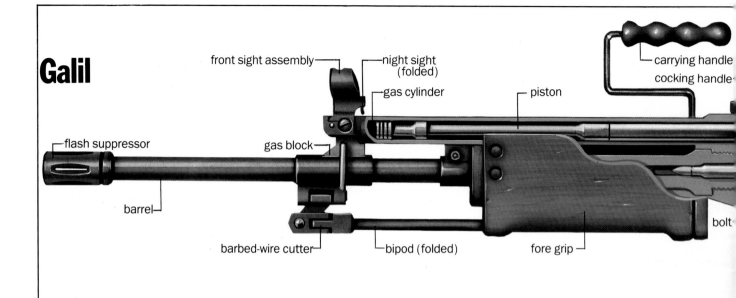

front sight assembly — night sight (folded) — carrying handle

gas cylinder — cocking handle

flash suppressor — gas block — piston

barrel — bolt

barbed-wire cutter — bipod (folded) — fore grip

planned during daylight. In the early evening, lead elements finally reached the village of Arnoun, the main obstacle before Beaufort. As the brigade's tanks took up their positions, fire poured down on them from the PLO Kastel Brigade in the village and castle beyond. The tanks and forward patrol unit (FPU) then began to advance through the fire, fighting short and bloody exchanges. As night fell, PLO firepower increased and Israeli casualties mounted. In the heat of battle the FPU command APC took a direct hit and the force commander was seriously wounded. Receiving no orders, the assault force stalled and the attack fell into disarray. As the Golanis desperately reorganised to pull out, a message on the radio net provided a ray of hope: 'No one move. Gonni's on his way.'

Until he completed his army service just a week before the invasion, Major 'Gonni' Hernik had been the FPU's commander. With the general call-up he had returned to the Golanis, and as news came through of the loss of the FPU's new commander, Gonni was immediately dispatched to take over. Speeding up the winding road to Arnoun, Gonni broadcast his personal call-sign, 'Vengeance Leader', putting new heart

into the hard-pressed soldiers. Gonni knew Beaufort well from exercises, and immediately took charge from the front. In the middle of the village his driver lost control of the APC and the carrier overturned. Despite a painful blow to the back, Gonni seized his Galil assault rifle and ran 700m to catch up with the rest of the attacking force. Reorganising his troops, Gonni quickly reassessed the situation. The original plan for a mounted assault using APCs and tanks was dropped because of the dark. Instead the Golanis would attack the castle on foot from a forward starting point. Keeping the APCs together in the pitch black as they approached the forward starting point proved impossible, and so at considerable personal risk Gonni switched on his own vehicle's headlights as a reference point.

Once in position 200m from Beaufort, with PLO fire pouring down, Gonni deployed his men. Yuval and his crew were to spread out to the left to provide covering fire, while the tanks with Erez and his men forged straight ahead to take the southern defences. Motti and Abu were to subdue the northern defences the fortress itself, and a number of firing positions.

Above: Based on the Russian AK-47 and its Finnish variant, the Valmet M62, the Israeli-designed Galil assault rifle was formally adopted early in 1973 as the official service rifle of the IDF.

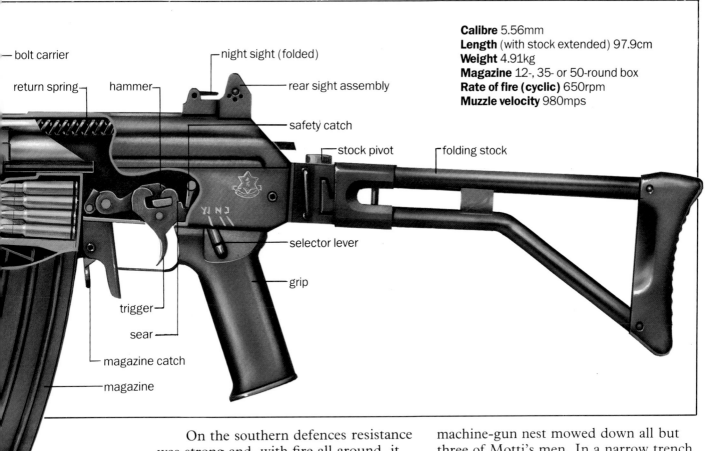

- bolt carrier
- return spring
- hammer
- night sight (folded)
- rear sight assembly
- safety catch
- stock pivot
- folding stock
- selector lever
- grip
- trigger
- sear
- magazine catch
- magazine

Calibre 5.56mm
Length (with stock extended) 97.9cm
Weight 4.91kg
Magazine 12-, 35- or 50-round box
Rate of fire (cyclic) 650rpm
Muzzle velocity 980mps

Below: The tough, realistic training of the Golanis was fundamental to their success in capturing the fortress.

On the southern defences resistance was strong and, with fire all around, it was almost impossible for the tanks to spot the sources of enemy fire. A PLO emplacement brought heavy fire to bear on Erez's unit, wounding Erez. Zwika, the commander of the tank unit, immediately organised a force to attack the emplacement, killing all the PLO there. Putting down a barrage of cannon and anti-tank fire, the same improvised force relieved a second unit which had come under heavy fire from the south. Only then could they turn their attention to the central bunker. Hurling explosives, grenades, and anti-tank shells into the bunker, the force finally silenced PLO fire. As the Golanis penetrated deeper into the stronghold, fighting was bitter. Hand-to-hand exchanges frequently occurred with no warning as groups encountered one another in the fortress.

Meanwhile, on the northern side, Motti and his 20 men charged straight into the fortress. Just half-way to his objective Motti realised grimly that only ten men still stood beside him. There was more firing, and more men fell. Suddenly, as they rounded a bend, they came face to face with Gonni. Gonni ordered the attack to continue, but a

machine-gun nest mowed down all but three of Motti's men. In a narrow trench Motti continued the attack alone, jumping from side to side, throwing grenades as he went. Gonni and a few others arrived, and together they cleared up the trench until only one heavily reinforced position remained. Motti hurled several grenades to no avail. As Gonni joined in he was cut down at close range. Motti was now left in charge and, in view of the heavy casualties sustained, was forced to deploy his men defensively.

From 2200 hours until first light the battle continued as a static action. Plans for the final push on to Beaufort were made. A unit under Tamir was to climb to the roof of the fortress and, having secured it, use it as a platform to give covering fire. Two units under Motti were then to mop up the trenches. As the Golanis went in, so they found that most of the Palestinians had fled under cover of darkness, climbing down a rope ladder from the fortress. The 'impregnable' Beaufort Castle had fallen, and the way was open into central Lebanon. In a typically courageous action, distinguished by bitter hand-to-hand fighting, the Golanis had once again done what they did best – taken the 'untakable'.

THE ARAB LEGION
The Jordanian Arab Legion

WITH just over 100 officers and men, the Arab Legion of Transjordan was formed in 1921 by the Englishman Colonel Peake. Until 1939 it served mainly as a gendarmerie and desert peace-keeping force, but in that year Peake was succeeded by Brigadier John Glubb. Glubb converted part of the by now enlarged Legion into a small but highly efficient army of Bedouins, led by officers contracted or seconded from the British Army. The remainder of the Legion were police. During World War II, the Legion guarded supply routes through Arabia to Russia, as well as innumerable Allied installations throughout the Middle East. It also fought alongside the British in Iraq and Syria in 1941, where the members of the Legion acquired the nickname 'Glubb's Girls' from their long khaki 'skirts' and hanging ringlets.

After World War II, the Legion was left with just three infantry battalions in the field. Glubb Pasha, as he became known, proceeded to double this number, but their equipment remained minimal. In the war of 1948, the Arab Legion, still under Glubb Pasha, captured the Old City of Jerusalem with just 500 men against 100,000 Israeli citizens in Jerusalem as a whole. By any normal staff-college assessment the whole thing was crazy, as one very distinguished British general was later to tell Glubb. 'True,' replied Glubb, 'but it worked'.

Under Arab pressure to sever links with Britain, and anxious to assert his independence from the increasingly powerful Glubb, the young King Hussein dismissed Glubb on 1 March 1956. With a small force, robbed of most of its leaders, the Jordanians now found themselves having to defend a 530km frontier against the numerous and well-equipped Israelis. Jordan was therefore forced to rely upon its Arab friends, and critically upon the Egyptian Air Force. With the air forces of Jordan and Egypt destroyed within hours of the outbreak of the 1967 War – on 5 June – the Arab Legion was in a position where it was outnumbered and outgunned. In this desperate situation the Legion acquitted itself well – particularly in the battle for Jerusalem against the Israeli paras.

The Israeli strategy for the capture of Jerusalem was to win the high ground around the city, and then to move to surround the Old City. With the Jordanians cut off from Ramallah in the north, Jericho in the east, and Bethlehem in the south, the Israelis would be able to establish local superiority. From this position they hoped to force Jerusalem to surrender. Defending the Old City was the 27th Infantry Brigade of the Arab

Above: Jordan Arab Army troops wait for the order to cross the border into Jerusalem in 1967.

Left: This sergeant of the Arab Legion in 1953 wears khaki battledress of British origin. Web equipment is of the 1937 pattern. The *shemagh* head-dress is held by a black *agal* to which the silver badge of the Legion is attached. Armament is the 9mm Sten Mk V sub-machine gun.

Previous page: A Bedouin of the Jordanian Arab Legion in full regalia scans the desert wastes ahead.

Legion, under the capable command of Brigadier Ata Ali. Although Ata Ali's forces were well dug-in, the Israelis had planned their artillery barrage well, and could rely on total air superiority. In particular, Israeli aircraft were able to prevent Jordanian relief forces from reaching the city. With the Israeli Jerusalem Brigade to the south, and a mechanised brigade to the north, the Jordanians were quickly cut off, whilst the crack Israeli 55th Parachute Brigade moved in on their positions. The fighting between the two elite forces was fierce and unremitting, but the men of the 27th were gradually forced back. In desperate see-saw battles through trenches, buildings, and on the roof-tops, the Jordanians bravely defended their positions, only for the paras to reach the wall of the Old City by mid-morning on 6 June. Cut off, with no air support and little artillery, the final nail in the Jordanians' coffin was hit home when the paras took the Augusta Victoria Hospital on Mount Scopus overlooking Jerusalem. By then, Ata Ali had realised that, no matter how bravely his men fought, defeat was inevitable. In a skilful manoeuvre, he withdrew his brigade before the Israelis could enter the Old City, thus saving lives and unnecessary destruction. Significantly, the capture of Jerusalem cost Israel almost half of its casualties in the Six-Day War. Although forced to withdraw, the Arab Legion had acquitted itself well, living up to its reputation as an elite force.

EGYPTIAN COMMANDOS

Commando groups of the Egyptian Army

AT 1415 hours on 6 October 1973, Egyptian commando squads sprinted for the water's edge on the west bank of the Suez Canal, dropped into their rubber assault boats, and began paddling furiously across the 200m-wide waterway. As jets screamed overhead on their way east, the commandos could see the Israeli defences of the Bar-Lev Line vanish in an inferno of bursting shells and drifting dust clouds. Here and there the Israelis returned fire, their automatic weapons and mortars stitching the water of the Canal. The Yom Kippur War was now under way.

After the defeat of the Arabs in 1967, the Israelis had pushed as far west as the Suez Canal. There they had established the formidable Bar-Lev Line, based around 30 strongpoints, or *moazim*. For the Egyptians the recapture of the east bank was essential not just in strategic terms, but also to salvage lost pride. For this they had spent years in training, and were prepared to receive high casualties. As a spearhead for this crucial attack, the Egyptians looked to the elite commando units.

The commandos had already carried out a detailed reconnaissance of the Israeli defences, and in addition to

Left: Egyptian commandos, unbowed by defeat, take part in a march-past in Cairo after the Yom Kippur War in 1973.

leading the crossing were expected to be helilifted into positions deep in the Sinai, where they would disrupt the anticipated Israeli armoured counter-attack. The burden placed on them was a heavy one.

The commandos crossed the Canal at carefully selected points between *moazim*. Once their boats touched the east bank, the crews scrambled ashore pulling assault ladders behind them up the steep sand ramparts for the follow-on forces. Moving rapidly, firing their Kalashnikovs and lobbing grenades ahead of them, they closed in on the Israeli strongpoints. Fighting was fiercest around Quay, at the southern end of the Line. Built on a 2m-wide breakwater, it was almost impossible to approach. Only one commando team, armed with flamethrowers, succeeded in penetrating the defences there, but none survived the assault. Elsewhere resistance was lighter, with many of the defenders cowering in their bunkers after the artillery bombardment, leaving the weapon pits unmanned. For the first time in its history, members of the Israeli Army allowed themselves and their wounded to be captured. The crossing had been hugely successful, not least because of the thorough planning and training of the commandos.

As Israeli tank commanders pressed on to relieve the Bar-Lev Line, so they fell victim to artillery assault, mines laid by the commandos, and above all to commando ambushes. Using portable anti-tank weapons, the commandos took a heavy toll of the tanks which six years earlier had been so successful. Within just 24 hours, Major-General Mandler's

armoured division, the only counter-strike formation of the IDF in the Sinai, had lost a staggering 170 tanks.

The commandos' presence was most heavily felt in the northern sector, no more so than in the epic struggle for the Budapest strongpoint. Not part of the main Bar-Lev Line, Budapest lay some 11km east of Port Fuad, and was protected by a broad belt of swampland to the south. Initially consisting of a mere 18-man garrison, the Israelis had quickly reinforced Budapest with a tank troop. On the afternoon of 6 October an Egyptian task force of 16 tanks and 16 APCs, jeeps and lorry-mounted infantry, launched their attack on Budapest with air and artillery support. This was repulsed with the loss of seven tanks and eight APCs, but under cover of the fighting a commando unit was put ashore 2km east of Budapest, isolating the strongpoint. Aware of the attack on Budapest, the Israelis attempted to reinforce the garrison at midnight with eight tanks from Major-General Adan's newly arrived armoured division. What the Israelis were not aware of was the presence of Egyptian commandos east of the fort, nor that these commandos had been busy mining the only approach road. As the first Israeli tank hit a mine, so the commandos fired flares, and under their harsh light destroyed two more tanks with ATGWs (anti-tank guided weapons). The Israelis were forced to withdraw. At first light they restarted their advance, but were halted by a belt of mines stretching the width of the sandbank. At only 500m range the commandos fired more ATGWs,

History of the Egyptian commandos

The creation of the Egyptian commandos owed much to one of the country's most famous soldiers: Saad el-Din Shazli. Shazli began forming paratroop units after the 1956 War, the first unit becoming operational in 1959. In 1960 Shazli himself commanded an Egyptian paratroop battalion serving with the UN forces in the Congo, and paratroop and commando units later saw action in the Yemen civil war on the Republican side.

During the build-up to the Six-Day

War, the 33rd and 53rd Commando Battalions were airlifted to Amman to take out Israeli air bases in the event of war, but suffered in the general disaster befalling the Jordanian Army. Further experience was gained with small-scale raids during the 'War of Attrition' in the late 1960s, experience put to use in February 1970 when the commandos successfully ambushed an Israeli patrol on the east bank of the Suez Canal. An Israeli naval auxiliary vessel was also blown up by commando frogmen in the Israeli port of Eilat.

Between 1970 and 1973 Shazli, as the Army's Chief of Staff, supervised the expansion of the commandos, so that by

October 1973 he could deploy two paratroop brigades (the 140th and 182nd), two heliborne assault brigades, and seven commando groups, three of which were attached to operational commands (the 127th, 129th and 133rd), while the others remained at GHQ's disposal. With the Middle East peace process in the 1970s, Egyptian defence policy shifted away from the destruction of Israel to self-defence with a highly mobile intervention force capable of reacting to crises in the Middle East and North Africa. Central to this second role are the parachute brigade and seven commando groups of the current Egyptian Army.

The anti-terrorist role

At 2015 hours on Sunday 24 December 1985 all was quiet aboard EgyptAir Flight 648, the hijacked Boeing 737 at Malta's Luqa airport. In the cockpit the leader of the hijackers was sitting with the captain, Hani Galal, and co-pilot Emad Monib, when suddenly a light flashed on the control panel. The light revealed that the rear cargo-bay door was being opened. Quickly turning off the light, praying the hijacker had not seen it, Monib glanced at the captain. Both men knew that it could mean only one thing – that a rescue attempt was under way.

With the rise of international terrorism in the 1970s, elite units had been formed throughout the world to combat the growing threat. In Egypt the task had been assigned to the Sa'Aqa (Lightning) commando group. In 1975 the group had successfully rescued another 737 at Luxor airport, though they were less than successful in March 1978 when attempting to rescue a hijacked DC-8 at Larnaca airport, Cyprus, mainly as a result of poor co-operation with the Cypriot authorities.

Within hours of the hijack of Flight 648, a Hercules transport carrying 25 commandos was dispatched to Luqa. Landing at 0930 hours, it was clear to the commandos that they would have to act quickly when Hani Galal's voice dramatically described over the radio the shooting of seven hostages and the threat to 'execute' more (though it later emerged that only one passenger had been killed and seven wounded). Within hours a plan was hastily formed. A 'shaped' device was to be exploded in the rear baggage area as a diversion while the main force clambered onto the wings, blew open the emergency hatches, and shot the hijackers. The noise of the cargo-bay door opening, however, alerted the hijackers, and as the commandos entered the aircraft, they found one door had been booby-trapped with a grenade. The hijackers threw more grenades amongst the passengers before being shot dead.

At the end of the hijacking, 59 of the 98 passengers were dead, largely due to the smoke which filled the plane after the explosions. All of the hijackers were dead, but the cost had been high.

Above: Egyptian commandos killed by the Cypriot National Guard in 1978.

disabling a further vehicle. Again the Israelis withdrew. Reinforced by a mortar battery and an infantry company, they attacked yet again later that morning. In their concealed locations, invisible to the tank crews, the commandos waited until the Israeli infantry were clearly outlined against the sandbank before unleashing a devastating barrage of automatic fire. This resulted in 15 Israelis killed and a further 30 wounded.

That same night a large commando group was inserted 30km east of Budapest, and it caught one of Adan's armoured brigades reversing off their transporters. In their attack the commandos destroyed two tanks and a half-track, going to ground when the Israelis counter-attacked, only to re-

emerge later to destroy another vehicle. Elsewhere, though, the commandos were less successful. Many of those helilifted into the Sinai to disrupt Israeli communications suffered heavy casualties and, despite showing considerable courage, were eventually countered by the Israelis. In the largest insertion an entire battalion of commandos being helilifted was spotted by Israeli Phantoms, and 14 of the helicopters were shot down.

In the 1973 Egyptian attack, then, the commandos played a crucial role. They were extremely successful in crossing the Canal and piercing the Bar-Lev Line; they inflicted heavy casualties on Israeli armoured reinforcements; and they delayed the Israeli counter-attack by their disruptive activities deep in the Sinai. Despite the eventual success of the IDF, the Egyptian commandos had proved themselves a force to be reckoned with, and even in the late stages of the war they grasped honour from the jaws of defeat by engaging the Israeli paras and fighting them to a standstill at Ismailiya.

Below: A commando lies low and surveys the terrain near the Bar-Lev Line.

Crossing the Bar-Lev Line
Egyptian commandos, October 1973

On the afternoon of Yom Kippur, 6 October 1973, the troops manning the Bar-Lev defensive line along the Suez Canal in Israeli-occupied Sinai were the victims of a surprise assault spearheaded by crack squads of Egyptian commandos. By the following day most of the Bar-Lev Line was in Egyptian hands.

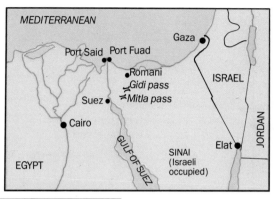

Sinai bridgehead

As the Egyptian 2nd and 3rd armies cross the canal to consolidate the bridgehead, further commando insertions are made near the Mitla and Gidi passes.
7 Oct Despite further commando landings on the coast, the Budapest stronghold remains in Israeli hands.

Key
Egyptian forces
Israeli forces
Lituf ■ Israeli strongholds
□ Israeli command posts

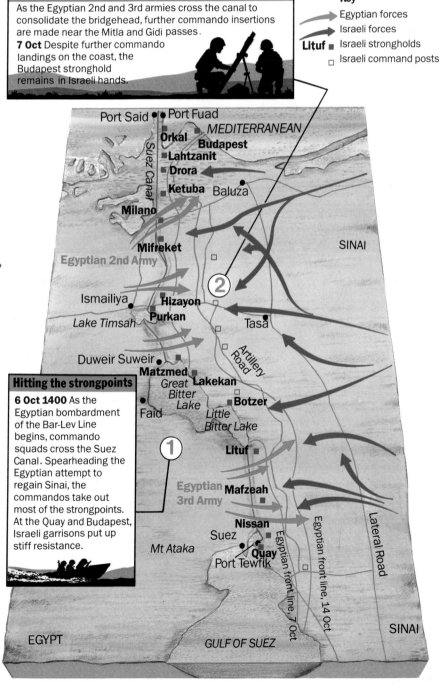

Hitting the strongpoints

6 Oct 1400 As the Egyptian bombardment of the Bar-Lev Line begins, commando squads cross the Suez Canal. Spearheading the Egyptian attempt to regain Sinai, the commandos take out most of the strongpoints. At the Quay and Budapest, Israeli garrisons put up stiff resistance.

5·FORCES IN SOUTHERN AFRICA

SINCE the early 1960s the sub-continent of southern Africa, which consists of ten territories to the south of Zaïre and Tanzania, has been the scene of continuous military conflict. Some of these countries, such as Angola and Mozambique, have known nothing but war since that time. Others, such as Malawi and Zambia, have been comparatively untouched. None of these countries, however, has completely escaped the ravages of war.

Two of these wars, those in Angola (1961–74) and Mozambique (1964–74), can be

described as colonial wars in the sense that in both countries nationalist guerrillas were fighting to gain independence from an imperial power – Portugal. The Portuguese responded by building up their troop levels to 50,000–60,000 in each territory, so as to check the guerrillas militarily, and by pursuing 'social promotion' programmes designed to win over the Africans. For a poor nation fighting three wars simultaneously (they also faced nationalist guerrillas in their west African possession of Portuguese Guinea between 1963 and 1974), the Portuguese were very successful in each territory. The wars accelerated strains within the Portuguese armed forces, however, and in April 1974 the army overthrew the Portuguese government, and the new regime gave independence to all the African territories.

Another of southern Africa's protracted conflicts, that in Rhodesia (1966–79) was a colonial war in a different sense. Rhodesia was nominally a British colony, but in practice political power lay in the hands of a white-settler government under Ian Smith – a regime which had seized independence in November 1965. Smith's Rhodesian Front (RF) government aimed to maintain white rule in Rhodesia, but it

Left: A member of the Rhodesian Light Infantry during an operation in the bush.

was challenged by two African nationalist movements that campaigned for majority African rule, these being the Zimbabwe African People's Union (ZAPU) led by Joshua Nkomo, and the Zimbabwe African National Union (ZANU) led by the Reverend Ndabaningi Sithole. Both movements decided to wage guerrilla war against the government.

During the late 1960s ZAPU and ZANU, using Zambia as their base, infiltrated their guerrillas across the Zambezi river into northern Rhodesia, but these incursions were easily defeated by the Rhodesian security forces. In December 1972, however, ZANU's military wing, the Zimbabwe African National Liberation Army (ZANLA), launched a new offensive in the north-east. ZAPU's military wing, the Zimbabwe People's Revolutionary Army (ZIPRA), built up a powerful army in Zambia, and mounted guerrilla operations in western Rhodesia. In late 1976 the leaders of ZAPU/ZIPRA and ZANU/ZANLA, Joshua Nkomo and Robert Mugabe (who had deposed Sithole), formed the Patriotic Front alliance (PF).

As the war intensified, the RF government's limited military resources became dangerously stretched and in March 1978 Smith sanctioned a coalition government with moderate black nationalists including Bishop Abel Muzorewa, who was elected premier in April 1979. The PF continued fighting, however, until later that year Britain successfully promoted a political settlement. A ceasefire was declared on 28 December 1979 and fresh elections were held in early 1980, resulting in a resounding victory for the ZANU party. In April 1980 Rhodesia became formally independent as Zimbabwe.

There have also been two other long-running conflicts in the region – the struggles for control over the South African-administered territory of South West Africa (referred to by the UN as Namibia since 1968) and over the white-ruled Republic of South Africa. Conflict began in South West Africa in August 1966, when the South West Africa People's Organisation (SWAPO), the territory's main African nationalist movement, began its guerrilla war against the South African authorities. After the accession to power of the MPLA in Angola, however, SWAPO was able to operate from that country, and to receive training and weapons there from Cuba, East Germany and the Soviet Union. The threat to South Africa itself similarly escalated after Portugal's departure from Africa. South Africa's leading African nationalist movement, the African National Congress (ANC) had carried out a sabotage campaign during the early 1960s, but most of its members were either killed or jailed or they fled into exile. After independence in Mozambique, however, the ANC's military wing Umkhonto we Sizwe (Spear of the Nation) was able to resume its campaign, using Mozambique as a base from which to launch its attacks.

Pretoria, however, responded defiantly. Using its economic wealth to strengthen the South African Defence Force (SADF), Pretoria adopted a forward strategy, launching cross-border raids into surrounding states so as to destroy the guerrilla bases and make the host governments think twice about giving sanctuary to the guerrillas.

PORTUGUESE FORCES OF INTERVENTION

As Forças de Intervenção

Composition of the Portuguese 'forces of intervention'

In order to defend their African territories against nationalist guerrillas the Portuguese deployed some 75 per cent of their metropolitan army in Africa, the majority of these troops being conscripts doing their national service. The conscripts, however, were not usually involved in anti-guerrilla warfare. Instead they performed garrison duties in strategic centres and carried out 'social promotion' programmes such as building schools and clinics so as to win over the local population.

The guerrillas were met in combat by the 'forces of intervention' – professional soldiers of the Portuguese Army, heavily supported by local black recruits. These elite fighting units included paratroopers, Marines, commandos and naval fusiliers. The Portuguese also raised local formations in their African territories, such as the Comandos Africanos, the Grupos Especiais (GE) and the airborne Grupos Especiais de Paraquedistas (GEP), of which anything up to 90 per cent were black Africans. In addition to the units fielded by the army, the Portuguese secret police organised a force known as the Flechas (Arrows), which acted as a long-range reconnaissance group in Mozambique. Many of the Flechas were guerrillas who had been captured and 'turned' (persuaded to change sides) by the Portuguese.

T HE Portuguese 'forces of intervention' usually divided a colony into a number of territorial or theatre commands – in Angola there were five and in Mozambique three. Units were made available at theatre level for the interventionary role. Below theatre level, tactical responsibility was shared by sector commands, and further subdivided into battalion and company commands. Intervention forces could also be made available at local level for specific tasks such as immediate reinforcement and convoy escort, or similar mobile roles.

Precise tactics were determined by the nature of the terrain, which varied in Angola, for instance, from jungle in Cabinda to open savannah in the east. Much also depended on the season, since all the colonies were subject to the tropical or semi-tropical climatic cycle of a cool dry season – April to September in both Angola and Mozambique – followed by a hot rainy season in the remaining months. Large-scale operations by the Portuguese were only possible in the dry season, while their guerrilla foes preferred to operate in the rainy months when thicker vegetation and low cloud cover reduced the threat from the air – the Portuguese had complete air superiority until surface-to air missiles became available to the guerrillas in the early 1970s.

Air power offered the opportunity of attacking guerrilla infiltration routes and also provided a quick-reaction force. Ultimately, though, the Portuguese needed to get to grips with the guerrillas on the ground, and in this respect

Portuguese strategy was transformed by the introduction of French-built Alouette helicopters in 1966. The elite units now had far greater mobility. By 1971 some 60 Alouettes were available, each mounting either a machine gun or a 20mm grenade launcher, and each capable of carrying five men. Parties could now be dropped to reinforce ground patrols and to block guerrilla escape routes. The value of these helicopters was proven when, after large-scale operations in eastern Angola in 1966, 1968 and 1972, the Angolan nationalists eventually decided to abandon infiltration from Zambia and try operating from the north.

Heliborne operations, however, were only a part of the Portuguese response to guerrilla activity. In other respects, technology was not of paramount importance to Portuguese counter-insurgency; for example, three squadrons of cavalry were deployed in Angola from 1966. They were used to protect the flanks of advancing troops in difficult terrain, and when supplied by helicopter could mount extended patrols. This deployment of cavalry proved effective, the horse having the added advantage of acting as a shock-absorber when troops strayed into a minefield.

The mine was the most effective weapon used by the guerrillas, accounting, for instance, for over 50 per cent of Portuguese casualties in Angola in 1970. The newer and more sophisticated mines could not be located by mine-detectors, few of which were available to the Portuguese in any case, and so the security forces resorted to the *pica* or sharpened stick. Depending on the width

Left: With his G3 assault rifle at the ready, a Portuguese soldier moves carefully through hostile Angolan bush country on the trail of guerrillas. Sign language alone was used during these bush patrols, and this was so successful that the Portuguese became known as the 'death walkers'.

G3A3

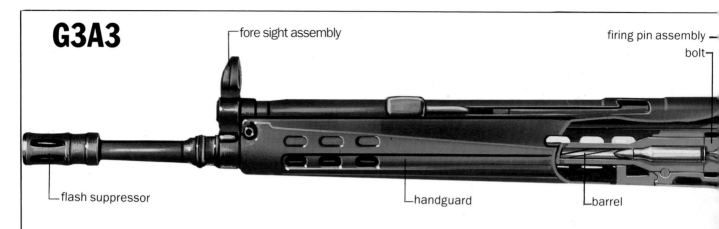

fore sight assembly

firing pin assembly

bolt

flash suppressor

handguard

barrel

Calibre 7.62mm
Length 102.5cm
Weight (loaded) 5kg
Magazine 20-round box
Cartridge 7.62 x 51mm NATO round
Rate of fire (practical auto) 100rpm
Muzzle velocity 780-800mps
Maximum effective range 400m

of the track to be cleared, one or two men ahead of a patrol would carefully use *picas* to feel the ground for soft areas that might indicate recent digging. If one was found, these *picadores* would then probe the area for the unmistakable, hollow 'clonk' of a mine. Other members of the patrol would remain vigilant as this was often a moment of ambush. Having located a mine, the *picadores* would then ensure that no second mine was placed alongside the first to trap the unwary.

The Portuguese improvised by using special trucks with sandbagged floors and tyres half-filled with water to lead convoys and deflect mine blast, though in the long term extensive road tarring made it more difficult for the guerrilla to lay his mines undetected. Other simple responses improvised by the Portuguese included ringing their own positions with empty beer bottles, an early-warning system which was just as effective as sensors. A standard anti-ambush technique was to hurl grenades into the bush when dismounting from vehicles under fire, in case guerrillas were lying in wait close to the track to catch the Portuguese as they took cover. Apart from mines, the ambush was the guerrillas' most deadly weapon – the frequent bombardments with mortars or

122mm rockets from long range were rarely effective.

The Portuguese discovered that small operations on foot offered far better chances of thoroughly disrupting guerrilla activities than large-scale sweeps, since the latter tended only to shift the guerrillas to somewhere else. In 1968 one observer in the heavily forested Dembos mountains in Angola found that 30-man patrols of three to five days' duration had become the norm. On a typical operation of this kind each of the 30 men in the patrol would have a distinct function, and would also know the duties of the two men directly in

Above: A unit of the 16,000 Portuguese troops deployed in Mozambique to oppose infiltration by guerrilla forces. These men are armed with standard Nato 7.62mm semi-automatic weapons.

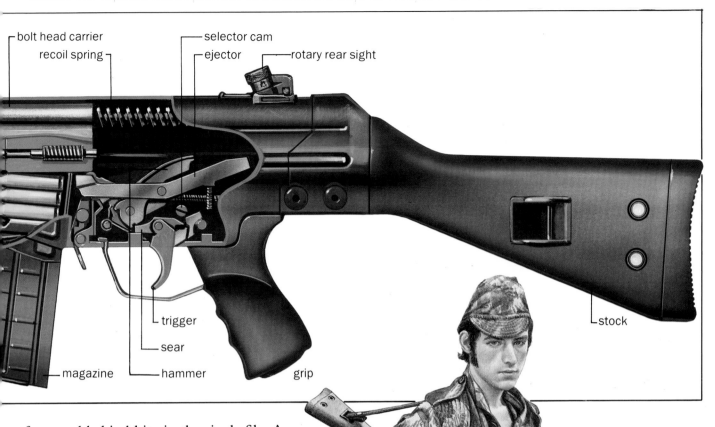

bolt head carrier — selector cam — ejector — rotary rear sight
recoil spring

trigger
sear
magazine   hammer   grip   stock

front and behind him in the single file. A
variety of weapons would be carried,
often three heavy machine guns and a
bazooka or mortar or, alternatively, three
mortars and a recoilless rifle. Those who
were not responsible for the heavier
weapons would carry ammunition, their
rifles and, from 1969, two Instalaza rifle
grenades. Strict silence would be
maintained, the only form of
communication being sign language. The
Portuguese would bind all metal parts of
their uniforms and equipment in cloth,
and they wore canvas boots with rubber
soles to minimise any sound of movement
over the rotting vegetation on the jungle
floor. So effective were these precautions
that the guerrillas in Angola came to
describe the men of these patrols as the
'death walkers'.

Such operations helped keep in
check the nationalist guerrillas in Angola
and Mozambique. The Portuguese
eventually left these territories, of course,
but this was not as a result of military
defeat. In fact, until the time of the April
1974 *coup d'état* in Portugal, the
Portuguese troops had proved themselves
to be the superior fighting force and the
forces of intervention in particular had
been remarkably successful in carrying
out their brief.

Above: The West German
Heckler and Koch G3A3
assault rifle, which is
manufactured under
licence in Portugal. The
G3 is constructed from
metal stampings, and its
stock and forward
handguard are both
made of tough plastic.

Left: Operating in
Angola in 1975, this
Portuguese paratrooper
wears fatigues cut from a
French camouflage
pattern. The cap is a
distinctive feature. Black
army boots are worn but
civilian footwear was
popular. Armament is
the G3A3 assault rifle.

RHODESIAN FIRE FORCE

The Rhodesian Light Infantry

ON Thursday 21 June 1979, just after breakfast time, the call-out siren at Grand Reef airfield, near Umtali in eastern Rhodesia, began its wail. As always the effect was instantaneous. Suddenly there was a flurry of activity as young commandos clutching rifles and machine guns burst out of their flimsy, bullet-holed huts. Some of these commandos were clad in shorts, tee-shirts and tennis shoes, while others were pulling on faded and torn camouflage coveralls as they ran. A few wore bush hats or bandannas cut from

The Fire Force role

The Rhodesian Light Infantry (RLI) was formed in 1961, in response to the Rhodesian government's need for front-line white units. Three years later the RLI took on the structure of a commando battalion, consisting of three company-sized infantry commandos similar in organisation to a British Army company. Later, in 1976, it expanded to include a Support Commando and in the following year began training for airborne operations. Each of the Commandos was divided into four Troops, the Support Commando fielding a Mortar, an Anti-Tank, a Reconnaissance and an Assault Pioneer Troop.

The total combat strength of the RLI fluctuated over the years, varying from 250 to 350 at any one time. A large proportion of its personnel, especially in No 3 Commando, were foreigners who volunteered for service out of political conviction or simply for adventure. This gave the RLI notoriety as a sort of Foreign Legion of southern Africa, but the foreign volunteers – from countries such as South Africa, Britain, France and the USA – brought with them invaluable experience gained from service with some of the world's finest units. When the RLI was disbanded soon after the cessation of hostilities, much of this experience was passed on in turn to the SADF.

Although it was a relatively small unit, the RLI accounted for a high proportion of enemy casualties, being used extensively in the Fire Force role. This was a technique developed by the Rhodesians to offset their lack of numbers by deploying mobile, quick-reaction forces to intercept the guerrillas, thereby taking the war to the enemy instead of allowing him to attack at will. Typically, Fire Force consisted of a Commando of the RLI, with the Troops working on a rotating basis. Ideally there would be a minimum of three four-man sticks available for immediate deployment by 'G-Cars' (Alouette helicopters), and another four four-man sticks available to parachute in from a 'Para-Dak' (DC-3 Dakota). Each stick packed a formidable punch, carrying 7.62mm FN rifles, a 7.62mm FN MAG light machine gun and grenades of various kinds, while firepower support was available from the G-Cars, which were armed with twin-mounted .3in Browning machine guns, and the 'K-Car' (the command chopper) armed with quad-mounted Brownings or with 20mm cannon. Further firepower was provided by a Lynx aeroplane, armed with Brownings, rockets and napalm, and in the case of an emergency a helping hand could be given by jets such as Vampires, Hunters and Canberras.

Left: A Rhodesian infantryman takes aim with his FN rifle.

combat scarves, others carried black, British-type paratroop helmets. All were festooned with an amazing array of personalised web gear, ranging from standard Rhodesian military issue, captured Chinese and Soviet-issue pouches stitched onto leather or web belts, to civilian hunting-jacket webbing. Long, shining belts of ammunition hung around the shoulders and chests of the machine gunners and further supplies of ammunition peeked from bulging pouches and packs. Pistols, machetes and knives dangled from belts or hung from shoulder straps.

Approaching a group of wooden huts, the men slowed to a walk and began to disperse. Those carrying para helmets entered one of the huts, while the rest continued towards several Alouette III helicopters parked in protective enclosures constructed from 40-gallon (182-litre) oil drums packed with earth.

As NCOs hurried away to the briefing hut opposite the chopper pens, the men relaxed, sitting or standing around as they waited for their 'stick' (small squad) leaders to return from the briefing with a few details scribbled into notebooks. It was not unusual for a call to be cancelled, but there was no stand-down on this occasion. A short time previously Selous Scouts had moved into the war zone along the eastern border, in the operational area designated Thrasher, and had set up observation posts with a view to detecting guerrilla infiltration. Guerrilla groups were indeed spotted, and reports were sent in recommending that an RLI Fire Force operation be put in motion. A lance-corporal soon appeared from the briefing hut, ordering his troops to kit up.

The orders were simple and to the point. First, four four-man 'stop groups' would be flown in by helicopter. If they could deal with the enemy, then all well and good. But if difficulties arose, then paras would be called in. Their task would be to sweep through the bush and, like beaters at a pheasant shoot, force the 'terrs' (terrorists) to break and run in the direction of the stop groups.

The commandos were soon heading towards their designated objectives. The stop groups were deployed without incident and shortly afterwards the 'Para-Dak' (DC-3 Dakota) was called in and kept on stand-by. It circled the DZ (dropping zone) time and time again, two rows of eight anxious men waiting inside its fuselage. Suddenly one of the three

Above: A patrol on a 'search and destroy' mission is landed in the bush by an SA 319B Alouette III helicopter.

Below: RLI commandos parachute in to flush terrorists out of the bush and in the direction of ambushes set up by stop groups.

Air Force dispatchers on board stood up and faced the commandos. He was receiving radio messages from troops on the ground. 'There's been a contact,' he shouted, 'The K-Car [command chopper] is taking flak. . . . Seven-Nine [Ground Force] is requesting a paradrop'. At this the troopers stamped out their cigarettes and tightened their chin-straps.

As the Para-Dak began to descend for its run-in, the 16 troopers rose

unsteadily to their feet and snapped their static lines to the double overhead steel cables, automatically checking their equipment and that of the man in front. 'We're going to drop you in one run-in so get out as fast as you can', shouted the dispatcher, adding that they must be prepared for strong cross-winds. As the aircraft dropped below 400 feet, the troopers responded to their orders: 'Action stations!' and then 'Stand to the door!' and finally 'Go!'

The drop was not exactly easy. There was indeed a strong cross-wind and to make matters worse the Para-Dak had gone so low that the first trooper was already on the ground before the last three had jumped from the aircraft. Two NCOs were injured in the jump and had to be casevaced (evacuated as casualties). The remaining 14 troopers, once down, immediately sought to locate the other members of their four-man sticks and take stock of their surroundings. In fact it was a typical setting – they saw a little kraal (hut village), set on the edge of a few mealie (maize) fields, against a background of heavily wooded, rocky hills, called 'gomos' by the troops.

The Alouettes that had brought in the stop groups choppered the paras

Above: Additional support is provided by a napalm drop from a Lynx aircraft onto a guerrilla position.

Right: An Australian trooper takes a closer look at an enemy SKS rifle while men of the Support Commando wait to be lifted out by helicopter at the end of a raid into Mozambique.

forward to the base of a particularly large gomo. They spent the next few hours negotiating the slopes of this hill. Sweltering under the weight of their kit, they crept along cautiously, keeping a wary eye on the thick bush in case guerrillas should be waiting in ambush.

Meanwhile, high atop the gomo, the lieutenant commanding the stop groups had halted his men for a few minutes' rest. Tired, they stood in silence, gazing at the magnificent panorama below them. Then suddenly, from down in the valley, came the sound of gunfire. They heard the unmistakable, intermittent crackle of MAG automatic fire, followed by an eruption of sound as the booms of FNs on top of MAG fire all but drowned out the pop-pop of AK-47 assault rifles. Green and red tracers arced skyward, indicating that a contact had been made. 'Lynx strike going in', someone said. All heads turned towards the familiar little aircraft as it came in along the valley, summoned by chopper sticks who had clearly encountered substantial resistance. Firing its .3in Brownings, the Lynx coursed upward as a mushroom of bright orange flame enveloped the ground below it. The attack procedure was repeated several times until, ammunition exhausted, the Lynx returned to base to rearm.

While this was happening the paras continued with their sweep, searching along the crest of the gomo, and then moved slowly down the other side. Here they linked up with the stop groups, who,

it transpired, had killed several guerrillas and taken one prisoner. While four men were detailed to locate and search the enemy dead, two sticks climbed down into a dried-up river bed and, pushing the enemy captive before them, ordered him to call upon any hidden comrades to surrender.

As the group wound its way round a bend in the river, another contact was initiated, prompting the search detail behind to take cover for a few moments. One of the detail's men, listening in on his radio set, gave a running commentary on events up ahead for the benefit of his team mates. The shooting then ceased abruptly, plunging the bush into an eerie silence. The search detail, having located four dead bodies huddled together, then proceeded to strip them of their weapons. The booty included an RPG-7 rocket launcher with several 40mm rounds and a Chinese-made Tokarev pistol. The latter was promptly confiscated by the radioman, while another trooper removed several bracelets from one of the corpses to add to his collection of battle trophies.

Moving off, the search party advanced cautiously along the river bed, sifting through the carnage wrought by the two forward sticks until finally the search-and-destroy operation was tied up in that particular area. The forces then

linked up and continued to sweep down the remainder of the gomo until they arrived at a kraal set in a clearing at the gomo's base. Suddenly there was an excited yell and a flurry of movement as everyone dispersed. A trooper appeared with two young Africans he had discovered hiding behind a wardrobe in one of the kraal's thatched huts. Weary RLI troopers shouted questions at the youths in English, repeating them in the native language, Shona.

The terrified captives denied any association with the *makadanga* – the terrorists. All the same, the troopers searched the hut and, finding nothing, set it on fire so that the guerrillas would not

Below: Armed with FN rifles and an FN MAG, troops of the RLI Support Commando relax on completing a mission.

be able to use it. Their suspicions soon proved to be justified. Minutes later the troopers were forced to scurry for cover as the air filled with exploding ammunition that had been hidden in the roof of the hut and detonated by the heat of the flames. Then, in the thick of the confusion, two guerrillas were spotted in the bush near the main body of the RLI men. A brief moment of pandemonium ensued but, after a flurry of shots, the troopers added an AK-47 and a Simonov SKS carbine to their pile of captured weaponry. The area was then quickly secured and the remainder of the kraal set on fire.

The RLI men now took the opportunity to relax. It had been a long and tiring day and they were keen to return to base. Not long afterwards the familiar sound of the Alouettes could be heard, as the RLI's transport came in low over the tree tops. The men ran towards the waiting choppers and climbed in, the captives huddled between the troopers. As the helicopters began their journey back to Grand Reef, the RLI troopers could congratulate themselves on a successful mission. They had killed 12 guerrillas and captured four, the final capture being made by a lone stick on the other side of the gomo, without incurring any serious casualties themselves.

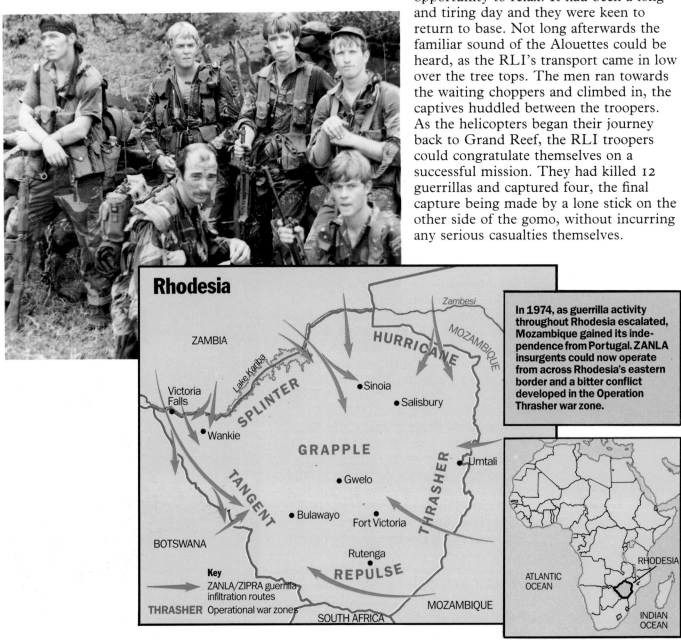

Rhodesia

In 1974, as guerrilla activity throughout Rhodesia escalated, Mozambique gained its independence from Portugal. ZANLA insurgents could now operate from across Rhodesia's eastern border and a bitter conflict developed in the Operation Thrasher war zone.

ZAMBIA

Lake Kariba

Zambesi

MOZAMBIQUE

HURRICANE

SPLINTER

Victoria Falls

Wankie

Sinoia

Salisbury

GRAPPLE

TANGENT

Gwelo

Bulawayo

Fort Victoria

Umtali

THRASHER

BOTSWANA

Rutenga

Key
ZANLA/ZIPRA guerrilla infiltration routes

THRASHER Operational war zones

REPULSE

MOZAMBIQUE

SOUTH AFRICA

ATLANTIC OCEAN

RHODESIA

INDIAN OCEAN

RHODESIAN SELOUS SCOUTS

The Selous Scouts Regiment

THE Selous Scouts had only a short operational history, but under the inspired leadership of Major (later Lieutenant-Colonel) Ron Reid Daly, its members won a fearsome reputation as the best bush soldiers on the African continent. Their primary mission was to infiltrate areas affected or dominated by guerrillas and send back vital information to the conventional forces earmarked to carry out attacks on the enemy. In this role they performed magnificently.

Their success reflected to a great extent the quality of their training. Volunteers who came forward to join the regiment were subjected to selection and training courses that in some respects were tougher than those of any other elite unit. The selection course was so punishing that of 60 volunteers 40 or 50 would drop out during the first couple of days. Those volunteers who qualified for the training course were then put through pure hell. They were expected to endure a gruelling fitness programme and to live off the land by surviving on such delicacies as a rotting baboon carcass. These trials of strength and stomach were strenuous if not almost barbaric, but they gave the recruits a taste of the hardships they might have to endure in the bush and thereby saved many a life.

The survivors from this course went on to a special camp to undergo the 'dark phase', in which they learned to look, act and talk like the guerrillas. Using information gleaned from dead or captured guerrillas, the instructors drummed into the recruits details about the guerrillas' methods of operation, uniform, weapons and equipment. The end product was that the Scouts could pose as guerrillas, forming 'pseudo-groups' to infiltrate guerrilla areas. Black Scouts of course had a natural advantage and therefore spearheaded such groups, but even the whites could pass themselves off as guerrillas at a distance – for instance, by wearing the appropriate clothing, carrying the right weapons and by blacking up all exposed flesh.

Successful recruits were quickly sent into the bush, usually in sticks of four or five men led by a white officer, to seek

out the enemy. As it was essential to remain undetected, these teams were usually dropped by covered lorry or helicopter, at night and well outside the target area. From their drop-point the Scouts would move in on foot and set up a well-concealed observation post (OP) in a location affording a good all-round view. At this stage the Scouts' punishing training paid dividends and bush skills came into their own, for the Scouts had to survive without outside support for many weeks, finding food and living undetected before finally making contact with the enemy without revealing their real identity.

In order to make contact with the guerrillas the Scouts used information gathered by attached police Special Branch units. While the white officers stayed at the OP, emerging only at nights to hear reports, give orders and relay messages back to base, black Scouts disguised as guerrillas would move into a village and try to meet with the local contact-man. Contact-men gave the guerrillas food, shelter and information. Finding them was always easier if the pseudo-group contained 'turned' terrorists with first-hand knowledge of the areas in question.

The usual pattern was for the pseudo-group to be accepted by the

Above: Armed with FNs, two Scouts look for signs of guerrilla activity.

Previous page: Combat wear was casual. These men wear non-regulation shorts and canvas training shoes.

History and equipment of the Selous Scouts

The Selous Scouts Regiment was named after Frederick Courteney Selous, a famous hunter who had helped Cecil Rhodes open up much of what became Rhodesia to white colonisation. The regiment began life in late 1973 as a small and predominantly white force called the Tracker Combat Unit. It expanded into a 1000-strong force con-

sisting mostly of blacks, including guerrillas captured and 'turned' by the security forces. Redesignated the Selous Scouts in March 1974, the regiment acted primarily as a combat reconnaissance force, which gathered intelligence on the enemy by fielding deep-penetration patrols and pseudo-groups (security-force personnel acting as if guerrillas), and when necessary it also acted in a hunter-killer role.

Many members of the Selous Scouts were natural trackers and hunters, being men from the countryside, and these abilities were strengthened by an extremely tough training course. The Scouts usually carried FN FAL 7.62mm rifles, though other weapons, notably captured AK-47 assault rifles, were also used. Members of the regiment often dressed casually, discarding their army issue camouflage uniforms for shorts, tee-shirts and track shoes, but their casual appearance belied their dedication and professionalism. Much of the credit for their success must go to their commander, Lieutenant-Colonel

Ron Reid Daly, who drew on the experience he had gained with C Squadron of the SAS in Malaya to build up from scratch a highly effective unit.

However, the supposed special treatment of the Scouts and their unorthodox methods caused resentment amongst members of the regular army. Some high-ranking officers believed that the Scouts were too much of a law unto themselves, and that on occasions they had compromised operations by other units and endangered the lives of army personnel. Reid Daly himself had several brushes with the military authorities, culminating in January 1979 in a blazing public row with his superior, the army commander Lieutenant-General John Hickman. The Scouts' commander was court-martialled for insubordination and, although receiving only a minor reprimand, decided to resign his command, thus ending his association with the regiment he had worked so hard to create. Not long afterwards, in early 1980, the unit was disbanded by the Mugabe government.

contact-man and, once it was, to arrange meetings with other local guerrilla groups at a particular time and place. This was not always easy and the Scouts had sometimes to go to extreme lengths to demonstrate their loyalty to the guerrilla cause – for instance, by launching mock attacks on Protected Villages (PVs) or white-owned farms. Once meetings had been arranged, the Scouts themselves would not attack the guerrillas, because this would have blown their cover. They would instead call in a Fire Force team, which would arrive suddenly and wipe out the enemy.

Another Selous Scouts speciality was cross-border reconnaissance. Some teams tracked guerrilla groups for anything up to a week. The Scouts looked out in particular for disturbed vegetation, sole prints in the dust and even traces of urine; the best time for following spoors was early in the morning or late in the afternoon, when the sun's slanting rays highlighted the slightest sign of movement. The Scouts themselves had to be careful not to alert the enemy to their presence in the bush. They were prohibited from shooting animals and had instead to live off game found dead or caught silently, together with edible plants and roots. Fires, if lit at all, were made from bone-dry kindling that did not give off smoke. At night the fire would be placed in a pit dug in the ground so that the embers would not be seen by the enemy.

In addition to their role as pseudo-groups and trackers the Selous Scouts were also deployed in a hunter-killer role, usually in conjunction with elements of the regular army, in cross-border raids on guerrilla camps and bases. Probably the most famous of their raids was that carried out in August 1976 on a base at Pungwe/Nyadzonya in Mozambique. A force of 72 Scouts, in 10 Unimog trucks and three Ferret armoured cars, drove calmly into the camp, fooling the guerrillas into thinking that they were friendly forces. By the time the guerrillas realised their error, the Scouts had opened up with everything they had. When the firefight was over, some 1200 guerrillas lay dead, while only five Scouts were wounded. Other raids of this sort followed during the next three years of the war.

In their short history the Selous Scouts inflicted huge losses on the enemy and yet, because of the inevitable secrecy that surrounded their operations, few Rhodesians knew of their worth. It was not until the end of the war, when Rhodesia's Combined Operations Centre issued a statement crediting the Scouts with responsibility for 68 per cent of enemy dead, that the scale of their success became known. In less than seven years of almost continuous war the Selous Scouts themselves lost only 36 men killed in action, but they accounted for several thousand guerrillas.

Above: Lieutenant-Colonel Ron Reid Daly.

Below: The Scouts were very skilled trackers.

SOUTH AFRICAN RECCE COMMANDOS
The Reconnaissance Commandos

THE South African Special Forces, which are controlled by Headquarters Special Forces at Voortrekkerhoogte, are organised into naval and military branches. The small naval element is made up of two components. One is the shipborne element, trained to guard naval and mercantile shipping while in port and to conduct clandestine attacks on enemy craft. The second component is a marine group that can operate from surface warships and submarines. The larger,

military, group is composed of a highly-skilled fighting and training cadre of white officers and soldiers, with the equivalent of two battalions of black troops organised on a company basis; some of the black troops are former guerrillas, 'turned' by the security forces.

The kernel of the Special Forces is the white Reconnaissance Commandos, who also provide most of the officers in the black units. The Recces are all volunteers, either regular soldiers who have transferred from other arms, or

The role of the Recces

The Reconnaissance Commandos – not

to be confused with the Commandos or local militias – are the central component of South Africa's Special Forces. Also known as the 'Recce Commandos', 'Recondos' or just 'Recces', they specialise in deep-penetration missions inside enemy territory, gathering intelligence, tracking enemy units and attacking strategic targets. They are South Africa's equivalent of the British SAS, the US Green Berets and the now disbanded Rhodesian Selous Scouts.

Like these equivalent units, the Recces are a small and highly selective unit, choosing only the very best men. Recces receive a comprehensive training programme that includes parachuting, skydiving, deep-sea diving, mountain climbing, unconventional and unarmed combat, and advanced explosives. Officially Recces wear standard SADF combat dress – sand-coloured jackets and slacks, with high-ankled boots and bush hat – and use standard SADF weapons like the FN 7.62mm rifle, but for missions behind enemy lines they often discard SADF uniform and carry non-SADF arms. It has been reported that Recces operate outside the standard operational structure of the SADF, being responsible directly to the chief of the SADF himself.

Left: With the sun low in the sky, a commando patrol returns to base after looking for evidence of activity by SWAPO guerrillas.

Right: Armed with a 7.62mm FN MAG machine gun, a Recce prepares to go out on patrol.

national servicemen recruited directly on their entry to the forces. Recruits to the Recces must be South African citizens and, as well as being exceptionally fit and strong, must have a high leadership potential, respectable background and be of metriculation level in terms of education. All are stringently vetted before being accepted.

Before being drafted, all prospective national servicemen are asked if they wish to volunteer for the Special Forces. If they do, they fill in a questionnaire which reveals the depth of their motivation and their qualifications. If the answers reveal that they are above average physically, psychologically and intellectually, they are entered for a special pre-selection examination and

undergo rigorous tests which eliminate those who are unable to achieve the very high standards demanded. They must perform physical feats which are beyond the capabilities of most young men without special work-up training – for instance running 200m carrying a man in a fireman's lift in one minute – and there are also pyschometric tests to determine their character potential, in particular whether they will be able to stand the strains of prolonged operations behind enemy lines.

Those national servicemen who pass these tests then join the Recces' mainstream production line. The basic training lasts for three months. It includes an individual acclimatisation course for four weeks, a one-week selection course that tests the trainee under simulated battle conditions, and parachute training. After the preliminary course has been completed, the men then do eight months of special orientation for their role. They are instructed in the handling of mines and explosives, demolition methods, bushcraft, survival, boating, sailing, battle tactics, signals and first-aid. There is comprehensive training on both their own and foreign weapons and time is spent practising liaison with the air forces used in their support. Those who fail at any stage – and quite a high proportion of them do – are returned to their unit or, if they are national servicemen who came straight to

Special Forces training, they are sent to the technical service corps such as the Signals, Ordnance, Intelligence or the Military Police.

The parachute course in particular is a very hard test. During the initial two weeks the trainees do ten 40-minute periods daily, which include a high content of endurance training and body-building. The next phase is the actual parachute training, but only between 50 and 60 per cent of the young hopefuls who set out on the initial course of the South African Parachute Brigade graduate to that level. The Recces make their first static-line jumps from 150m, then go on to become experts in free-falling. Some of them train to be high-altitude, low opening (HALO) specialists.

Once trained, the newly qualified commando joins his operational unit; he will remain with it for the unexpired portion of his two years if he is a national serviceman. Recces receive additional allowance for having passed their stringent training and they also get extra pay during active operations. If a Recce reaches the rank of sergeant, he may apply to be considered for promotion to officer status. At the end of the service period both regulars and national servicemen are transferred to the Second Battalion of the Reconnaissance Commandos, the Citizen Force (CF) unit in which they can continue to use their specialist skills until their reserve

Above: South African helicopters come in to land in arid Namibian territory.

commitment has ended. Young national servicemen can apply to become regulars.

The Recces have been employed repeatedly in the protracted conflict against SWAPO. They were involved in the 1975–76 'Angola March' and later took part in Operations Sceptic (1980), Protea (1981) and Daisy (1981). Since then they have been involved in a multitude of clandestine, short-duration, hit-and-destroy attacks. Their targets were reached variously by parachute, on foot, in vehicles, by helicopter or across water. When deployed in the bush the white-cadre Recces use the base of a conventional front-line support unit during protracted operations, but in short-lived 'take-out' attacks they parachute in direct from their home base and then extract themselves when their mission has been accomplished. The black troops operate as self-contained units or in small groups for the duration of the operations and are then withdrawn to their base camps.

Operating in areas which are entirely populated by blacks, the white cadre is careful to disguise itself and for this reason white Recces on active service black-up all exposed flesh. In some instances pseudo-teams will go into action disguised as guerrilla groups and carrying Soviet weapons such as the AK-47 and the RPD machine gun. Some Recces use the 7.62mm FN MAG machine gun, but most carry the FN FAL NATO rifle with a folding stock. At the belt they carry a blackened stiletto, a water bottle, two days' concentrated rations, ammunition pouches and immediate first-aid.

The Recces take great pride in belonging to the fittest, toughest and most highly-trained outfit in the SADF. As individuals they are highly specialised and very formidable fighting men, and as units they enjoy an unequalled reputation for successful military operations in the harsh and punishing conditions of the African bush.

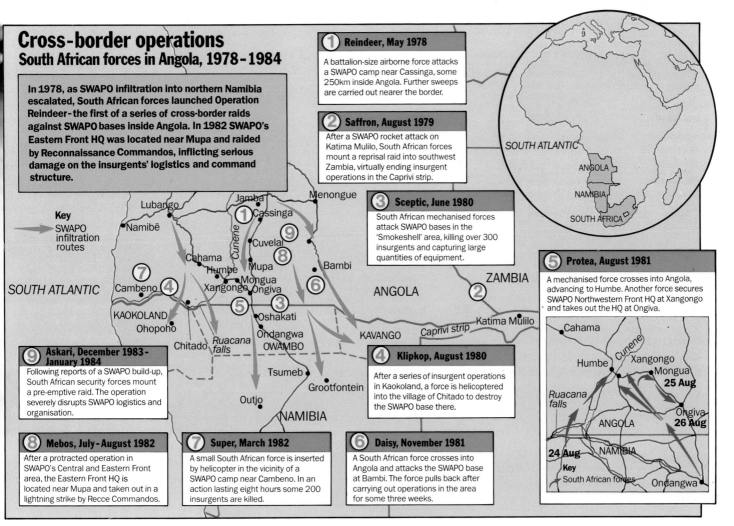

INDEX